I0887552

Hollywood Bloodshed

Hollywood Bloodshed

Violence in 1980s American Cinema

James Kendrick

Southern Illinois University Press
Carbondale

Printed in the United States of America

18 17 16 15 5 4 3 2

Library of Congress Cataloging-in-Publication Data
Kendrick, James, 1974–
Hollywood bloodshed : violence in 1980s American cinema / James Kendrick.
p. cm.
Includes bibliographical references and index.
ISBN-13: 978-0-8093-2888-8 (alk. paper)
ISBN-10: 0-8093-2888-7 (alk. paper)
1. Violence in motion pictures. 2. Motion pictures—United States. I.Title.
PN1995.9.V5K46 2009
791.43'655—dc22 2008032416

Printed on recycled paper. ♻

The paper used in this publication meets the minimum requirements of American National Standard for Information Sciences—Permanence of Paper for Printed Library Materials, ANSI Z39.48-1992. ∞

Contents

Illustrations

Preface

THIS PROJECT WAS ORIGINALLY sparked by two seemingly separate but ultimately interrelated fascinations: the role that screen violence plays in our complex attraction to and enjoyment of movies, and the ostensibly sharp divide that separates Hollywood cinema of the 1970s from Hollywood cinema of the 1980s. The amount of scholarship about American film in the 1970s is voluminous, and it is axiomatic for many to declare it one of the richest and most evocative periods of cinema not only in the United States but in the world. Meanwhile, the decade of the 1980s, when written about, has been frequently dismissed as a period of artistic and ideological retreat in which movies became simplified and empty—vacuous entertainment for an increasingly conservative culture that had elected a former movie actor to the most powerful position in the world. Similarly, violence in movies of the 1960s and 1970s, which is frequently viewed as a kind of formative moment in the aesthetic and ideological development of screen bloodshed, has been scrutinized quite heavily, as has screen violence of the 1990s. However, scholars have written comparatively little about screen violence in the 1980s, which is ironic, given its prevalence on American movie screens during the Reagan era.

Thus, it seemed to me that the intersection of screen violence and the shifts in American filmmaking at the juncture between the 1970s and the 1980s could offer rich possibilities in terms of exploring how movies ebb and flow with the times. As a lens, screen violence provides an intriguing perspective for exploring the constantly shifting nature of Hollywood cinema—the aesthetic, social, and industrial continuities and changes, some which are subtle, some of which are radical. In short, I was interested in screen violence not so much for its own sake but for what it could tell us about what was happening culturally and institutionally in Hollywood.

Of course, characterizing any given era in Hollywood history is always a dangerous endeavor because each historical period, however defined and delineated, is invariably rife with contradictions, volatility, and diversity. Each era has "characteristic" films, filmmakers, and production trends that are used in summation as convenient shorthand, but they consistently fail to capture the depth and complexity of what the Hollywood film industry represents at any given time. Such is the case with the two eras that are contrasted in this book: the 1970s and the 1980s. The former is conventionally understood as an era of experimentation, social consciousness, artistry, and boundary-pushing, while the latter is often seen as a period of conservative ideological entrenchment and commercial conformity. Each era is usually viewed through the prism of its political culture, with the 1970s seen as an era of upheaval and disorientation, while the 1980s is seen as a period of focused conservatism. And, on some level, both characterizations are right, but to stop there is to see only a fraction of the whole.

Digging just slightly beneath the topsoil reveals that the fabled New Hollywood of the late 1960s and 1970s, the same era that produced such critical landmarks as *The Graduate* (1967), *The Godfather* (1972), *The Exorcist* (1973), *Chinatown* (1974), *Nashville* (1975), and *Taxi Driver* (1976), was routinely dominated at the box office by sentimental romance (1970's *Love Story*), musicals (1971's *Fiddler on the Roof* and 1978's *Grease*), disaster epics (1974's *The Towering Inferno*), and science fiction (1977's *Star Wars*). Thus, we can see in only that cursory overview that, as Peter Lev puts it, "for sheer diversity of aesthetic and ideological approaches, no period of American cinema surpasses the films of the 1970s" (xvii). Similarly, while we like to see the so-called Reagan era as a period overrun by the "Lucas-Spielberg Syndrome" and conservative blockbuster filmmaking, a slightly deeper investigation unveils a twisting maze of contradictions and heterogeneity that includes a noted increase in the exhibition of documentaries (Plantinga) and the rise to prominence of controversial filmmakers such as David Lynch, Spike Lee, Abel Ferrara, David Cronenberg, and Oliver Stone.

Yet, in writing the many histories of Hollywood, it is quite natural to fall back on the practice of periodizing, which by its nature tends to privilege the historical "breaks" that separate one period from another. However, as Murray Smith argues, it is important that, in trying to understand the historical trajectory of Hollywood's development and the changes in its various structures (industrial, aesthetic, ideological), it is crucial to recognize continuities in addition to breaks. The constant goal of Hollywood filmmaking, and thus the primary continuity that has crossed every significant historical break, including the one between the 1970s and the 1980s, has been "the maximizing of profits through the production of classical narrative films" (M. Smith 14). This one goal binds together the history of Hollywood production, from the silent films of the 1920s, to the CinemaScope spectaculars of the 1950s, to the auteur-driven revisionist genre films of the 1970s, to the digital-effects-laden blockbusters of the 1990s and today. Therefore, as Smith notes, it is most useful to focus on "smaller-scale changes and shifts, at both the institutional and aesthetic levels, within a more broadly continuous system of American commercial filmmaking" (14).

It would seem, then, that this book's focus on screen violence in the decade of the 1980s, often in counterpoint to the violence of films in the 1970s, would contribute to the reification of periodizing as the optimal means of understanding Hollywood history. Separating out the 1980s as a decade somehow distinct from the 1970s and the 1990s is too convenient, and it is not my aim. Rather, the focus on the 1980s is meant to underscore, not erase, the continuities between what came before and what came after without losing sight of the significant changes that did occur. In looking at the 1980s, this book focuses on how aesthetic and industrial practices involving the representations of screen violence underwent changes and shifts at varying scales and on different levels, thus creating connections among the various decades. On the surface, there is a great disparity between the characteristics associated with violent films of the 1970s and those of the 1990s, and this book explores what happened in the years in between as a way of linking them back together, focusing on the often hidden articulations and small-scale changes, rather than on just the large-scale historical breaks, in how violence on screen was depicted.

Chapter 1 is a historical overview of violence in the cinema, beginning with the silent era but focusing primarily on the enormous increase in both quantity and levels of graphic detail beginning in the late 1960s with the end of the Production Code and the implementation of the Motion Picture Association of America's (MPAA) rating system. While this story has been told before, particularly by Stephen Prince (*Savage Cinema*; *Screening Violence*; "Graphic Violence") and David A. Cook ("Ballistic Balletics"), it is important to lay this historical groundwork before focusing on the 1980s and the screen violence of that decade. One way in which this historical overview differs from those told before is its primary focus on the rise of the "New Hollywood" and the connection of its most revered auteurs with depictions of violence and on how their particular violent style ended when that "New Hollywood" was eclipsed by the blockbuster era.

Chapter 2 focuses on the 1980s, beginning chronologically by covering the controversies that opened the decade. There are continuities that span historical breaks, and even though the cinema of the 1980s is often discussed and described in stark opposition to the cinema of the 1970s, the early years of the 1980s had much in common with the previous decade despite the large cultural shift to the Right. Thus, violent films like Brian De Palma's *Dressed to Kill* (1980), William Friedkin's *Cruising* (1980), and

Sam Fuller's *White Dog* (1982), which were more in tune aesthetically and ideologically with the previous decade, ran into myriad problems and controversies in marketing and theatrical distribution. The lessons learned from these films and their various difficulties help explain why the industry was so intent on avoiding controversy—not by removing violence from movies but by finding ways to package it so that, on the surface, it appeared less controversial.

The final four chapters focus on case studies of specific kinds of violence that characterized Hollywood in the 1980s and on the ways in which filmmakers and studios packaged them. Again, this is not an encyclopedic coverage of all the kinds of violence that characterized Hollywood films of the 1980s but rather a series of specific case studies that explore a select few of the various articulations among screen violence and producers, consumers, and the culture at large.

Chapter 3 shifts to the "pure action" genre and focuses on the rise of the powerful and highly visible producer and his role in packaging violent entertainment. The director-auteurs of the 1970s lost much of their power in the 1980s and were replaced by producers in the public's understanding of who was largely in control of Hollywood filmmaking. This chapter looks particularly at Don Simpson and Jerry Bruckheimer as self-styled packagers of pure action violence and at the ways in which their films negotiated the kinds of violent subject matter that were troubling in 1970s films like *The French Connection* (1971) and *Marathon Man* (1976) and made them palatable and acceptable to a more conservative-minded audience in films like *Beverly Hills Cop* (1984) and *Top Gun* (1986). While certain aspects of these action films remained consistent between the two decades, there was a discernible ideological shift in how violence functioned in the narratives. Thus, central to this discussion is also the way in which action films of the 1980s rewrote the rules first laid down in the western genre, from the male hero fighting for what's right to the male hero fighting simply to win, which mirrors on a meta-level the producers' view of the motion picture industry and their role in it.

Chapter 4 offers a counterpoint to the reductionism of the pure action genre by focusing on the cycle of films about the Vietnam War that dominated the latter half of the 1980s. Vietnam films offer a particularly intriguing glimpse into the competing ideologies of the Reagan era in their attempts to recuperate and make sense of a war that had divided the American culture for decades. My contention in this chapter is that, rather than categorizing the 1980s Vietnam films as right-wing revenge films or realistic combat films, it is more useful to consider them in terms of how they direct violence narratively and ideologically. Thus, we can examine these films in terms of being externally violent, in that the violence is directed at a foreign enemy and/or the corrupt—and therefore un-American—bureaucracy that caused the United States to lose the war, or inwardly violent, where violence is directed inward at the U.S. military or even American culture itself.

Chapter 5 looks at the violence of the horror genre, which has been a popular topic of analysis from a number of angles, including gender (Clover), subversion of social hierarchies (Paul), and political ideology (R. Wood, *Hollywood*), to name just a few. However, this chapter moves away from analysis of the film texts themselves and instead focuses on how the explicit gore that characterized the most popular horror films of the 1980s (for example, 1982's *The Evil Dead* and the *Friday the 13th* and *A Nightmare on Elm Street* series) was packaged through fan magazines such as *Fangoria* and was understood by the genre's specialized audience. Surprisingly little has been written about the rise of the horror fan magazine during the 1980s and the role it played in articulating screen violence, the horror genre, and fandom. Mark Kermode has written briefly about *Fangoria,* which he describes as "the Sex Pistols of horror fanzines, loud, noisy, visually graphic and absolutely guaranteed to send your parents apoplectic with righteous indignation" ("Teenage Horror Fan" 59). While Henry Jenkins notes that science fiction fans make up a "scandalous category" of people, horror fans are viewed as that much more extreme and therefore "illegitimate" given the disreputable nature of their objects of pleasure (16). This chapter investigates the articulations among these fans, the film texts they love, and the fanzines that captured and dispersed their enthusiasm. As David Sanjek argues, these fanzines cannot be dismissed, because they "constitute an alternative brand of film criticism, a school with its own set of values and virtues" (316).

Chapter 6 looks at how the MPAA dealt with the complexities of screen violence in the 1980s by creating a new rating, PG-13, to distinguish those films that existed in the previously unmarked space between more kid-friendly PG-rated films and adult-oriented R-rated films. The PG-13 rating was yet another form of packaging screen violence—a brand that marked the violence of certain movies as just illicit enough to entice curious viewers but not so illicit that some people (that is, children) had to be kept from viewing it outright. Central to the creation of the PG-13 rating was hugely successful producer/director Steven Spielberg, whose films *Indiana Jones and the Temple of Doom* (which he directed) and *Gremlins* (for which he served as executive producer), both of which were released to large box-office grosses in the summer of 1984, were primarily responsible for blurring the lines between how screen violence can function in "children's" and "adult" entertainment. As both of these films were clearly aimed at young audiences, the role they played in the subsequent creation of the

PG-13 rating tells us much about the 1980s conception of childhood and what role violent entertainment can and should play in it.

Finally, the conclusion bridges the gap between 1980s and 1990s Hollywood cinema by examining the concomitant emergence of new forms of screen violence—dubbed "new violence," "neo-violence," and "postmodern violence" by critics and scholars—and the rise of independent studios as a viable market force to contend with the hegemony of the major Hollywood studios, arguably for the first time since the "instant majors" in the late 1960s. Many of the most notable and economically successful independent films of the early 1990s engaged screen violence in a way that most films had not for the past decade. In a sense, it was like a return to the 1970s in which brash young filmmakers fought to make a name for themselves by "reinventing" American cinema, often by reworking traditional representations of violence.

Acknowledgments

ANY BOOK—BUT PARTICULARLY a first book and one that has been several years in the making—will inevitably bear the imprint of many people. The one you hold in your hands is no different, and while I cannot even begin to do justice to everyone who has left his or her mark on the following pages, I would like to acknowledge some of them individually.

I owe immeasurable gratitude to the professors at Indiana University who were so influential in shaping me as a scholar: Chris Anderson, Barbara Klinger, and Eva Cherniavsky, all of whom continued to offer advice, encouragement, and support as I pursued the long, sometimes frustrating road toward publication. I am especially grateful for the guidance and support of Joan Hawkins, who was particularly instrumental in my development as a scholar and whose unfailing generosity in reading and critiquing new material has been invaluable. My good friend Jon Kraszewski has been with me daily via e-mail as this project has progressed over the past several years; I am deeply indebted to him for his willingness to read chunks of the manuscript and offer nonstop encouragement and advice through the peaks and the valleys. In this regard, I also owe a debt of gratitude to my peers in graduate school, who over the years knowingly or unknowingly contributed to my work in both class discussions and casual conversations. My discussions over the years—both serious and not—with Bob Rehak, Jake Smith, and Chris Dumas were particularly helpful in shaping my thinking and ideas.

I could not have completed this project without the support of the Department of Communication Studies at Baylor University, and special thanks go out to my division chair, Michael Korpi, and my department chairs, Karla Leeper, Bill English, and Dave Schlueter, who were always ready and willing to offer whatever support and resources I needed. My colleagues Corey Carbonara, Chris Hansen, Justin Wilson, Joe Kickasola, and Brian Elliott listened to me talk about my ideas and offered exactly the kind of support I needed to keep the project rolling.

Several parts of this book, but especially chapter 5, benefited significantly from research I conducted at the Oral History Research Collection at Columbia University's Butler Library. To this end, I must first thank

Richard D. Heffner for his generosity with his time and for allowing me access to his personal papers and oral histories, which for the first time have given researchers an inside look at the mechanisms of the Motion Picture Association of America's ratings system. The research would not have been possible without the University Research Grant I received in the spring of 2007 from the vice provost for research at Baylor University, nor without the dedicated librarians at the Butler Library who helped me take advantage of my time there, despite it being the middle of spring break. I would also like to thank the staff at the Cushing Memorial Library and Archives at Texas A&M University for their help while I paged through years and years of *Fangoria* magazines. My thanks to them for collecting and taking such good care of what so many others would view as disposable cultural detritus.

I am especially grateful for the editors at Southern Illinois University Press, Karl Kageff and Bridget Brown, who believed in this book when it was just a proposal, and Kathleen Kageff, who saw it through the publication process. I would also like to thank the two anonymous readers for their concerted effort and thoughtful responses to my work. Their insightful critiques and suggestions urged me to question more and dig deeper.

I would, of course, not be here without my family, and my thanks and love go out to my parents for all they have done for me throughout my life. I must offer a special thank you to my father, who probably had no idea that the genesis of this book and my academic career really began back in the spring of 1991 when I was a junior in high school and he brought home from the office a copy of *Newsweek* with a cover story about media violence as a way of encouraging me to step back and think about my sometimes dark pop-culture fascinations. The fact that I begin the introduction of this book by discussing that issue is testament to how it has stuck with me.

Finally, I would like to thank Cassie, my wife and best friend, who has been right with me through the long and sometimes difficult process of writing this book. She has sparked me intellectually, motivated me emotionally, and given her full and unquestionable support to my ambitious endeavors, even when that meant sitting through movies she never would have wanted to watch on her own. But, most important, her love and commitment have kept me grounded in what's truly important, and for that reason this book is dedicated to her.

Hollywood Bloodshed

INTRODUCTION

THE MAINSTREAMING OF HOLLYWOOD SCREEN VIOLENCE

"VIOLENCE GOES MAINSTREAM"—or so declared the bold headline on the cover of the April 1, 1991, issue of *Newsweek* magazine. As visual accompaniment to this declaration, the editors chose to run a dramatic, close-up image of the face of Hannibal Lecter, the fictional serial killer played by Anthony Hopkins in Jonathan Demme's recently released and hugely popular *The Silence of the Lambs* (1991). All we can see is the bridge of Lecter's nose and his intently wide-open, penetrating eyes, alight with a feverish intensity that makes it immediately clear why "Hannibal the Cannibal" had already become a pop-culture icon, as both mythic nightmare and subversive antihero. At the same time, those eyes, positioned as they are just beneath the sensational word "violence" in ragged font, indict the reader and his or her fascination with violent subject matter: Are those Hannibal Lecter's eyes penetrating his next victim, or are they our own, gazing in rapt excitement at the latest bout of Hollywood bloodshed?

At the bottom of the cover, a sub-headline pointedly asked, "Movies, Music, Books—Are There Any Limits Left?," suggesting that mediated violence had escaped whatever cage to which it had previously been confined and was now breaking taboos and crossing the previously demarcated limits that separate "us" from the base instincts that define the uncivilized "others" from whom we need to be protected. The accompanying article says just as much: "Sure, ultraviolent fare has always been out there—but up until now, it's always been *out there*, on the fringes of mass culture. Now it's the station-wagon set, bumper to bumper at the local Cinema 1–2–3–4–5, that yearns to be titillated by the latest schlocky horror picture show" (Plagens, Miller, Foote, and Yoffe 46). The title of the *Newsweek* article—"Violence in Our Culture"—subconsciously paints screen violence as an invading force, a contagion, breaking into "our" previously protected spaces and infecting them.

In sounding the alarm about the breakdown of limits and the "appalling accretion of violent entertainment" (Plagens, Miller, Foote, and Yoffe 46), *Newsweek* had its finger firmly on the pulse of American entertainment at the dawn of the 1990s, especially mainstream Hollywood movies, many of

1. Cover of *Newsweek*, April 1, 1991. Cover copyright *Newsweek*, 1991 Newsweek, Inc. All rights reserved. Used by permission and protected by the copyright laws of the United States. The printing, copying, redistribution, or retransmission of the material without express written permission is prohibited. Image from *The Silence of the Lambs*, copyright 1991 Orion Pictures Corporation. All rights reserved. Courtesy of MGM Clip+Still.

which were undeniably violent. However, the magazine was wrong in asserting that violence was "going mainstream" in the spring of 1991. Rather, violence had already *gone* mainstream, and the films, television shows, rock and rap albums, and books cited throughout the article were, in fact, just a particularly explicit manifestation—darker shades, you might say—of what had, in some form or another, been long accepted by the general American population: In all its many shades, screen bloodshed *is* entertainment.

In fact, some two and a half decades earlier, *Esquire* had sounded a similar alarm with its infamous cover image of a beautiful model with a Band-Aid over her left eyebrow just beneath a seemingly simple, direct question: "Why are we suddenly so obsessed with violence?" Numerous authors, critics, and pundits attempted to answer that question throughout the special issue of July 1967, including *Bonnie and Clyde* (1967) screenwriters David Newman and Robert Benton, who inflamed the generation gap by suggesting that anyone who couldn't enjoy "the fun" of violence was out of step with the times (55). In the same issue, journalist Tom Wolfe coined the term "porno-violence," which he used to describe a kind of mediated violence in American entertainment that was not confined to a single point of view or a particular moral perspective. Despite this term's pejorative nature and its failure to catch on in the national dialogue, "porno-violence," as defined by Wolfe, is really quite appropriate in describing the role of violence in popular entertainment. As John Fraser argues in *Violence in the Arts,* the complexity of mediated violence is immense, and it can fulfill and has fulfilled numerous and varied functions: "violence as release, violence as communication, violence as play, violence as self-affirmation, or self-defence, or self-discovery, or self-destruction, violence as a flight from reality, violence as the truest sanity in a particular situation, and so on" (9). Violence is not a single entity, and it cannot be contained, although that is precisely what the Hollywood studios attempted to do during the 1980s: not eliminate screen violence but control it and tame it—shade it in such a way that it could work for them.

This book is about the varied roles screen violence played in the U.S. film industry during the 1980s—a crucial decade in Hollywood's economic and industrial development. Given the immense popularity of a wide variety of violent films and that decade's standing as the bridge on which the parameters of our current Hollywood system were negotiated, it is particularly important to understand how representations of violence functioned during this time. Thus, the book's focus is on the films produced by mainstream Hollywood, which is generally defined as the large movie studios that are members of the Motion Picture Association of America and "consistently account for 80 to 90 percent or more of the total receipts from the distribution of theatrical movies to theaters and the variety of other media in the United States" (Waterman 15).[1] As J. David Slocum argues, "The history and recurrence of film violence, certainly in Hollywood productions, represents not only an account of shifting cinematic standards and cultural values regarding the use of force and aggression, but an element in the ongoing negotiation of the place and meaning of cinema itself in society" ("Film Violence" 650). After the economic turmoil of the late 1960s and early 1970s, the Hollywood studios were looking for stability, which is reflected in the way violence is presented in films of that era.

The changes in the industry during the 1980s were so transformative that Stephen Prince argues that they rank alongside the coming of sound in the 1920s and the breakup of the industry's oligopolistic ownership of production, distribution, and exhibition in the late 1940s (*New Pot of Gold* xii). During this time, the industry evolved from the late 1960s and 1970s "New Hollywood," an era dominated by young, film-school-trained auteurs and their incorporation of European aesthetics into traditional genre films, to the 1980s "New Hollywood" (sometimes referred to as the "New New Hollywood"), which is characterized by the high-concept blockbuster and an industrial reorganization around media mergers, transnational conglomerates, multiple avenues of exhibition, and emerging ancillary markets. Hollywood was no longer the producer of what Robin Wood calls "incoherent texts" (*Hollywood* 46), which reflected the ideological crises of the 1970s; rather, the industry was moving into what Andrew Britton calls "Reaganite entertainment," which found its most indelible form in the "clean" blockbuster aesthetic molded by hands-on producers like Don Simpson and Jerry Bruckheimer. This is not to say that the films of the 1980s were monolithic in focus, commercial strategy, or ideological intent. However, there were certain powerful production trends like the "blockbuster aesthetic" that created the illusion of an era dominated by simplistic commercial entertainment infused with Reagan-era social and political culture, which may explain why so many scholars have shied away from analyzing this period. As Prince states, "If we move past the received wisdom on eighties Hollywood, we see instead a volatile era, volatile in terms of the industry's restructuring and reorganization and in terms of the connections and relationships between its products and the society that alternately assimilated and attacked them" (*New Pot of Gold* xvii).

This book explores the relationship of cultural changes in the 1980s to the various ways in which screen violence was depicted by filmmakers, packaged by studios, and understood by audiences. "Packaging," in this sense, refers both to how filmmakers packaged violence textually through narrative, character development, and aesthetic style and to how studios packaged many of the films themselves as a commodity through marketing and mediated discussion in newspapers and magazines and on television. It is closely related to Justin Wyatt's argument about "high concept" movies: "High concept functions as a form of differentiated product primarily through two routes: through an integration with marketing and merchandising and through an emphasis on style" (*High Concept* 19). Thus, the films discussed in this book are but one element in a larger articulated web of discourse that shapes and influences how we understand particular instances of screen violence.

What Is Screen Violence?

In any book about screen violence, it is important to ask a central, but often neglected, question: What, exactly, is screen violence? Defining this concept is a notoriously tricky endeavor, littered with rhetorical mines and conceptual pits, not to mention the ever-present shadow of common sense. Defining screen violence can be so exasperating, in fact, that one is tempted to follow the model James Naremore used in defining film noir by saying there is simply "no completely satisfactory way to organize the category" (9). Screen violence is similar in that, like film noir, it has been discussed and understood in multiple contexts—historical, ideological, rhetorical—that structure and define its meaning. Simply put, the term "screen violence" means different things to different people at different times. For example, screen violence that offended sensibilities in the 1940s not only might seem tame by contemporary standards but might even elicit laughter.

In this book, I will employ what Slocum has termed "the least elaboration" of violence to define it: "an action or behavior that is harmful or injurious" ("Introduction" 2). Of course, even this seemingly simple and intentionally vague definition has plenty of caveats and addendums. For example, the harm can be physical, psychological, or sociological, and in some instances it need not be done since the threat of harm can be just as disturbing as the harm itself. Violence can also be systematic or structural (for example, racism, sexism, and the like) rather than the product of an individual causal agent, and it can be directed at anything, from human beings, to animals, to inanimate objects. Importantly, Slocum notes that the term itself—violence—is essentially a label that is applied to preexisting behaviors or actions through a web of complex social processes: "Legitimacy as a critical category is thus crucial not only for the actions it validates as violent within a given culture but for the behaviors that it excludes from popular discourses of violence" (3). Similarly, Nancy

Armstrong and Leonard Tennenhouse write, "To regard certain practices as violent is never to see them just as they are. It is always to take up a position for or against them" (9). Martin Barker argues even more specifically that the term "violence" as we currently understand it emerged in the social context of the late 1950s and early 1960s as a response to social changes and political unrest. Thus, violence is never an unloaded marker and must always be understood within multiple, shifting contexts.

Because films are inherently visual, there is an important distinction that needs to be made between "violence" and "graphic violence," terms that are commonly used to distinguish between two distinctly different visual representations of violent behavior. Shoot-outs in old westerns, for example, are considered to be violence even if there is no overt display of blood or suffering. Graphic violence, on the other hand, refers to unmistakable on-screen representations of the damage to the human body that result from violent acts. In this sense, "violence" refers to the action, and "graphic violence" refers to how the results of that action are depicted. When violence is depicted graphically, the audience is able to view the filmmaker's approximation of actual bodily injury. No longer is it enough to see an actor fall down in order to demonstrate that he has been shot; instead, we see the actual explosion of a blood squib to suggest the body being violated—literally torn apart—by the bullet.

We can see the difference between violence and graphic violence by comparing different versions of William Shakespeare's *Macbeth*. When the play is traditionally performed onstage, the majority of the violent action (murder and sword fights to the death) is minimized or kept offstage entirely, away from the audience view. So, when Macduff and Macbeth engage in their final duel, the stage directions usually read "exeunt fighting," which indicates that the actors are fighting offstage. However, in Roman Polanski's 1971 film version, the violence is brought to the cinematic center stage. Polanski graphically renders that which had been previously kept from the audience's sight, such as Macduff beheading Macbeth. This is an example of a physical act being transformed from violence to graphic violence, with the primary difference being the amount of actual physical, bodily damage the audience is allowed to witness. As we will see, this distinction between violence and graphic violence is the primary characteristic that is used to divide classical from contemporary screen violence, which means that Hollywood did not necessarily become more violent as the years wore on, just more graphic.

From the 1970s to the 1980s: Changes and Continuities

The year 1968 was one of the most tumultuous in U.S. history, described by many as the peak of what is commonly understood as "The Sixties." It

2. Macduff's (Terence Bayler) beheading of Macbeth (Jon Finch) in Roman Polanski's 1971 film version of Shakespeare's play is a good example of a physical act being transformed from violence to graphic violence. Polanski depicts that which had been previously kept from the audience's sight in most theatrical productions. DVD still.

was the year of the Tet Offensive in Vietnam, when popular opinion of the war began to break down; violent clashes between antiwar demonstrators and police outside the Democratic National Convention in Chicago; U.S. athletes Tommie Smith and John Carlos raising the Black Power symbol after winning medals at the Summer Olympics in Mexico City; the Orangeburg Massacre in which three student demonstrators were shot and killed by patrolmen and twenty-seven others were injured; and racially charged riots in Washington, D.C., Baltimore, and Trenton. In the fall of that year, President Lyndon Johnson and the U.S. Congress responded to the high-profile and widely mediated assassinations of civil rights activist Martin Luther King Jr. and presidential hopeful Robert Kennedy, as well as to the rising tide of violent crime in the United States, by convening the National Commission on the Causes and Prevention of Violence. A significant component of the commission was the Task Force on Mass Media and Violence, whose purpose was to conduct hearings in order to determine the effects on the public of media portrayals of violence. One of the people called to testify at the hearings was Jack Valenti, who only a year and a half earlier had been appointed president of the MPAA, the U.S. film industry's trade organization. As the public face of Hollywood, Valenti's primary goal in testifying at the hearings was to defend the film industry, which not only was in dire financial straits at the time but also was under intense criticism for fostering a climate of violence in the United States with increasingly graphic and bloody films that went far beyond what had previously been seen on the silver screen.

In a prepared statement that he read before the commission on the morning of its fourth day of hearings, December 19, 1968, Valenti stated:

> Today, we must understand the following: films explore more deeply into the human condition than they ever did before. . . . There is a new breed of filmmaker. And mark you well this new filmmaker, because he's an extraordinary fellow. He's young. He's sensitive. He's dedicated. He's reaching out for new dimensions of expression. And he is not bound—not bound—by the conventions of a conformist past. I happen to think that's good. Moreover, this new style in filmmaking is matched by a new audience. It is seeking new fulfillment. Its members are better educated. (qtd. in National Commission on the Causes and Prevention of Violence 193)

Thus, although Valenti spent most of his time before the panel discussing the newly adopted MPAA rating system and whether or not it could be effectively enforced, he also boldly defended Hollywood filmmakers and their challenging films on the grounds of artistic development and political engagement, as well as on their connection to a youth audience that was seeking alternative film experiences. Valenti conceded that artists do have responsibility to both their art and society in their portrayals of violence, that there is a balance at which "violence which is honest" tips over into "portrayals which are excessive and overweighted" (192). However, his main point was that filmmakers need to be free of all constraints, especially governmental constraints: "The screen must be free if it is going to flourish" (192).

Fast-forward twelve years. The Vietnam War had ended, but the country had yet to deal with its legacy in any significant way. Republican Ronald Reagan, a former movie star whose political career began when he cooperated with the House Un-American Activities Committee's investigation into Hollywood politics in the late 1940s, had just been elected president, and there was a subsequent reinvigoration of the tensions of the Cold War, shifting from the Carter administration's détente to Reagan's aggressive rhetoric about the dangers of the "evil empire." Riding Reagan's popular coattails, the Republican Party had also just gained control of the Senate for the first time in twenty-five years. A significant portion of the country was gripped by a mood of renewed conservatism that had been gaining power during the previous decade by filling in the gaps left by the unrealized ideals of the 1960s. The Moral Majority and other right-leaning religious groups were launching successful campaigns against virtually everything the Left had achieved in the previous decade, from women's liberation, to abortion rights, to the acceptance of homosexuality. And national attention was increasingly focused on the "money culture" of "nouveau riche speculators, financiers, entrepreneurs, and corporate chieftains" (Taylor 9).

For Hollywood, it was a watershed moment in which the vaunted "New Hollywood"—whose brash young auteurs such as Francis Ford Coppola, Brian De Palma, Martin Scorsese, and William Friedkin had produced a succession of challenging, often violent films—was increasingly out of step with the cultural mood. And, in an almost exact reversal of his statement before the commission in December 1968, Jack Valenti, the public voice of Hollywood, sounded the industry's disapproval in an article in the *New York Times* in July 1980: There is "a greater gulf today than there was 10 years ago between the creative filmmakers and the public. The political climate in this country is shifting to the right, and that means more conservative attitudes toward sex and violence. But a lot of creative people are still living in the world of revolution" (qtd. in P. Wood D14).

As Valenti's comments indicate, at the beginning of the 1980s, the Hollywood studios, virtually all of which were owned by diversified international conglomerates, were shifting from strong support of the "extraordinary . . . young . . . sensitive . . . dedicated" directors who were not bound by a "conformist past" to lamenting that those same directors were unwilling to conform themselves to a new era by retreating from the "world of revolution." Therefore, the New Hollywood and all it stood for became problematic for the film industry, which for its entire history had attempted to present its best face in the public arena. In a sense, the New Hollywood filmmakers were becoming embarrassments to the industry—revolutionary spirits mired in a fleeting past tense of left-wing political and artistic change—and they subsequently lost virtually all the power they had wielded so mightily only a few years before. As Peter Biskind notes, "The American directors of the '70s, with few exceptions, burned out like Roman candles after an all-too-brief flash of brilliance, cut off in mid-career" (409). Most of these artists were resentful of the changing times and how it affected their careers. Brian De Palma, who was one of the few New Hollywood directors who managed to maintain his controversy-provoking, violent artistic sensibilities well into the mid-1980s, lamented at the turn of the decade, "I sense a repressive era beginning in the country again" (qtd. in P. Wood D14).

Although calling the era "repressive" borders on hyperbole, in the 1980s there was little room at the Hollywood studios for filmmakers like Arthur Penn, whose finger had been so firmly pressed on the outsider pulse of the late-1960s zeitgeist, or Robert Altman, who was consistently able to reenvision Hollywood's most cherished genres in ways that uncovered their misguided mythological foundations. Such filmmakers had helped the studios out of their financial crises in the late 1960s, but, as it turned out, the future lay in predominantly safe, uncontroversial, big-budget blockbusters that were necessarily devoid of intentionally challenging ideas, particularly those that in any way might be considered radical. As *New York Times* and *Washington Post* Hollywood correspondent Sharon Waxman notes in *Rebels on the Backlot,* this mindset resulted in a film industry where "the tastes of the moguls at the top . . . ran to the middlebrow and the feel-good ending. The tastes of the people who worked for them ran to keeping their jobs, and the best way to do that was to avoid risk whenever possible" (xvi).

Because representations of violence had been so crucial to the meteoric rise of many of the directors of the 1970s, it is not surprising that violence became one of the central controversies surrounding their work in the 1980s. It is not that films became any less violent in the Reagan era; in fact, one could argue that Hollywood films were more violent than ever. The change was in the dominant ideologies behind the representations of violence, which made it increasingly difficult to make films like *Taxi Driver* or *Chinatown* anymore, films that used violence ambivalently to explore the darker recesses of American culture. The major studios' willingness to dabble in aesthetic and ideological experimentation, especially when it came to violence, was coming to an end as conservative formulas gained a stronger foothold in the industry amid a flurry of media coverage that questioned the role of violence in entertainment. For example, in the span of just over a year (1982–83), the *New York Times* ran articles with headlines that declared "Bloodbaths Debase Movies and Audiences" (Maslin, "Film View") and asked such questions as "Is the Violence in 'Blade Runner' a Socially Destructive Element?" (Collins), "How Should We React to Violence?" (Canby, "Film View"), and "Is There a Moral Limit to the Violence in Films?" (Goodman). Meanwhile, the *Saturday Review* put four of the most well known of the New Hollywood auteurs (Martin Scorsese, Brian De Palma, Paul Schrader, and Walter Hill) on the cover of its October 1980 issue with the headline "The Brutalists: Making Movies Mean and Ugly."

The change in how screen violence was depicted was partially due to a power shift in the film industry, as producers began to regain the control they had turned over to directors during the 1970s. As David Ansen wrote in 1985, "Right now Hollywood is undergoing a power shift of enormous significance. The old-fashioned, creative producer is back, and he (and sometimes she) is a hot commodity. No mere check signer, this hands-on new producer models himself on the likes of Selznick and Dore Schary and Alexander Korda and Sam Spiegel, producers who put their imprint on a movie, producers whose names often surpassed the directors they hired and fired" ("Producer"). Thus, representations of violence that did not fit into the blockbuster formula favored by these hands-on producers, many of whom signed multimillion-dollar deals with the major studios, were considered increasingly risky.[2] Judging by the studios' output in the mid-1980s, executives were increasingly unwilling to green-light violent, ideologically challenging projects, or else they demanded that they be reworked to fit their perception of what their audience wanted. For example, as we will see in chapter 3, John Milius's *Red Dawn* (1984) was changed at the insistence of MGM/UA CEO Frank Yablans from its original conception as a dark, *Lord of the Flies*–inspired antiwar story into a more conventionally reactionary action film.

Part of this was likely a response by the studios to changes in the audience, which *New Yorker* critic Pauline Kael sensed in the late 1970s. In her 1978 essay "Fear of Movies," she noted that American film audiences were comprised primarily of "the kids [who] want to get Greased over and over and the literate adults [who] go off to their cozy French detective comedy" (141). For Kael, this meant the death of disturbing, provocative films—the ones that, in her mind, expressed the greatness of the movies: "their power to affect us on so many sensory levels that we become emotionally accessible, in spite of our thinking selves" (137). In the late 1960s and throughout the 1970s, Kael was at the forefront of the American film vanguard, championing tough, violent films like *Bonnie and Clyde*, *Carrie* (1976), and *Taxi Driver*, and she expressed dismay at the shift in what she termed "'more discriminating' moviegoers" who "don't want that sense of danger" and instead "want to remain in control of their feelings" (137). Kael explicitly marked the shift in terms of screen violence, noting that "audiences hiss the sight of blood now. . . . They seem to be saying, 'I don't need this!' They hiss the blood as if to belittle it, to make it less menacing" (141). She connected this directly to the end of the Vietnam War, which is frequently associated with the rise in screen bloodshed, noting that "people had probably had it with movie violence long before the war was over, but they didn't feel free to admit that they really wanted relaxed, escapist entertainment" (142). She also connected the audience's waning interest in tough violence to television, "with its car crashes and knifings and shootings that have no pain or terror in them, and no gore" (147). Filmmakers were catching on to this shifting tide against troubling violence, as well, evidenced in Paul Schrader's joke to John Milius that he had exchanged "violence for design" (qtd. in Biskind 383), which is precisely what he did with 1980's slick and stylish thriller *American Gigolo*.

Universal Pictures learned this directly when it held a public test screening of John Landis's gory horror-comedy *An American Werewolf in London* (1981). The studio's concerns about the level of gore in the film were confirmed when a significant number of the test audience left before the film was over and angrily clustered around the executives' limousines (Bart and Guber 238). Landis and his editor then toned down the violence—the eventual theatrical version was just bloody enough to draw in horror fans but not repulse too many other viewers—and the film became a modest hit at the box office.[3] Similarly, *Los Angeles Times* film critic Charles Champlin blamed the box-office failure of John Frankenheimer's terrorism thriller *Black Sunday* (1977) on the film's violence: "The audience was a little weary of explicit violence, and I think it just—Its moment in time was just wrong for it; that's why it didn't do better, I don't think it had anything to do with the rating. I think the film was extremely well made, but it was just too graphic, I think, and that was the problem with it" (qtd. in Heffner, "Reminiscences," vol. 4, box 5, 689). Audience concern about violence was also evident in a poll conducted by the *Los Angeles Times* in 1987. While nearly 40 percent of the 1,826 respondents indicated an equal amount of concern with the levels of sex, violence, and profanity, 27 percent singled out violence as their primary concern versus 20 percent who singled out sex and only 6 percent who singled out profanity ("Poll Supports Changes").

We can also see this perceived shift in audience tastes and desires reflected in the strengthening of restrictions against screen violence in the late 1970s and throughout the 1980s. In 1978, Richard D. Heffner, who was chair of the Classification and Rating Administration (CARA) from 1974 to 1994, wrote a letter to Sydney Gruson of the *New York Times* in response to the newspaper's request that Heffner write an article to commemorate the rating system's tenth anniversary. In the letter, Heffner noted a specific change in how violence was being judged at the end of the 1970s:

> There has been a switch in recent years, however, and that is what has to be judged today, not the patterns of the past. So what nudity that automatically drew an R years back frequently gets PG-rated today while violence is rated R today that was not restricted before. I can testify to this change, for it has occured [*sic*] during my own tenure as Chairman. And one becomes aware of it when one spends more time in analyzing current films and their ratings than in rehashing out-dated complaints about the classification system. It's why some old-fashioned types claim that I'm a dirty old man for insisting that on screen the human body doesn't always have to be rated R. And it's why a noted filmmaker who couldn't shake his new film's R-for-violence denounced me during an unsuccessful appeal of his rating as "the mortician of the film industry."

> But all of this isn't a function of a Rating Board that's turned dirty-minded; or of members who have somehow gotten fanatical about violence. Rather, it's a result of what we perceive to be changing parental attitudes towards nudity, sex and violence. Parents do seem to be somewhat less concerned now than a decade ago about a bare breast and a suggestive word . . . [ellipses in original] and much more fearful of gore and violence. It is the latter, after all, no longer the former, that is perceived as threatening our very lives. And the Rating Board's responsibility is to reflect this shift in parental emphasis in deciding what part of the rating spectrum from G to X it should assign to this film or that. (Heffner to Gruson, August 14, 1978, in Heffner, "Reminiscences," box 1)

A year later, in a letter to Frank Wells, president of Warner Bros., Heffner warned against being too complacent in light of a recent opinion poll showing positive attitudes toward the major studios:

> That's why I think violence—in word as well as in deed, in language as well as in action—is bound to give the industry more and more trouble. Do you really think otherwise? I believe such violence is more and more anathema to sensitive or at least frightened parents who feel less and less in control over what their kids say and do, and what others say and do to them. And our concern must be that frightened parents will turn to other, perhaps more effective, authorities to do what they cannot do, to make us do what their concerns have not led us to do. (Heffner to Wells, November 15, 1979, in Heffner, "Reminiscences," box 1)

As we will see, Heffner's fears about the potential of audience backlash against screen violence became a reality in the early 1980s when groups picketed the release of films such as *Dressed to Kill* and *Cruising* and parents and critics alike were appalled by the levels of violence allowed in supposed children's films like *Gremlins* and *Indiana Jones and the Temple of Doom*. These exceptions aside, CARA's increasingly harsher ratings on violent films throughout the 1980s was consistently supported by the rating system's Appeals Board, a dozen-member group drawn from the studios; the National Association of Theater Owners (NATO); and the Producers Guild of America—in essence, the major constituent parts of the mainstream U.S. film industry (Vaughn). Thus, their willingness to support CARA in tougher ratings for violent films is indicative of an overall industry desire to skew movies and the violence in them toward a more conservative mainstream.

In addition to changes in audience desires and demographics, the shift in the kinds of movies that filled American theaters in the 1980s was also thoroughly intertwined with changes in the way in which audiences viewed them. Timothy Corrigan argues that economic and technological changes in the film industry in the late 1970s and early 1980s—particularly "the conflux of inflated corporate economics, the multiplication of 'small,' specialty movies to complement blockbusters, and the development of the VCR and other view technologies" (*Cinema* 27)—irrevocably altered moviegoing habits, creating a nostalgia for a time of "humanistic representations and, more importantly, for a filmic and narrative image as the place where meaning is made for the viewer" (24). At the same time, there was a change in moviegoing itself, as viewers no longer went "out to the movies" as a form of social ritual but rather used movies "as a backdrop for their own social activities" (31).

Thus, in the 1980s, it was more difficult for moviegoing to function as a subversive, revolutionary act as it had in the late 1960s. The majority of accessible films did not offer satisfaction on that level, and the very act of moviegoing itself had changed into just one of many escapes from the domestic space, not a ritualistic engagement. The rise of the New Hollywood had coincided neatly with the rise of the youth movement. Young people steeped in existentialist literature, left-wing politics, and antiwar sentiments who were likely to attend rallies, marches, and protests were also among the most avid consumers of New Hollywood cinema, which was viewed as American art film in the vein of Jean-Luc Godard, Luis Buñuel, Michelangelo Antonioni, and other European auteurs. As Justin Wyatt notes, the viability of independent cinema—those films that offered something different, something radical—was largely dependent on the economic turbulence and lack of stability that threatened the studios in the late 1960s, and once they regained their stability in the 1980s, there was less incentive to cater to the counterculture market ("Roadshowing"). By the 1980s, most of the radicals of the late 1960s and 1970s were boomer parents living in the suburbs, and those who had maintained any sense of radicalism were increasingly marginalized in a conservative, synergized movie marketplace that favored "children's films conceived and marketed largely for adults—films that construct an adult spectator as a child, or, more precisely, as a childish adult, an adult who would like to be a child" (R. Wood, *Hollywood* 163). Such films were aimed at the broadest possible audience and designed to continue making money through ancillary markets, particularly the emerging home-video market (see also Krämer, "Would You Take Your Child").

Of course, "the audience" is a tricky concept in film studies because there is the temptation to generalize a single audience for any given time and place when there are always at least two distinctly different audiences: the one the studios and filmmakers imagine when creating and marketing their films and the actual, multivaried groups of human beings who go to the movie theater or, as was increasingly common in the 1980s, the video store. While great strides have been made in recent years in the area of historical reception studies, and more and more scholars are doing primary research on actual audiences, when discussing film history it is more often than not necessary to reduce the audience to faceless statistics or to reconstruct the audience imaginatively through secondary texts, a process that has as many pitfalls as benefits.

In terms of the former approach, there are a few general statements we can make about movie audiences in the 1980s from numbers alone. From a purely economic standpoint based on yearly ticket sales, the theatrical movie audience was quite stagnant. In 1980, ticket sales at U.S. theaters were 1.02 billion, and in 1989 they were 1.26 billion, suggesting that the studios had effectively saturated the theatrical marketplace and were not drawing in new audience members. This was a trend that had been ongoing since the late 1960s, when ticket sales had flatlined at roughly the 1 billion mark (Murphy 5). Thus, in terms of simple numbers, the U.S. audience was and had been steady for two decades, which meant that the studios were competing with each other for the same viewers.

However, this in no way indicates who the studios *thought* was going to the movies, a concept that is much more important when discussing what films they chose to make and how they marketed them. By the 1980s, movie producers arguably knew more about their audiences than at any other point in the history of the cinema. Market research, although dating back to the second decade of the twentieth century, did not become an integral part of the film industry until the 1970s, and by the 1980s it had become common practice (Wyatt, *High Concept*).

Starting in the 1950s, Hollywood had begun to cater its product more and more to youth audiences, particularly older adolescents and teenagers whom the industry recognized as consumers with disposable income whose buying habits made them trendsetters for the culture at large (Doherty). Buoyed by market research, this mentality had a firm grip on the industry by the 1980s, as all indicators suggest that studios saw the movie audience in the early part of the decade as young—generally between eighteen and twenty-five, with teenagers making up 25 percent of the audience—and not particularly interested in "serious" movies. The focus on a younger audience was also heightened because almost 50 percent of teenagers went to the movies at least once a month, whereas only 25 percent of adults attended movies with such frequency (Pampel and Fost). The 1980s was also the decade in which the opening weekend box-office returns became absolutely crucial to a film's profitability. If a film didn't open big, it was almost always doomed to a mediocre box-office performance, if only because the *perception* of its opening weekend failure kept new viewers away. Since teenagers and adolescents were more likely than adults to be part of that opening weekend audience, "pleasing them [could] make or break a big-budget movie" (49). Hollywood did take notice of older viewers in the latter half of the decade, as polls began to show the "graying" of the audience and the gap between younger and older moviegoers narrowing dramatically (Harmetz, "Figures"). The studios responded with more mature films aimed at adult audiences, although these tended to take the form of "sophisticated comedies" such as *Broadcast News* (1987), *Moonstruck* (1988), and *Reversal of Fortune* (1988).

Yet, even though the Hollywood studios have attempted to eliminate uncertainty about their audience as much as possible through decades of test marketing and research, they have continued to rely heavily on intuition and guesswork (see Prince, *New Pot of Gold*). Part of this is because of the long lead time involved in producing a major motion picture: It could be two or three years between preproduction and opening night, and much can change in even that relatively short amount of time. In fact, despite increased emphasis on research and test marketing, Hollywood in the 1980s was characterized by "the uncertainty and instability about the reception of a product that has too many audiences or too vague an audience" (Corrigan, *Cinema* 22–23). Hence, producers attempt to "undifferentiate" the audience, thus "forcing a massive alteration of the conception of an audience . . . [by] appealing to and aiming at not just the largest possible audience (the more modest strategy of classic films) but *all* audiences" (20–21; see also Schatz, "New Hollywood"). This is particularly crucial in terms of how Hollywood films represented violence, because the studios' conception of the mainstream U.S. audience helped to dictate what role screen violence played in their films.

The Continuity of Screen Violence

Even with all the aesthetic, ideological, and economic differences—both large and small—between Hollywood of the 1970s and Hollywood of the 1980s, there were important continuities. For example, most of the characteristics used to describe Hollywood in the 1980s—the focus on blockbusters, the corporate mentality at the expense of artistry, the centrality of emerging ancillary markets and alternative venues of distribution on television and video—all have roots in the 1970s. And, despite their surface differences, both eras were heavy with change. Peter Lev and Stephen Prince might very well be writing about the same decade when the former describes the 1970s as "a period of uncertainty and change . . . [that] was remarkable for its pluralism, its heterogeneity" (185) and the latter describes the 1980s as an era in which "heterodoxy is the norm—a profusion of styles and subjects—tied to the medium's conditions of popularity, its need to appeal to diverse audiences" (*New Pot of Gold* xv).

Cutting across that heterogeneous spectrum of film production in both decades was an even more important, overarching continuity that persisted in spite of the various changes in the industry: screen violence. Screen violence was one of the vital elements, if not *the* vital element, of Hollywood's financial success. In fact, the rise in screen violence through the 1970s and 1980s is one of the most consistent traits of Hollywood cinema. When David Waterman compiled trends over a thirty-five-year period (1967–2001) in the genres of top-performing U.S. films, he found that so-called violence-prone genres (action, adventure, science fiction, thriller, horror, crime, and war) steadily rose from just over 40 percent of Hollywood's output in 1967 to 70 percent by 2001. During that time, both action and adventure films more than doubled in output, from 16 percent to 42 percent and from 14 percent to 30 percent, respectively. These quantitative data show that, at least in terms of types of movies produced, the 1980s was actually a more violent era at the movies than the 1970s, with roughly 65 percent of the output in 1987–1991 being "violence-prone" compared to a little over 50 percent in 1972–1976 (Waterman 228–29).

Thus, while there were many changes in the film industry from the 1970s to the 1980s, the importance of screen violence to Hollywood's success remained because the industry found ways to repackage it to fit the times. Specifically, studios used the high-concept economic imperative to contain screen violence, regardless of the genre or filmmaker intent. Screen violence in popular films of the 1970s was often defended on the grounds of individual artistic vision and appeals to the meaningful connections between the cinema and the increasingly fragmented nature of U.S. society in the wake of the turbulent 1960s. Violent films of the 1980s found little success with such a defense and were instead insulated within a commercial rhetoric of harmless, action-oriented escapism. That the decade of the 1980s opened with a flurry of extremely public battles over screen violence waged by grassroots organizations (the subject of chapter 2) is testament to the slippery nature of the art/society defense and how the acceptability of screen violence fluctuates constantly along with changes in public sentiment, which in turn are influenced by historical events, government policies, and the rhetoric employed by the film community itself.

The first years of the 1980s generally marked the end of the kind of violent films that had characterized much of the 1970s. Complex, ambitious, and potentially controversial films by noted "New Hollywood" auteurs like Coppola's *Apocalypse Now* (1979), De Palma's *Dressed to Kill,* Michael Cimino's *Heaven's Gate* (1980), and Scorsese's *Raging Bull* (1980), all of which caused studio executives significant consternation, were the last vestiges of what has been termed "the golden age of screen violence" (Slocum, "Introduction," 19). Even after the violence in *Heaven's Gate* was trimmed during the notorious re-edit following its disastrous premiere, sneak previews of the film in February 1981 showed that "the violence of the battle sequence was still far too brutal for most moviegoers and that the rape sequence before it—graphic in the sense of violation it imposed on the audience as well as Isabelle Huppert—was everywhere accompanied by (mostly) female walkouts" (Bach 382). And, as much as United Artists president and CEO Andy Albeck admired *Raging Bull* (his response after his first screening of the film was simply, "Mr. Scorsese, you are an Artist"), he never had faith in its box-office potential, even though the finished film reflected six months of script rewrites to make the brutal Jake LaMotta a more understandable character (Bach 347). The 1980s closed with violent movies that were packaged as something of a completely different sort—mainstream, high-concept, audience-pleasing blockbusters like Steven Spielberg's *Indiana Jones and the Last Crusade,* Richard Donner's *Lethal Weapon 2,* and Tim Burton's *Batman,* all of which ruled the summer of 1989 and became the top three highest-grossing films of that year. Together, they sum up how violence was being employed in the majority of U.S. films during the 1980s: as one of many components in the high-concept package explicitly designed to attract as many of the most sought-after demographic as possible while simultaneously avoiding controversy and public outcry.

The changes in screen violence in the 1980s were intertwined with larger changes in both American culture and the Hollywood industry. On the face of it, the 1980s was an era of increasing cultural conservatism. The surface manifestations of symbolic politics created the impression that the country had made a hard swing to the Right, something that the Hollywood studios, ever conscious of their audience base, were sure to notice. Even though there is plenty of evidence that the 1980s had not spelled the absolute death of progressive politics, the impression was that the country as a whole was more conservative than it had been in decades. And, as we have already seen, Richard Heffner and other industry insiders were becoming more and more aware that parents were increasingly concerned about violence at the movies. As Sherill C. Corwin, who was then CEO of Metropolitan Theaters, wrote in a note to Heffner, which Heffner subsequently cited in defense of CARA's having given an R rating to *Blade Runner* (1982), "If we're going to save our collective asses from the censor, we'd better recognize film violence as one of the things that parents hold most against us" (qtd. in Heffner, "Reminiscences," vol. 5, box 5, 899). As a result, the socially conscious, disturbing, and provocative violence that characterized so many films of the 1970s—*The French Connection, Deliverance* (1972), *Taxi Driver*—was being replaced by "safer," though not necessarily less explicit, forms of screen violence. Much of the screen violence deployed in the 1980s was for thrills and entertainment, epitomized best in the rise of the "pure action genre" (the subject of chapter 3). High-concept films such as *Beverly Hills Cop, Top Gun*, and *Die Hard* (1988) were slick and high energy and used violence as an audience-pleasing solution to global problems, which is precisely what Tom Wolfe saw coming back in 1967: "The new pornography is the fantasy of easy triumph in a world where status competition has become so complicated and frustrating" (112). Similar films existed in the 1970s, especially the wave of reactionary vigilante films led by *Dirty Harry* (1971), *Walking Tall* (1973), and *Death Wish* (1974), but those films were characterized by a level of grit and environmental realism that is consciously lacking in high-concept films of the 1980s, which focused much more on fantasy than on inflaming real-life fears about serial killers, urban decay, and increasing crime. While Scorpio, the villainous hippie-killer in *Dirty Harry*, tapped into both mainstream fears about the darker side of the counterculture and the still-unsolved Zodiac killings in the San Francisco Bay area, few if any found any real-life analogous fears raised by the specter of Victor Maitland (Steven Berkoff), the wealthy, drug-smuggling Aryan art dealer in *Beverly Hills Cop*.

The centrality of violence to U.S. filmmaking has a long and storied history, but starting in the late 1960s with the changing political mood and the removal of the Production Code, which had imposed strict limits on how violence could be represented, it rose to new levels on many fronts. Screen violence was more graphically depicted, and it was a primary component of more films. Most important, it was the crucial ingredient that virtually every one of the "New Hollywood" auteurs utilized to establish himself as a major filmmaker. From Coppola's *The Godfather*, to Spielberg's *Jaws* (1975), to Scorsese's *Mean Streets* (1973), most of these heralded directors first made their mark choreographing graphic violence in complex and sometimes troubling ways. Much of this changed in the 1980s as the industry sought to package violence as mass commodity, which it did with great success.

This was accomplished using a variety of methods and film styles, from the hyperaction extravaganzas cooked up by producers Don Simpson and Jerry Bruckheimer, to the kids-in-danger scenarios of Spielberg's "children's" films, to the increasingly outrageous makeup special effects ghastliness of horror films. While different in their own ways, these forms of screen violence were all calculated to draw in the right audience (primarily youth looking for escapism) while generating the least amount of controversy possible—no small feat. While the films of the 1980s were not necessarily less violent quantitatively or qualitatively than their 1970s counterparts, they were often perceived as being so because of their slick packaging and willful dismissal of any serious intent (at least on the surface). For example, in making the 1987 hit *Lethal Weapon*, which teamed Mel Gibson as a possibly psychotic police detective with Danny Glover as his older, more conservative straight-man partner, director Richard Donner purposefully played down explicit violence in favor of a more classical approach: "I tried to make it more like an old-fashioned western. Sure there were a lot of deaths, but they died like they died in westerns. They were shot with bullets, they weren't dismembered. I like action and a strong story line. I like to turn my head away in suspense, not in disgust. I think the audiences feel like I do, and that's why people like the film and come back to see it a second time" (qtd. in Darnton). Thus, Donner insulated the film's ample violence (which includes numerous shoot-outs, car chases, hand-to-hand fighting, and a scene in which Gibson is tortured with electrical shocks) within a buddy-cop story line and a throwback appeal to violence that is exciting, not disturbing, even if it is significantly bloodier and more visceral than the old westerns of Donner's childhood. Thus we can see how, despite the wide variety of screen violence employed in the 1980s, the majority of it was meant to enthrall, not disturb, and the new producers packaged it with remarkable efficiency.

There were certainly ruptures in this system—films like *Salvador* (1985), *Blue Velvet* (1986), *Angel Heart* (1987), and *Henry: Portrait of Serial Killer* (produced in 1986, but not commercially released until 1990)—that employed screen violence to challenge generic expectations, social mores, and conventional ideologies. Yet, films like these that featured hard, disturbing violence were few and far between and were more often than not the product of independent filmmakers and small production companies whose goal was to differentiate their product from the Hollywood mainstream. And, in many instances, these films had significant difficulties getting into the theatrical marketplace. For example, *Salvador*, Oliver Stone's character study of real-life photojournalist Richard Boyle that overtly condemned U.S. foreign policy in El Salvador, was originally supposed to be distributed by Orion Pictures, which had most recently released James Cameron's hit action film *The Terminator* (1984). However, after screening the film in late-cut form, Orion turned it down due to its extreme levels of violence (CEO Mike Medavoy walked out in the middle of the screening). Much of the film's violence, which had already been a source of friction between Stone and producer John Daly, was eventually toned down, but even then no distributor would touch it, and the film's production company, Hemdale, eventually had to release the film itself (Riordan 171–74).

Thus, although films like *Salvador* that featured hard, thought-provoking violence certainly existed in the margins of the Hollywood system, it was usually difficult to get them produced and distributed. And, while many of them gained notice both critically and commercially, their primary role was still as counterpoint to the dominance of the mainstream aesthetic, which tended to promote violence as escapist thrill rather than consciousness-provoking enigma. Or, as Mike Leaveck, communications director for Vietnam Veterans of America, put it in a 1986 article in the *San Francisco Chronicle*, many violent films in the 1980s were "trying to reassert the black-and-white view of global politics. We're trying to simplify our view of the world, to make things comfortable. Hollywood is just learning that they can make some money on this" (qtd. in Beale).

And so they did.

1

A BLOODY RENAISSANCE

SCREEN VIOLENCE AND THE RISE OF THE NEW HOLLYWOOD AUTEURS

THE IDEA THAT THE LATE 1960s and most of the 1970s represent a period of radical change in the American cinema is a given in virtually all recountings of postclassical Hollywood film history. According to David A. Cook, "The American film industry changed more between 1969 and 1980 than at any other period in its history, except, perhaps, for the coming of sound" (*Lost Illusions* 1). Thus, this era is viewed as a historical rupture of massive proportions, a time during which Hollywood production practices, ideologies, audiences, and the films themselves changed so drastically that the subsequent years were labeled the "New Hollywood." The reasons for this revolutionary transformation of the industry are numerous: the recession that put the major studios in severe financial straits and made them vulnerable to takeover by international conglomerates, the demise of the longstanding Production Code and its replacement with the Motion Picture Association of America rating system, the box-office failure of so many formerly successful genres (particularly the musical and the western), and changing audience demographics, not to mention the various corollaries between changes of attitude in Hollywood films regarding sexuality, criminality, and politics and the social upheaval taking place in the streets of America.

In the midst of this industry-wide turmoil rose a new generation of filmmakers who were fundamentally different from their classical Hollywood predecessors. Rather than old-school artisans who had worked their way up through the system, learning the trade of filmmaking from those above them, the so-called Film School Generation was composed of young, brash, self-proclaimed artists who were raised on television and who had studied film in school. Well-versed in the history and aesthetics of world cinema, these filmmakers were in tune with the youth market that made unexpected hits out of fringe films like *Bonnie and Clyde* and *Easy Rider* (1969), and they were primed to revolutionize the American cinema.

Which, in a way, is exactly what they did, creating an "'American film renaissance' of sorts" (Schatz, "New Hollywood" 14). The reservation inherent in that statement—the idea that it was a renaissance "of sorts"—reflects its relatively short duration and the fact that it was eventually subsumed back into the conservative ideological agenda of the industry in the 1980s. Robert Kolker has usefully characterized the New Hollywood of the Film School Generation as a temporary intervention in the tradition of Hollywood filmmaking. At the same time, "despite the influence [of the French New Wave], no 'new wave' in America occurred, no movement. That brief freedom . . . was really a freedom to be alone within a structure that momentarily entertained some experimentation" (9).

However, experimentation did take place, and out of this willingness to experiment, in terms of both reworking the old and bringing in the new, was a reimagining of the role of violence in the cinema—visually, narratively, and thematically. The New Hollywood filmmakers reimagined screen violence by bringing it to the fore of their most important films in ways that both highlighted and subverted the established and understood narrative and thematic tropes of violence in Hollywood filmmaking; at the same time, they gave it a brash visual intensity and level of gut-churning graphic realism that had, with only a few exceptions, never been seen before. Thus, the screen violence of New Hollywood films had the dual edge of radically reworking old and comfortable themes and narrative structures while also introducing what can only be described as "a new way of seeing" violence on-screen. Although these new forms of screen violence are central to the films of virtually every major figure of the New Hollywood, scholarship has made violence at best secondary in the study of their careers. Here I will argue that these new and innovative depictions of screen violence were of primary importance to these young filmmakers and served as a concrete means for them to distinguish themselves from their classical Hollywood forebears. It marked their arrival as the bold, visionary leaders of the New Hollywood.

In this chapter, I will first offer a brief historical overview of representations of violence in the American cinema, starting with the silent era and ending with the rise of the New Hollywood directors in the late 1960s and their dominance throughout the 1970s. I am using the term "auteur" not in the highly romanticized sense of the *politique des auteurs* ("the policy of auteurs") suggested by François Truffaut in his seminal essay "Une certaine tendance du cinema français," in which he advanced the idea that films should be viewed as personal artistic expressions (although New Hollywood directors can also be viewed as auteurs in Truffaut's sense). Rather, I use it in the sense advocated by Timothy Corrigan, which recognizes the utility of the idea of authorship in the cinema but sees that it is as bound up with "industrial desires, technological opportunities, and marketing strategies" as it is with an individual vision or coherent set of stylistic or thematic practices ("Auteurs" 40). This was particularly true in the late 1960s, when Hollywood was in an economic slump and needed a viable strategy to bring audiences back into the theaters. One of these strategies, then, was the conferring of the auteur status on a group of young filmmakers who became "stars" in their own right. As Corrigan notes, the auteur status "aim[s] to guarantee a relationship between audience and movie whereby an intentional and authorial agency governs, as a kind of brand-name vision whose aesthetic meanings and values have already been determined" (40).

My primary contention is that representations of violence were central to the formation of the auteur status and subsequent reputations of the majority of the New Hollywood filmmakers, including Arthur Penn, Francis Ford Coppola, Steven Spielberg, Martin Scorsese, Paul Schrader, and Brian De Palma. Granted, there were some directors associated with this group, including Hal Ashby, Bob Rafelson, Peter Bogdanovich, and Robert Altman, whose careers were not defined by their use of violence. However, even some of these filmmakers experimented with screen violence in their early films, reworking classical norms and drawing direct connections with current events. For example, in *Targets* (1968), his directorial debut, Bogdanovich creates a chilling portrait of a seemingly normal young man whose shooting spree is reminiscent of Charles Whitman's 1966 attack from the clock tower at the University of Texas. In *M*A*S*H* (1970), a military satire that used Korea as a barely disguised stand-in for Vietnam, Altman created revolutionary humor by juxtaposing anarchic jokes with the grisly mise-en-scène of a frontline army hospital. Upending the typical separation of painless comic violence and New Hollywood viscera, Altman's camera never flinches from the oozing gore of the surgery room as the comical army surgeons, caked in blood, try to stop squirting arteries and extract shrapnel from shredded bodies.

Part of the mythos of the auteur is the perception that he or she can mold particular conventions, which is what drew the New Hollywood auteurs to screen violence. When screen violence was released from the strictures of the Production Code in the late 1960s, vast new potentials for violent representation were opened up that had, until that point, been restricted. Screen violence was thus something the New Hollywood auteurs could give their own imprimatur, to prove that they had complete control over the medium and to distinguish themselves from the masters of the classical Hollywood era. To put it simply, screen violence was how they left their mark.

Violence in the American Cinema, 1896–1959

Violence has been a fundamental component and successful selling point in the American cinema since Thomas Alva Edison and William Kennedy Laurie Dickson invented the first motion picture camera, the Kinetograph, in 1890. As Thomas R. Atkins points out, "There is plenty of evidence to indicate that violence, real and recreated, has always been a popular subject with moviegoers" (5; see also French 60). These include the brief newsreels and short films at the end of the nineteenth century that, following the path blazed by sensationalistic penny papers and yellow journalism, dealt directly with war, crime, assassinations, and executions, as well as films of boxing matches (real and re-created), cockfights, natural disasters, and other forms of chaos. This fascination with violent spectacle led to some truly disturbing early films, including the Edison Co.'s *Electrocuting an Elephant* (1903), in which Topsy, a three-ton Coney Island elephant, was electrocuted in front of the camera lens, the primary purpose being to illustrate the dangers of alternating current, which challenged Edison's direct current for dominance in the newly emerging electrical marketplace.

One of the most popular forms of early cinema was the historical recreation, and not surprisingly these tended to lean toward violent moments in history. The Edison Co.'s 1894 film *The Execution of Mary, Queen of Scots* made the most of its unambiguous title by using stop-motion substitution to depict the queen's beheading beneath the blade of an executioner's ax in what appeared to be a seamless single shot, which illustrates early cinema's fascination with both violent spectacle and the various means in which the cinematic apparatus could be manipulated to create the illusion of realistic violence. The Spanish-American War also provided plenty of excuses to restage violent encounters in order to depict the "savagery" of the Spanish and thus support American involvement in the war. Such films included *Cuban Ambush* (1898) and *Shooting Captured Insurgents* (1898), the latter of which is a surprisingly disturbing documentary-like recreation of insurgents being executed by gunfire. Early cinema also mixed the modalities of comedy and graphic violence (G. King); for example, in Cecil Hepworth's *Explosion of a Motor Car* (1900), a car full of people inexplicably explodes, resulting in the comical raining of dismembered body parts on an investigating officer.

With the development of more sophisticated narrative films, such as Edwin S. Porter's *The Great Train Robbery* (1903), the medium's fascination with, and proclivity for, violence became even more direct. Even in this nascent stage, filmmakers were already playing with notions of identification and how screen violence functioned narratively, thematically, and visually. As Charles Musser argues, the infamous emblematic shot in *The Great Train Robbery*, which featured actor Justus D. Barnes firing his six-shooter directly into the camera, "added realism to the film by intensifying the spectators' identification with the victimized travelers" (354–55). Porter's use of such a direct and assaulting violent image as his emblematic shot, which functioned in early cinema to establish narrative, genre, and tone—to serve, in fact, as a metonym for the entire film (Hayward 98)—is a clear indicator of the centrality of violence in the minds of the earliest cinematic pioneers.

As silent films became more narratively and thematically complex, they continued to develop means of integrating violence into both the story lines and the visual spectacle. D. W. Griffith's *The Birth of a Nation* (1915) was replete with violent images, from large-scale battle sequences, to a character committing suicide by jumping off a cliff, to threats of rape. A large portion of the one-reelers Griffith made for the Biograph Company were violent reenactments of Civil War battles and Indian raids, the latter most notably depicted in *The Battle at Elderbush Gulch* (1914). However, it was Griffith's next feature-length film, the gloriously ambitious *Intolerance* (1916), that is the real eye-opener in terms of just how explicit screen violence could be in the silent era. While most scholars have noted how the silent era was quite permissive in terms of depicting sexuality and (particularly female) nudity prior to the formation of the Motion Picture Producers and Distributors of America (MPPDA) in 1922 and its subsequent attempts to control movie content, the existence of on-screen gore is not often mentioned. Yet, in the battle sequences in *Intolerance*, Griffith gives us full view of two decapitations, bodies being pierced by arrows, and an unedited shot of a character having a spear driven into his stomach, replete with gushing blood. As John McCarty notes, "Griffith was obviously not fooling around. He wanted his battle scenes to have the sting of authenticity, to be both brutal and shocking" (10). For the most part, *Intolerance* is the exception, rather than the rule, in depictions of graphic violence in the silent era, but the few seconds of explicit gore it offers show that the impulse to create vivid, brutal images is nearly as old as the cinematic medium itself.[1]

Other silent-era filmmakers also experimented with instances of graphic violence, including Lewis Milestone, who created one of the most indelible war images in his 1930 version of *All Quiet on the Western Front* when he depicted a soldier being hit by a grenade while charging the German trenches, leaving only his dismembered hands clutching a barbed

3. The brief glimpses of explicit gore during the Babylonian battle sequences in *Intolerance* (1916) show that the impulse to create vivid, brutal representation of violence on-screen is nearly as old as the cinematic medium itself. DVD still.

wire fence. While bullet strikes were often left to the imagination, some filmmakers found ways to visualize them directly. In *Hell's Angels* (1930), Howard Hughes depicted a character being shot in the back by actually shooting the actor with an ink-soaked plug of sponge rubber from a starting pistol (Cook, "Ballistic Balletics" 131).

The specter of criminality and its attendant violence was a constant lure for Hollywood, and the second and third decades of the twentieth century saw the production of numerous films whose stories of murder were ripped straight from salacious headlines, often starring the actual people whose lives were being depicted (F. Miller 23). The 1920s and 1930s saw a rash of gangster films (*Little Caesar*, 1930; *The Public Enemy*, 1931; *Scarface*, 1932) that had violence seething at their core, as well as a string of horror movies (*Dracula*, 1931; *Frankenstein*, 1931; *The Mummy*, 1932; *The Bride of Frankenstein*, 1935) produced by Universal Studios. Although the violence of these two genres was not explicitly forbidden by the MPPDA's original Production Code, which was adopted in 1930 in an effort to govern the content of movies, both constantly ran afoul of local and state censors and were eventually banned outright, the former in the United

States and the latter in Great Britain. When the MPPDA reworked the Production Code in 1934 with more explicit instructions on how to handle violence and gruesomeness and a renewed vow by the member studios to enforce them, instances of graphic violence like the ones glimpsed in *Intolerance* were all but outlawed.

Scholars most frequently focus on how the majority of the Production Code (in all of its incarnations) addressed issues of sexual morality (the longest section under the "Particular Applications" section amended to the Code in 1934 is "Sex," with nine specific subsections), as did the subsequent controversies when filmmakers clashed with the Code's enforcement mechanism, the Production Code Administration (PCA; see, for example, Leff and Simmons). However, on-screen violence was also addressed specifically under the last of the amended "Particular Applications," labeled "Repellent Subjects." This section warned filmmakers of the following:

> The following subjects must be treated within the careful limits of good taste:
>
> 1. *Actual hangings* or electrocutions as legal punishments for crime.
> 2. *Third Degree* methods.
> 3. *Brutality* and possible gruesomeness.
> 4. *Branding* of people or animals.
> 5. *Apparent cruelty* to children or animals.
> 6. *The sale of women,* or a woman selling her virtue.
> 7. *Surgical operations.* (qtd. in Leff and Simmons 286)

Also, under "Crimes Against the Law," the opening section of the "Particular Applications," it explicitly states, "*Brutal killings* are not to be presented in detail" (284). This meant that the stylistic approaches used to depict violence had to be significantly curtailed, which resulted in Hollywood movie violence that was largely unrealistic and pain-free.

However, some instances of explicit violence still slipped through. For example, *Show Them No Mercy* (1935) was a rare film in which bullet strikes were graphically depicted on a victim by firing inked plugs at a clear screen in front of the actor being shot (Prince, *Classical Film Violence* 119). The enforcers of the Code also relaxed during World War II and allowed filmmakers to be more graphic in their depictions of war-related violence, even though such films still resorted to unrealistic visual codes such as the "clutch and fall" manner of gracefully collapsing after being shot. *Pride of the Marines* (1945) offers an interesting case study in this respect (155–58). It includes a number of surprisingly graphic moments of violence, including the use of an exploding squib to depict a character being shot in the arm. At another point in the film, a U.S. Marine named Johnny is shot in the head, which in and of itself was a rarity for Hollywood cinema. However, the bullet strike is also clearly depicted both visually (his helmet bends inward and a puff of smoke bursts out of the hole) and aurally (on the soundtrack we hear the thud of the bullet). This visual realism is temporarily interrupted by Johnny's actual death, in which he gently sinks to the ground. However, verisimilitude is then reasserted with a close-up of his dead face, which is "unmistakably a body done to death by violence, without the cosmetic gloss that typically surrounded violent death in [classic Hollywood] movies" (157). Other war films of that era depicted forms of violence that would have normally hit the cutting room floor at the insistence of the PCA, including an enemy soldier being clearly bayoneted and an African American soldier being nearly decapitated in *Bataan* (1943).

The increased graphic nature of screen violence in World War II films, which the PCA allowed given the historical circumstances, inevitably carried over into the postwar era. As James Naremore notes, "It was violence, not sex, that accounted for the most visible changes in the standards of motion-picture censorship during the 1940s and early 1950s" (102). The visible changes in screen violence are particularly evident in the rash of postwar crime films (many of which are included in the category of film noir) such as *Brute Force* (1947), which features a sadistic guard beating a prisoner with a length of rubber hose and culminates in the machine-gunning of dozens of people in a scene that prefigures *The Wild Bunch*'s (1969) apocalyptic finale by more than twenty years; *Kiss of Death* (1947), in which a deranged gangster pushes a disabled woman in a wheelchair down a flight of stairs to her death; *Raw Deal* (1948), in which the villain throws a flaming fondue into a woman's face; *Gun Crazy* (1949), which predates *Bonnie and Clyde* with its romanticized story of an outlaw couple on the run; *Border Incident* (1949), which depicts an undercover policeman being slowly run over by a tractor; *The Big Heat* (1953), whose most notorious scene of sexual sadism depicts Lee Marvin hurling a pot of scalding hot coffee into a woman's face; and *Kiss Me Deadly* (1955), which begins with a woman being tortured to death with a pair of pliers (offscreen, of course, although her anguished screams tell us as much as we need to know) and ends with the femme fatale being burned alive by an exploding atomic device.

As these examples illustrate, although the specifics of the Production Code limited the graphic display of on-screen violence from the 1930s until the Code's final dismantling in the late 1960s, violence was always present. It might not have been as gory, graphic, or realistic as contemporary screen violence, but it was there. After all, violence, in one form or another, is the basis of all drama. Thus, it can never be removed entirely

4. The climactic machine-gunning of dozens of inmates in *Brute Force* (1947) prefigures the apocalyptic finale of *The Wild Bunch* (1969) by more than twenty years. DVD still.

from any entertainment realm that relies on drama as its foundation. It can only be toned down, disguised, hidden from view, or denied. But, it is always there, which is why, as one can see from the exact wording of the Production Code, there is no decree that violent subjects had to be avoided altogether, as some other subjects were (for example, "sex perversion," "white slavery," and "pointed profanity"). Violence could remain a staple element of Hollywood films, so long as it was "treated within the careful limits of good taste." Thus, brutally violent acts like strangulation (as in, for example, *Double Indemnity*, 1944), dismemberment (*Rear Window*, 1954), torture (*Kiss Me Deadly*), or bodily mutilation (*The Searchers*, 1956) were depicted using a complex series of aesthetic strategies described by Stephen Prince as "substitutional poetics," which emerged directly out of the regulatory pressures exerted by the Production Code (*Classical Film Violence* 205). Thus, unlike other production processes and aspects of film style that developed in response to necessary economic strategies and concerns for narrative efficiency, the depiction of violence in the classical

Hollywood era was shaped almost entirely by the filmmakers' need to adhere to the tenets of the Code.

According to Prince, there were a number of primary visual codes employed by filmmakers during the classical era to depict violent actions that were crucial to the narrative but were too gruesome to show directly. These codes were part of the "unstable equilibrium" of classical film violence: owing to changes in style and various periods in which enforcement of the Production Code was either relaxed or strengthened, films of this era contained both direct and indirect violence. Nevertheless, these visual codes were routinely used to convey violent action, so much so that they have become part of the "deep structure" of cinema and continue to be used even after the fall of the Production Code and the opening of restraints on screen violence in the late 1960s. Thus, these codes cross all boundaries, including genre, historical period, and filmmaker (*Classical Film Violence* 220).

The most inartistic and direct visual code is spatial displacement, which "removes the viewer from a vantage point where violence may be directly witnessed" (Prince, *Classical Film Violence* 208). This was accomplished in various ways, the most common being either a direct cut away from the violent action or moving the camera so the action was no longer in view, thus relegating the violence to offscreen space. Rather than simply hiding the violence, filmmakers also used strategies such as metonymic displacement, "in which the occlusive or evasive composition contains some object or action that stands in for the violence that is occurring out of view" (220). Prince offers an example from *Scarface* in which a bowling pin spinning and falling stands in for the collapsing body of Gaffney (Boris Karloff) as he is shot offscreen by Tony Camonte (Paul Muni) and his gang. Indexical pointing is a similar concept, except that what we see on-screen has a direct connection to the violence that is taking place offscreen. A good example of this is "shadow play," in which we see a violent action rendered only as shadows on a wall, which allows us to see exactly what is happening, although indirectly (Prince cites several good examples, including the initial killing in *Scarface* and the killer ape strangling Dr. Mirakie in 1932's *Murders in the Rue Morgue*). Other strategies include substitutional emblematics, which evolved out of the proscription against showing the physical, bloody wounding of the body and thus displaced that violence onto other objects (for example, the drive-by shootings in numerous gangster films that tore property to shreds), and emotional bracketing, which allowed the viewer to "recover and catch his or her breath following an episode of violence that is intense, startling, or with serious consequences for the narrative and one or more of its major characters" (244–45). Although not all films of the classical era used all of these visual codes to depict violent actions, together they formed the dominant means by which violence was conveyed prior to the 1960s.

The Rise of Graphic Violence: 1960–1970s

While direct, graphic presentations of violence are scattered throughout the history of Hollywood cinema, the 1960s is often singled out as the period when movie screens were increasingly awash in the reddish glow of free-flowing blood and gore. The use of substitutional poetics persisted, but filmmakers grew more and more brash and confident in their ability to show violence directly, rather than displacing it onto other visual elements or eliding it completely. It is not that there was an increase in violent content; instead, "it [was] the form and intensity of violence that . . . changed, rather than its quantity" (French 61). For the first time, mainstream movie audiences saw blood squibs used to show the actual moment of impact when a bullet hit a body, and watched as characters had their throats slit, bodies disemboweled, heads cut off, and any number of other graphically depicted physical violations, all in bright Technicolor on larger-than-life widescreens. And audiences responded in large numbers at the box office.

The incremental shifts in the explicitness of screen violence throughout the 1960s were clear to those who were experiencing them firsthand (particularly youth audiences enraptured by exploitation horror films and imported art-house fare), although it was really in the last years of the 1960s that the door to graphic violence in the mainstream cinema was flung wide open and, crucially, stayed open. Why, after more than forty years of general restraint, did the mainstream Hollywood movie industry rapidly dive headfirst into depictions of graphic violence? And, more important, why did audiences—no longer just youth and fringe audiences, but the mainstream, as well—respond to it so immediately? The answer is complicated, with reasons that are both direct and indirect, within the Hollywood industry and outside of it.

The most obvious and direct reason for this change in how violence was represented on-screen was the dissolution of the Production Code and its replacement with the rating system in 1968. An indirect—and, arguably, more important—reason was the climate change in America with the Vietnam War, the civil rights movement, urban riots, public assassinations, an escalation in street crime, and antiwar protests. Also, the rising youth audience was central to the increasingly violent films because they made them successful at the box office. And, finally, it is important to point to the effects of the general economic state of the film industry, which was suffering through a massive industry-wide recession starting in

1969. The confluences and interaction of these four factors unexpectedly led to the willingness of the major studios and American audiences to not only stomach unprecedented representations of violence but eventually to embrace them as a recurrent element of popular American cinema. And this violence was absolutely central to the rise of the New Hollywood auteurs and the cementing of their artistic and commercial reputations throughout the tumultuous 1970s, which is why so many of them had difficulties adjusting when industry and social attitudes changed in the more conservatively minded and economically stable 1980s.

The End of the Production Code

As we have seen, the Production Code, which was established by the MPPDA (later renamed the Motion Picture Association of America in 1946), had exerted significant control over motion picture content since the 1930s. However by the early 1950s, the Code was coming under increasing attack for being outdated and useless, particularly in its strictures against representations of sexuality.

In the 1952 court case *Burstyn v. Wilson*, the motion picture medium was finally given protection as free speech under the First Amendment (the decision was later referred to as the *Miracle* decision after the Italian film that spurred the case). Throughout the 1950s and early 1960s, the Production Code was challenged again and again by filmmakers with artistic and economic clout. Immediately following the *Miracle* decision, Otto Preminger, declaring the Production Code "antiquated," distributed his comedy *The Moon Is Blue* (1953) without a Production Code Seal of Approval. This had been done before (notably by Howard Hughes in 1946 with *The Outlaw*), but the difference here was that Preminger's film turned a profit, showing that the PCA's threat of economic sanctions against films shown without a seal of approval was losing its bite. Preminger did the same thing again in 1956 with *The Man with the Golden Arm*, a frank depiction of drug addiction. But the final nail in the coffin of the Production Code was MGM's successful run with Michelangelo Antonioni's *Blow-up* (1966), which was distributed under a separate non-MPAA subsidiary in order to avoid fines (see Lewis, *Hollywood* 146–48).

In response to this climate of prevailing change, the MPAA announced the creation of an age-based, exhibitor-enforced rating system. The rating system, which was officially put into effect on November 1, 1968, opened the door to violence in studio-financed movies. Unlike the Production Code, which had as its fundamental basis the idea that all movies, regardless of topic or intent, should be appropriate for a generic family audience, the MPAA rating system for the first time in the industry's history codified in a set of guidelines the idea that different movies are appropriate or inappropriate for different audiences based on their age.[2] Somewhat confusingly, however, the MPAA did not give up completely on the Production Code itself and instead retained a shortened version that contained eleven "Standards for Production" that read conspicuously like the greatest hits from the old Production Code of 1934. According to Stephen Farber, who was a member of the Rating Board for six months in 1970, these "Standards" were almost never raised in board discussions regarding the rating of a particular movie (*Ratings Game* 16), which leads one to believe that they were largely a form of public relations intended to maintain the public's belief that the MPAA still cared about traditional values, despite the radical changes in the content of movies produced by its studio members.

Nevertheless, those radical changes were a direct result of one of the first declared objectives of the new rating system, which, according to an official explanatory brochure printed by the MPAA in 1968, was "to encourage artistic expression by expanding creative freedom" (qtd. in Farber, *Ratings Game* 112). Filmmakers working for the studios took advantage of it almost immediately because they realized that movie audiences were not only ready for harder-edge fare but hungry for it. As Prince notes,

> The impetus for this new climate of creative freedom was the gale winds of social protest and counterculture values that swept through American society after 1966 and, of more immediate economic and institutional importance, the emergence of a sizable youth audience for motion pictures and of a younger generation of studio executives who were willing to flout motion picture conventions. (*Savage Cinema* 14)

In other words, the mainstream market was simply ready for something new, which, in this case, consisted of (among other things) graphic onscreen violence. The new freedom of violence was part of the culmination of what film historian Gerald Mast had termed "The Years of Transition," where the "conservative inertia of both Hollywood and its audience was first tested" (qtd. in Ray 131). If this was true of the tentative nature of change characterized by social-liberal films of the 1940s and 1950s, then the cinema of the late 1960s can be seen as an outright slap in the face to both conservative movie moguls who were still cemented in traditional Hollywood mythmaking and those audiences who had grown up with and were accustomed to that mythology.

A Violent Social Climate

Indirectly responsible for, but just as important to, the rise of graphic violence in the 1960s was the changing social climate in America. According to Philip French, "Violence on the screen tends . . . to take its character and form (if often obliquely) from the mood of the time and place in which it is made" (64). During the 1960s, violence in American society was an unavoidable—almost omnipresent—fact of life. "Violence was endlessly talked about, feared, skirted, flirted with" (Gitlin 316). As Tom Shachtman notes, "With each passing year the times themselves seemed to become more violent" (52). In fact, crime was reaching "near epidemic proportions" during this time period. Between 1965 and 1968, more than a dozen civil rights leaders were assassinated, gun homicides were increasing by 15–20 percent each year, and the rate of all violent crime doubled (52, 61–62).

Aside from the violence, the 1960s represented one of the most important decades in modern American history in terms of social change. Historian Eric Goldman asserts that the 1960s was "a watershed as important as the American Revolution or the Civil War in causing changes in the US" (qtd. in Ray 250). The laundry list of societal change that took place during that decade is impressive in its length and daunting in its cultural importance: the assassinations of such important figures as Martin Luther King Jr., John F. Kennedy, Robert Kennedy, and Malcolm X; large-scale protests against American involvement in Vietnam; the rise (and eventual fall) of widespread liberalism (Steigerwald); the women's liberation movement; the rise of youth culture and its relationship to drug culture and the reinscription of the American family (Hobsbawm); and the violence, turmoil, and eventual progress of the civil rights movement. Any one of those events is worthy of a detailed study on its own, but for the purposes of this argument, their importance lies in their cumulative effect. Taken together, all these rapid social changes reflected a kind of violence in and of themselves—an attack on previously held assumptions and traditional values that had defined the American way of life.

However, in a more direct sense, Americans were being bombarded with violent images outside of the movie theaters. Vietnam marked the first time television brought a war home to the American family and allowed it to play out in the suburban living room; "images without precedent seized the small screen" (Gitlin 298). With almost unlimited access, journalists (both print and television) and filmmakers went into the heat of battle in Southeast Asia and broadcast graphic images of the cost of war. According to Irwin Unger and Debbie Unger:

> They [reporters] strained for the vivid vignette that would stand out from the gray fact and rivet the reader's attention. They talked inevitably of blood, fear, rage, and destruction. TV, even more than print, reached for the striking image, and the cameramen

> scrambled to supply the networks with footage of shattered and burning buildings, bandaged American grunts, and heaped-up civilian bodies. (103)

Of course, violent images were not relegated to the television screens alone. The morning newspaper often carried disturbing and graphic images from the war, including Associated Press photographer Eddie Adams's infamous 35mm photograph of the moment of death when General Nguyen Ngoc Loan, head of the South Vietnamese national police, executed a Vietcong officer in the streets of Saigon. This picture not only made it to the front page of the *New York Times* but also ran as news footage on *The Huntley-Brinkley Report* (Unger and Unger 105).

Jack Valenti, president of the MPAA, emphasized the link between Vietnam's presence in the American home and what was happening on movie screens: "For the first time in the history of this country, people are exposed to instant coverage of a war in progress. When so many movie critics complain about violence on film, I don't think they realize the impact of thirty minutes on the Huntley-Brinkley newscast—that's real violence" (qtd. in Prince, *Savage Cinema* 25). What Valenti's rhetoric shows is not simply a reactionary defense of the new cinematic violence that pervaded American films in the late 1960s but a reflection of how events like the Vietnam War were seeping into the culture and helping to define our outlook. As Todd Gitlin notes:

> Vietnam, whose flattened TV images were the culture's cliché, was at once remote and queerly, heartbreakingly present. So were the ghetto firestorms. So violence and the threat of violence became stark and factual to us in an eerie way—as abstractions. Having stepped into the aura of violence, many of the middle-class young were stunned into a tolerance, a fascination, even a taste for it. (318)

These middle-class young viewers with a "taste" for violence were coming to movie theaters in record numbers. By 1968, a survey showed that 48 percent of the moviegoing public was comprised of eighteen- to twenty-four-year-olds (Knight 333).

Filmmakers of the late 1960s, especially Sam Peckinpah and Arthur Penn, did not see the blood-soaked newscasts of Vietnam footage as an excuse to heighten violence in the cinema; rather, they saw it as an imperative. According to social psychologist Kenneth Keniston, "*The issue of violence is to this generation what the issue of sex was to the Victorian world*" (qtd. in Gitlin 316; emphasis in original). Because the vast majority of the American public was, for the first time, witnessing the kind of damage bullets and shrapnel can do to the human body through the Vietnam footage shown directly in their living rooms, these filmmakers felt that they could no longer brush off death and violence. It could no longer be minimized on-screen, because that would be a disservice to the nature of violence itself. As film critic Pauline Kael notes in her review of *Bonnie and Clyde*, "The dirty reality of death—not suggestions but blood and holes—is necessary" (*Kiss Kiss* 69).

Sam Peckinpah, sometimes referred to as "Bloody Sam" because of the intense violence in many of his films, was by far the most outspoken filmmaker in connecting the strands of violence in American culture and violence in the American cinema. Peckinpah claimed that he used graphic violence in his films to make a point about violence itself: "I use violence as it *is*. It's ugly, brutalizing, and bloody fucking awful. It's not fun and games. . . . It's a terrible, ugly thing" (qtd. in Farber, "Peckinpah's Return" 8). Prince has made a long and detailed argument for the link between societal violence in the 1960s and filmic violence in Peckinpah's late-1960s and early-1970s films, most notably *The Wild Bunch* and *Straw Dogs* (1971). As Prince notes, "The sociocultural revolution within American society was generating a complex empirical and ideological support system that would legitimize and nourish Peckinpah's personal and creative inclinations" (*Savage Cinema* 11). In other words, Peckinpah's (as well as other filmmakers') graphic depictions of on-screen violence sprang from the particular era in which he was working. While some of this is undoubtedly related to the removal of Production Code–era restrictions on what could and could not be shown on American movie screens, Prince stresses that it was also the societal impetus that fueled the new violence: "The exceptional brutality in *The Wild Bunch* cannot be separated from the social climate in which it was made because it is inextricably a part of that environment, as were Peckinpah's intentions in representing violence on screen" (27).

While Prince tends to minimize this social influence on other directors of violent cinema in the same time period, it is hard to imagine that the overwhelming cultural revolution taking place in the United States and its accompanying social violence did not affect them as well. While not nearly as outspoken as Peckinpah, numerous other directors at that time also emphasized the relation of on-screen violence with its counterpart in real life. This could take different forms, including the perceived need to make screen violence more physically realistic. For instance, in his discussion of a particularly brutal murder sequence in *Torn Curtain* (1966), Alfred Hitchcock noted: "In doing that long killing scene, my first thought again was to avoid the cliché. In every picture somebody gets killed and it goes very quickly. They are stabbed or shot, and the killer never even stops to look and see whether the victim is really dead or not. And I thought it was time to show that it was very difficult, very painful, and it takes a very long time to kill a man" (qtd. in Truffaut 311).

On the other hand, some filmmakers felt that the violence in their films was directly related to the social violence of the 1960s. This was not far from Arthur Penn's mind when he conceived the final scene depicting the deaths of Bonnie and Clyde. He once noted: "America is a country of people who act out their views in violent ways. Let's face it: Kennedy was shot. We're in Vietnam shooting people and getting shot. . . . It is the American society, and I would have to personify it by saying that it is a violent one. So why not make films about it" (qtd. in Bouzereau, *Ultraviolent Movies* 11). In one shot in the final death scene, part of Clyde's head is clearly blown off, which Penn intended audiences to associate with the manner in which Kennedy had been assassinated (Biskind 35).

Film critics quickly picked up on this connection between screen violence and real-life violence, and it divided them sharply. Bosley Crowther, the long-standing critic for the *New York Times*, was steadfastly against the new screen violence, and he decried the use of violence in films like *The Dirty Dozen* (1966) and *Bonnie and Clyde*: "By habituating the public to violence and brutality . . . films of excessive violence only deaden the sensitivities and make slaughter seem like a meaningless cliché" ("Smash"). Pauline Kael, writing for the *New Yorker*, took a vastly different view of "excessive violence," especially as it was represented in *Bonnie and Clyde*: "Suddenly, in the last few years, our view of the world has gone beyond 'good taste.' Tasteful suggestions of violence would at this point be a more grotesque form of comedy than *Bonnie and Clyde* attempts. *Bonnie and Clyde* needs violence; violence is its meaning. . . . It's a kind of violence that says something to us; it is something that movies must be free to use" (*Kiss Kiss* 69). Caught somewhere in the middle was Joe Morgenstern, the critic for *Newsweek* who found himself in the uncomfortable position of having to retract his earlier review of *Bonnie and Clyde*, in which he had dismissed the film as a "squalid shoot-'em for the moron trade." In his retraction, he made a strong and articulate statement about the necessity of cinematic violence and the manner in which it should function:

> Violent movies are an inevitable consequence of violent life. They may also transmit the violence virus, but they do not breed it any more than the Los Angeles television stations caused Watts to riot. Distinctions can and must be made between violent films that pander and violent films that enlighten, between camp, comment and utter cynicism. And there is nothing like the movies for

giving us historical perspective on violence we have known, and in many cases loved. (82)

The Youth Audience

Most forms of increasingly graphic screen violence in the 1960s appeared mainly in genre films that played around the fringes of the mainstream motion picture business. All of these genres—the horror film, the spaghetti western, exploitation cheapies—which were made possible by the dismantling of the Production Code, were almost entirely the province of a new youth audience comprised largely of teenagers and college students who had emerged as a powerful market force in the 1950s and 1960s (Doherty).

A 1968 study by Daniel Yankelovich showed that 48 percent of box-office admissions went to sixteen- to twenty-four-year-olds, and 54 percent of that group were "frequent moviegoers." Yankelovich concluded, "Being young and single is the overriding demographic pre-condition for being a frequent and enthusiastic moviegoer" (qtd. in Doherty 231). Not surprisingly, the young had different tastes and tolerances than the older moviegoing demographic that made them more inclined toward edgier fare, which included increasingly graphic representations of violence. Along with this youth market came "a demand for a new kind of product which was largely defined by its *devaluation* in relation to the respectable and cultured adult mind" (Hoberman and Rosenbaum 115). Not surprisingly, such films frequently traded in visual representations of violence, whether outwardly horrific (for example, *Night of the Living Dead*, 1968), campy and satirical (for example, *Pink Flamingos*, 1972), or self-parodying (for example, virtually any film released by American International Pictures). This exposure to screen violence in popular, if often illicit, genre films made young moviegoers "experts" in their conventions, which undermined many of the fears that they would somehow be damaged by watching. As Jon Fraser notes, "The young may in some ways be more accurate than some of their elders in their perceptions of a good deal of fictional violence, and better able to distinguish between realistic and stylized violences, intentionally and unintentionally comic ones, and so on, than is often allowed for" (8–9). The youth audience was also more willing and eager to shift between high and low genres (Hawkins), allowing them to appreciate in their own way the differences between the stark, symbolic, and psychological violence in films by Michelangelo Antonioni and Ingmar Bergman and the graphic physical violence of B-grade thrillers and horror movies. As Joan Hawkins notes in her discussion of Pauline Kael's essay "Zeitgeist and Poltergeist, or Are Movies Going to

Pieces," the "loud and unmediated carnival spirit" that characterized the youth audience responses is "one way in which art house, avant-garde, and horror audiences were linked in this period" (59).

The Effects of the Recession

A fourth factor that affected the rise of graphic violence on American movie screens in the late 1960s was the economic recession that struck the industry and left it virtually paralyzed. Various industry estimates have put the collective studio losses from 1969 to 1971 at $300 to $400 million (Cook, *Lost Illusions* 9), which forced the industry to the edge of collapse. Weekly audience attendance was shrinking, reaching an all-time low in 1971 of 15.8 million (14),[3] while average studio profits fell from $64 million in the five-year span 1964–68 to only $13 million during 1969–73 (Dominick as qtd. in Schatz 15).

This was an especially painful development because it came on the heels of a decade of success characterized by a general boom in entertainment and leisure activities (Belton, ch. 4). In the 1950s, Hollywood's hegemonic dominance over mass entertainment had been threatened by the rise of television and other leisure activities like theme parks. But, once again proving its resilience, the industry had met the challenge by engaging in television production (Anderson) and by transforming the moviegoing experience into one of active recreation, with technological developments like 3-D, surround sound, and widescreen processes (Belton) and changes in exhibition with the rise of family-friendly drive-ins on one end and high-price, spectacular road-show event movies on the other. The decade-long period encompassing the mid- to late-1950s and early 1960s was bookended by two colossal megahits, *The Ten Commandments* (1956), which earned $43 million at the domestic box office, and *The Sound of Music* (1965), which made almost $80 million (Schatz, "New Hollywood" 13).

Thomas Schatz ("New Hollywood"), Richard Maltby, David A. Cook (*Lost Illusions*), and others argue that the recession at the end of the 1960s was a direct result of the overvaluation of earlier successes of that decade. Specifically, as Hollywood is wont to do, the industry tried to capitalize on its previous hits by churning out more of the same. Unfortunately, while that is a formula that has reaped massive profits before and since, in this situation it failed miserably because the shift in American culture in the late 1960s left audiences largely uninterested in the kinds of movies that had packed them into theaters several years earlier. By the time the studios realized this, however, it was too late. From 1966 to 1968, they engaged in a gluttonous spree of overproduction that was inspired by the rampant success of *The Sound of Music.* This resulted in a string of deadly box-office bombs that tried to mimic *The Sound of Music*'s formula, including *Doctor Dolittle* (1967, lost $11 million), *Star!* (1968, lost $15 million), and *Hello, Dolly!* (1969, lost $16 million) (Schatz, "New Hollywood" 14). The major studios' problem was further aggravated by the entry of two new "instant majors" in 1967, National General Corporation and Cinerama Releasing, which produced even more films that further crowded the already failing marketplace, drove up the price of talent by aggressively bidding for star power, and drove down distributors' box-office take to less than 30 percent by offering exhibitors especially good splits in order to compete (Cook, *Lost Illusions* 10).

As a result, the studios found themselves on the shakiest financial ground they had experienced since the period following the end of the Studio Era. The severity of this economic collapse can be gauged in the number of major studios that were, for the first time in history, bought up by large, widely diversified conglomerates that had previously had no interest in entertainment ventures. This period was, according to Maltby, "an upheaval in company ownership more substantial even than that of the early 1930s" (31). By the end of the 1960s, 20th Century-Fox, Disney, and Columbia were the only remaining majors to have survived the corporate takeover wave, as Paramount was bought by Gulf + Western in 1966, United Artists was bought by Transamerica in 1967, Warner Bros. (then Warner–Seven Arts) was bought by Kinney National Services in 1969, and MGM was bought by Las Vegas real estate mogul Kirk Kerkorian in 1969.

The net result was that, by the end of the 1960s, the studios were barely hanging on financially and were anxiously looking for "the next big thing." The desperation the studios felt is well summarized in film critic Roger Ebert's reminiscence of making *Beyond the Valley of the Dolls* (1970), the X-rated satire he scripted for independent maverick Russ Meyer:

> Remembered after 10 years, *Beyond the Valley of the Dolls* seems more and more like a movie that got made by accident when the lunatics took over the asylum. At the time Russ Meyer and I were working on *BVD* I didn't really understand how unusual the project was. But in hindsight I can recognize that the conditions of its making were almost miraculous. An independent X-rated filmmaker and an inexperienced screenwriter were brought into a major studio and given carte blanche to turn out a satire of one of the studio's own hits. (Ebert, "Russ Meyer" 43)

The takeovers by larger conglomerates and various strategies of restructuring kept the studios alive, but barely, and they knew that the spectacle blockbuster formula was no longer going to sustain them, particularly since they were cash-strapped and in no position to fund large-scale productions.[4] Thus, more so than at any time since the nascent period of the second and third decades of the twentieth century, Hollywood was open to innovation—in terms of taste, aesthetics, genres, and themes.

Violent Movies of the 1960s

American audiences saw blood in Technicolor red for the first time when U.S. distributors started importing films from Hammer Film Productions, Ltd., a minor British studio that specialized in updating the old 1930s Universal horror films in full color and with greater sexual suggestiveness and explicit violence.[5] Two popular Hammer films, *Curse of Frankenstein* (1957) and *Dracula* (aka *Horror of Dracula*, 1958), which found great success in the United States, forever changed the horror genre and what was not only acceptable but expected in terms of on-screen bloodletting.[6]

In addition to Hammer films, there were several other notable British imports that raised the gore threshold. Chief among these were two films by cinematographer-turned-director Arthur Crabtree. His 1958 science fiction/horror hybrid *Fiend without a Face* is about an attack by invisible "mental vampires" that suck the brain and spinal cord out of their victims, and it was lambasted by many critics at the time of its release because of its gore. When the fiends are shot, they ooze large glops of viscous matter and expire with a grotesque wheezing that, as one critic noted, sounds like a leaking bicycle tire. *Fiend* is quite gruesome even today, which makes it abundantly clear why teens looking for a good shock loved it and respectable adults hated it. The next year, Crabtree directed *Horrors of the Black Museum* (1959), which included an inspired, grisly killing device: a pair of binoculars that impale the viewer's eyes with retractable knives. Although we don't see the actual impaling (it takes place offscreen), unlike most American films of this time, Crabtree shows bright red blood running through the actress's fingers as she holds her eyes and screams, and he gives prominent screen placement to puddles of blood on the floor.

If the British films were upping the ante of screen violence in the horror genre, it was Italian films that did the same for that most American of genres, the western. Viewers caught glimpses of graphic violence in Sergio Leone's Italian spaghetti western trilogy *A Fistful of Dollars* (*Per un pugno di dollari*, 1964), *For a Few Dollars More* (*Per qualche dollaro in più*, 1965), and *The Good, the Bad, and the Ugly* (*Il buono, il brutto, il cattivo*, 1966), all of which were popular in American movie houses, although, as Jake Horsley notes, it was the "wantonness" of the violence, not its "intensity," that "caused such a stir among audiences and filmmakers" (25).

Meanwhile, the drive-in and grind-house circuit was showing fringe audiences the first truly explicit "gore" films, which were pioneered by Herschell Gordon Lewis, a former college-literature-professor-turned-director of nudie films who treated the dismemberment of the human body with the same exploitative, voyeuristic glee that he treated the naked female form. In fact, Lewis began his venture into graphic violence because on-screen nudity was becoming too common and he was looking for something new to exploit. Lewis's *Blood Feast* (1963), *Two Thousand Maniacs* (1964), and *Color Me Blood Red* (1965) went far beyond anything that had been seen on the screen before in terms of explicit gore. Much like traditional pornography, Lewis's movies were constructed around flimsy narrative structures that existed primarily to create situations in which people could be dismembered, gutted, beheaded, crushed, or otherwise killed in some imaginatively grisly manner; in effect, graphic gore replaced nudity as the movie's illicit promise to see something you couldn't see elsewhere. However, like sexually explicit films of the era, Lewis's blood-soaked cheapies were largely relegated to fringe audiences who sought out such sensationalistic material. They were successful at the box office, earning large profits for Lewis and his production partner, David F. Friedman, but they were hardly mainstream.

Graphic violence was first hinted at in a studio-produced mainstream film in 1960 with the brilliantly edited montage of Janet Leigh being stabbed to death in the shower in Alfred Hitchcock's *Psycho.* Granted, Hitchcock did not show any actual wounds, but his liberal use of flowing blood, grisly sound effects, and rapid-fire montage editing to give the illusion of slicing and physical penetration caused numerous critics to reject the sequence (and the film) in disgust.[7] It is important to note here that the first significant use of graphic violence in a widely viewed mainstream Hollywood film was by an eminent auteur. In effect, *Psycho* not only paved the way for more explicit violence in the American cinema but also offered a concomitant opportunity for that violence to be connected with the recognized artistic intent of the filmmaker (even if that connection was made belatedly), which the New Hollywood auteurs used to justify the use of violence in their own films a decade later, if on notably different artistic terms.

However, the film that truly introduced graphic violence on the big screen to the typical American audience was Arthur Penn's violently comical, counterculture-celebrating *Bonnie and Clyde.* The slow-motion machine-gun slaughter of the (anti)hero and heroine at the end of the film firmly cemented graphic violence into common practice, as did the unrivaled brutality and graphic depictions of death in Peckinpah's *The Wild*

Bunch. Thus, by the early 1970s, explicit screen violence was established as a commonplace in mainstream, studio-produced American movies; no longer was it relegated to the provinces of fringe, cult, exploitation, and foreign films so cherished by youth audiences. Graphic and often disturbing physical representations of violence, whether played straight or satirically, began to appear in movies in every conceivable genre, many of which were significant box-office and critical successes: *Night of the Living Dead*, *Catch-22* (1970), *Soldier Blue* (1970), *Dirty Harry*, *The French Connection*, *Straw Dogs*, *Deliverance*, *The Godfather*, *Ulzana's Raid* (1972), *Flesh for Frankenstein* (aka *Andy Warhol's Frankenstein*) (1974), *Death Wish*, *Jaws*, and *Taxi Driver*.

As screen violence shifted from the fringes of the industry to the mainstream, the Hollywood studios turned primarily to a new generation of largely untested filmmakers who were emerging out of various film schools, many of whom had been part of the youth audience in the 1960s that had made increasingly violent films more and more popular and financially successful. They were young, brash, and filled with a wealth of ideas about how they could change movies forever. Thus entered the now famous "Film School Generation," those New Hollywood auteurs whose decade-long tenure at the top of Hollywood left an indelible mark on virtually every aspect of Hollywood filmmaking, but none so much as how violence was represented on-screen.

New Hollywood Violence, Auteur-Style

Richard Maltby argues that "periods of economic instability in Hollywood appear also to be periods of relative instability in the movies' codes of representation" (32), and never was this more true in relation to Hollywood violence than in the late 1960s and early 1970s. After decades of being tightly controlled by the strictures of the Production Code, the expectations of favored genres, the rules of the classical Hollywood style, and the general resistance to change endemic to the economic stability of the Hollywood studio system, filmmakers not only found themselves relatively free to depict violence in ways previously unimagined but were also given the resources of the major studios to do so. They could depict violence in different tones, ranging from documentary-like realism to the darkly comedic and every shade in between. In one sense, then, the sudden rise of graphic screen violence was a literal return of the repressed—something that had been contained for decades and, once restrictions were eased, suddenly and ferociously (and literally) exploded. In another sense, though, the screen violence of this era is best understood in terms of sheer novelty, as something new that was desirous simply because it hadn't been seen before.

For both reasons, violence became central to the New Hollywood filmmakers' quest to reinvent Hollywood filmmaking—not by trashing the system completely but by reworking the components of classical Hollywood film to suit their own ends. In this sense, Robert Kolker is right not to associate the New Hollywood with something as radically disjunctive as the French New Wave, which literally dismantled the traditional French "cinema of quality" with discontinuous editing, ambiguous characters, handheld camerawork, and loose plotting. The auteurs of the New Hollywood revered both their American forebears (Howard Hawks, John Ford, Orson Welles, Alfred Hitchcock, Samuel Fuller) and influential foreign filmmakers (Jean-Luc Godard, François Truffaut, Federico Fellini, Robert Bresson, Akira Kurosawa, Ingmar Bergman), and they endeavored to leave their stamp on the industry by combining the two: the traditional formal strengths of the former with the sense of experimentation and daring of the latter. And, as it turned out, screen violence was perfectly suited to this task.

As with any element of film, violence is molded and shaped by filmmakers to fit their aesthetic and ideological purposes. Thus, the violence in a film by Sam Peckinpah is radically different from the violence in a film by John Milius, which is why it is so pointless to talk about "violence" as some monolithic entity. As noted earlier, violence in some form has always been a central element of storytelling in the American cinema, but because its graphic depiction and narrative and ideological functions had been mostly restricted until the late 1960s, it offered something new, something different the New Hollywood filmmakers could work with to help distinguish themselves from those who came before them; it was a way to get out of the shadow of Old Hollywood. As New Hollywood director Brian De Palma put it, "It's all terrain that's been explored before, and unless you invoke it in a different way a good idea is going to look like all the other stuff that's around" (qtd. in Childs and Jones 44).

A brief look at some of the films that "made" the reputation of the seminal figures of the New Hollywood—that is, the films that first got them noticed by both critics and audiences—illustrates just how violently they made their mark.

Arthur Penn and Sam Peckinpah

One must start, of course, with Arthur Penn and *Bonnie and Clyde* and Sam Peckinpah and *The Wild Bunch*. First, it is important to note that, although associated with the New Hollywood, Penn and Peckinpah, like Robert Altman and Stanley Kubrick, were not a part of the Film School Generation, because both of them had already been working in the film industry for more than a decade, and both had originally cut their teeth in television production in the 1950s. Penn had already directed four films when he made *Bonnie and Clyde*, beginning with the western *The Left-Handed Gun* in 1958, which re-envisioned Billy the Kid as a sympathetic young rebel (thus foreshadowing his vision of Bonnie and Clyde nine years later). Peckinpah had directed three films before *The Wild Bunch*, beginning with *The Deadly Companions* (1961). Both filmmakers had already explored most of their salient themes in their early films, including the roles of and responses to violence. However, both men were essentially "made" in the eyes of both the industry and audiences with *Bonnie and Clyde* and *The Wild Bunch*, arguably because these two films did more to revolutionize the depiction of violence in the cinema than any film since *Psycho.* It was only after the release of these two films that Penn and Peckinpah were genuinely conceived of as auteurs, despite having worked steadily in the industry for many years.

When people speak of either film, the discussion invariably revolves around the seemingly contradictory combination of beauty and brutality of their violence. The twenty-two-second montage depicting the deaths of Bonnie and Clyde was the most harshly violent sequence most American audiences had seen up until that time. Early in the film's conception, Penn, star and co-producer Warren Beatty, and co-writers Robert Benton and David Newman "all agreed that the violence should shock" (Biskind 34).

This scene was largely displeasurable for audiences on several levels. First, as Kolker argues, it "punished" the audience for having identified with outlaws for two hours. At the same time, though, countercultural audiences read the scene as a symbolic indictment of police brutality, as the machine-gunning of the unarmed Bonnie and Clyde was yet another example of excessive authorial response to those who would dare to challenge the system. Aesthetically, the scene was displeasurable in Roland Barthes's sense that it violated the audience's "repertoire of expectations" regarding how violent death would be depicted in a mainstream film, which works in either the "punishment of the audience" or the "indictment of the authorities" reading of the scene. That is, no matter how you read the scene symbolically, the violence was shocking.

Yet, however violent and displeasurable those twenty-two seconds were for early audiences, they were also undeniably innovative, conveying as they did both "the spastic and balletic qualities" of violent death (Crowdus and Porton 9) by combining various speeds of slow motion and using the recently developed technology of blood squibs to represent the physiology of bullet hits. Using four cameras running at different speeds, the scene took four days to shoot and represented the production's largest technical challenge. However, rather than trying to show how horrible and ugly violence is, Penn said, "I wanted to take the film away from the relatively squalid quality of the story into something a little more balletic. I wanted closure" (qtd. in Biskind 35). Thus, the violence of this sequence was radically inventive not only on an aesthetic level but also on a narrative level. It ultimately became the crowning achievement of Penn's career, a scene that left an indelible mark on film history and catapulted him, however temporarily, to the forefront of American filmmakers.

Peckinpah took Penn's achievement one step further in *The Wild Bunch*, filming the climactic (some would say apocalyptic) gun battle at the end with as many as six Panavision, Mitchell, and Arriflex cameras that were all running at the same time at different speeds with different wide angle, telephoto, and zoom lenses (Cook, "Fifteen Years After" 123). The whole sequence took eleven days to shoot and used more than three thousand squibs and more blank ammunition than was fired during the entire Mexican Revolution of 1913 (Bouzereau, *Ultraviolent Movies* 17). The final battle spans almost seven minutes and includes some 339 individual cuts; it has been called "the unparalleled montage event of cinema history" (Cook, "Fifteen Years After" 128). And, even though *The Wild Bunch* didn't perform particularly well at the box office (it was produced for $6.2 million and made $7.5 million in its first year of release), "many critics saw [it] as a work of genius, which gave the director renewed credibility in the industry and made it possible for him to write his own ticket for the first half of the 1970s" (Cook, *Lost Illusions* 82). Penn reaped similar benefits with *Bonnie and Clyde*, but even more so since that film was a genuine box-office hit.

Francis Ford Coppola

Similar to Penn and Peckinpah, the members of the emerging Film School Generation also gained notice by making particularly violent films. The first of these young directors to make a real impact on the industry was Francis Ford Coppola, who was hired by Paramount to helm *The Godfather* after numerous other directors had turned the project down. It wasn't Coppola's first film; in fact, he had worked steadily throughout the 1960s while earning a master of fine arts degree in filmmaking at UCLA. Like several other young directors of the era, he apprenticed under exploitation pioneer Roger Corman at American International Pictures, and one of his first films, directed when he was only twenty-three, was a little-seen black-and-white cheapie horror flick called *Dementia 13* (1963), which featured several ax murders, including a brief but graphic decapitation (this scene, however, was actually shot by director Jack Hill at the behest of Corman, who didn't feel that Coppola's finished picture was violent enough). Little notice was taken of his next three films, *You're a Big Boy Now* (1966), *Finian's Rainbow* (1968), and *The Rain People* (1969), none of which were box-office hits, but they did gain Coppola recognition among critics who appreciated his willingness to experiment.

The Godfather, however, was the film that not only catapulted Coppola to the forefront of all American directors but also single-handedly pulled Paramount out of its economic slump and helped revitalized the entire film industry, thanks to its enormous box-office haul ($85.7 million, making it the most successful film up until that time). Based on the best-selling novel by Mario Puzo, *The Godfather* was a notably violent film, featuring multiple assassinations, beatings, and the infamous decapitated horse head in the Hollywood producer's bed. However, Coppola didn't follow in Penn and Peckinpah's footsteps by aestheticizing the violence with complex choreography and slow motion. Rather, he relied on a more traditional stylistic approach, allowing the violence's visceral impact to emerge from the simple act of witnessing its lifelike brutality. The scene in which Sonny Corleone (James Caan) is mowed down with half a dozen machine guns in an ambush at a toll booth certainly has echoes of Bonnie and Clyde's violent undoing, but Coppola lets the bullets fly and the blood squibs erupt in real time, thus giving the sequence a jarring verisimilitude that underlines the film's greatest asset, which is the way it takes the grandiosity of myth and grounds it in a palpable, everyday reality. The violence in *The Godfather* is certainly epic in scope, particularly the much-heralded crosscutting sequence near the end of the film that moves fluidly between Michael Corleone (Al Pacino) standing godfather to his sister's newborn child and his henchmen violently dispatching all his enemies. Yet, there are also sequences of brutality that strike closer to home, particularly the grueling scene of domestic abuse endured by Michael's sister, Connie (Talia Shire). The fact that the characters in the film are believable and even sympathetic also adds to the resonance of the film's violence. As Vincent Canby wrote in his review of the film for the *New York Times*, "It is also more than a little disturbing to realize that characters, who are so moving one minute, are likely, in the next scene, to be blowing out the brains of a competitor over a white tablecloth."

Coppola's ability to convey violence in both artfully mythic and disturbingly grounded terms served him well for the rest of the decade, as every film he made in the 1970s was violent in tone and content: *The Godfather Part II* (1974), which continued the same themes as its predecessor; *The Conversation* (1974), which centered on Nixon-era conspiracy fears about covertly enacted retributive violence; and, of course, *Apocalypse Now*, which plunged even deeper than *The Godfather* into mythic violence by using the specter of Vietnam to stand metaphorically for the madness of humankind.

Martin Scorsese

Like Coppola, Martin Scorsese got his start apprenticing for Roger Corman, and one of his early films was the Depression-set *Boxcar Bertha* (1972), a violent gangster story that ended with one of the main characters crucified on the side of a railway car. Scorsese's status as an auteur, however, was firmly established with *Mean Streets* (1973), a semi-autobiographical tale of small-time hoods in Little Italy. Unlike in *The Godfather*, there are no mythical pretensions in Scorsese's film, and the violence is even more raw and unguarded, giving it an almost documentary-like verisimilitude. *Mean Streets* didn't do much at the box office, but critics eagerly took notice, and the film was the most talked-about entry in that year's New York Film Festival.

Three years later, Scorsese cemented his reputation with *Taxi Driver*, which won the coveted Palm d'Or at the Cannes Film Festival. In it, Scorsese exposes the underbelly of New York through Vietnam veteran Travis Bickle (Robert De Niro), a loner who is unable to comprehend the society in which he lives. He is the epitome of alienation, constantly trying to connect with others but never being able to. The film forces the viewer into the uncomfortable position of identifying with Bickle, a man who is clearly on the edge and about to go over; we are always with him, listening to his thoughts, seeing the world through his ravaged eyes, watching him talk to himself in the mirror. Eventually, he does go over the edge and proceeds on a vigilante rampage that, as *Bonnie and Clyde* and *The Wild Bunch* had before, set new standards for screen violence. The effects, which were designed and executed by Dick Smith, involved the top of a man's hand being blown off and then stabbed through the palm with a large knife, multiple squib effects, and splattering head shots. Beyond the shock of the effects themselves, Scorsese pushes home the results of the vigilante violence by allowing his camera to linger on the aftermath, taking in every blood spatter and dead body. The gore of this final sequence was so graphic, in fact, that Scorsese had the scene desaturated in postproduction to take away some of the impact in order to avoid an X rating.

Brian De Palma

Another Film School Generation filmmaker closely associated with screen violence, but for entirely different reasons, is Brian De Palma. (Technically, De Palma didn't go to film school but got his start making 16mm short films while a physics major at Columbia University; later, he was awarded an MCA-sponsored fellowship to Sarah Lawrence College.) De Palma courted controversy early, as his first feature film, the satirical comedy *Greetings* (1968), was the first X-rated film to have its rating appealed by its distributor ("First Appeal").

After a series of low-budget, independent comedies, De Palma, like other members of the Film School Generation, took his first step toward auteur status with an overtly violent film, in this case, *Sisters* (1973), a loving homage to Alfred Hitchcock that was made independently for less than half a million dollars. The film was highly regarded for its eye-grabbing style; shot mostly in tight, enclosed rooms, De Palma employed complex tracking shots, long zooms, fast-cut editing, and a now-famous use of precisely timed split-screen effects. This marked it as significantly different from his previous efforts, which were largely improvised. Every facet of *Sisters* was carefully planned because "De Palma's goal was to create a surreal atmosphere as well as shock the audience with violent scenes" (Bouzereau, *De Palma Cut* 33). It was clearly a breakthrough film, as noted by Canby in the *New York Times*: "Mr. De Palma, best know for his anarchic comedy ('Hi, Mom,' 'Get to Know Your Rabbit'), reveals himself to be a first-rate director of more or less conventional material that has associations not only with 'Repulsion,' but also with Hitchcock's 'Psycho.'"

Like many of Hitchcock's films, *Sisters* is obsessed with voyeurism, a theme that De Palma would return to often. It is also a graphically violent film; much like *Psycho*, it uses a knife murder a third of the way into the film as a catalyst for a sudden switch in identification. Unlike *Psycho*, though, De Palma's knife murder shows the blade penetrating the victim's body again and again in a gruesome montage. De Palma clearly drew more from Hitchcock than just an appreciation for the effect of well-timed violence, though; he also utilized Hitchcock's sense of suspense and black humor, and *Sisters* gets surprising mileage out of a sustained gag involving the body of the victim being hidden in a foldaway couch.

For some, De Palma's true breakthrough film was the richly gory high school gothic thriller *Carrie*. Based on Stephen King's first novel, it features an apocalyptic bloodbath inside a high school gymnasium after the titular character is picked on one too many times and unleashes her telekinetic fury. De Palma envisioned *Carrie* as a serious film, one that he hoped would stir up the same nationwide controversy that *The Exorcist* (1973) had three years earlier (Bouzereau, *De Palma Cut* 45). The film was ultimately a hit, grossing fifteen times its $1.8 million budget, although De Palma was upset that United Artists had distributed it as a teen-oriented Halloween movie. However, this didn't mean that critics didn't take notice, particularly Pauline Kael, who was one of De Palma's most vociferous champions. She noted in her review that De Palma "had mastered a teasing style—a perverse mixture of comedy and horror and tension" (*When the Lights Go Down* 208), thus highlighting not only De

Palma's new auteur status but the centrality of his unique spin on horror violence. Like Canby, Kael compared De Palma to Roman Polanski and Hitchcock but ultimately elevated him above them: "*Carrie* becomes a new trash archetype, and De Palma, who has the wickedest baroque sensibility at large in American movies, points up its archetypal aspects by parodying the movies that formed it—and outclassing them" (209). *The Fury* (1978) trod similar ground but upped the ante by ending the film on the shockingly gory note of seeing John Cassavetes' entire body explode.

Others: William Friedkin, Michael Cimino, Steven Spielberg, Mike Nichols

In addition to those already mentioned, one could point to others, including William Friedkin, who made his name with the gritty and violent police drama *The French Connection*, which won the Oscars for Best Picture and Best Director, and the seminal horror film *The Exorcist*, which was notable for its frighteningly effective use of documentary techniques to lend an air of realism to its fantastical story of demon possession. Another case in point is Michael Cimino, who gained worldwide acclaim for his sophomore effort, the Oscar-winning film *The Deer Hunter* (1978). It was the first major studio film to deal explicitly with Vietnam, although Cimino was criticized in some circles for his inaccurate depiction of the war, particularly the Vietcong's sadistic use of forced games of Russian roulette, which Cimino defended as being metaphorical (Simon).

Even those filmmakers not usually associated with gory films often experimented with violence. Steven Spielberg, for example, originally gained notice for his suspenseful TV movie *Duel* (1971), and immediately afterward he was tapped by producer Philip D'Antoni to direct *Cruising*, the violent story of an undercover cop infiltrating the underworld of gay clubs in New York to find a serial killer (it was eventually directed by Friedkin in 1980) (Clagett 189). But it was really the blood-soaked *Jaws*, which was one the biggest commercial hits of the 1970s, that made Spielberg a household name. Although rated PG, *Jaws* is a graphically violent film, featuring a severed arm, a young child being devoured by a shark as torrents of blood explode from the water, and an extended, grueling scene in which the shark hunter Quint (Robert Shaw) is eaten alive from the waist down. The violence was so intense, in fact, that the film's PG rating was accompanied by an addendum on the advertising one-sheet that read "May be too intense for young children."[8]

Another example is Mike Nichols, who is most commonly associated with *Who's Afraid of Virginia Woolf?* (1966) and *The Graduate*, films that helped expand the limits of dialogue and the depiction of sexuality in American films. However, his follow-up was an ambitious adaptation of

5. The shark hunter Quint (Robert Shaw) is eaten alive by the monstrous great white at the end of *Jaws* (1975), one of several scenes in Steven Spielberg's summer blockbuster that led to an addendum to the film's PG rating: "May be too intense for young children." DVD still.

Joseph Heller's *Catch-22*, which features scenes of explicit violence that veer from the blackly comedic (a man being unexpectedly cut in half by the propeller of a low-flying plane) to the starkly disturbing (a long-withheld revelation of an injured airman whose intestines are hanging out of his stomach).

Thus, even those New Hollywood filmmakers who had established themselves with nonviolent films were drawn to more violent material, thus illustrating the centrality of screen violence in this era of filmmaking. In this sense, it is impossible to separate the "renaissance" of American filmmaking in the late 1960s and early 1970s from the rise of graphic screen violence. The former helped enable the latter, yet the scintillating and thought-provoking manner in which the young directors depicted violence contributed to both their auteur status and their box-office clout. Violence was both a means to an end (box-office success, auteur status) and an end in itself (insofar as it was something new and fresh that most audiences had not experienced before).

By the mid-1970s, Hollywood was well on its way to recovering from its near financial collapse of the late 1960s, and with the release of *Jaws* in 1975 and then *Star Wars* in 1977, the industry had found its new formula for success: the blockbuster. Unfortunately, this meant that many of the heralded auteurs of the New Hollywood would have to either adjust to the new system or find themselves increasingly on the outs. This was a lengthy process that extended into the early 1980s, and, as the next chapter will show, many of these filmmakers continued trying to make the kinds of films that had characterized the New Hollywood renaissance but found it increasingly difficult to do so, particularly where violence was involved.

2

RETREATING FROM THE WORLD OF REVOLUTION

CONTROVERSIES OVER SCREEN VIOLENCE AT THE DAWN OF THE REAGAN ERA

MOVIES HAVE ALWAYS BEEN battlegrounds on which various cultural wars have been waged, but in the 1980s those wars sharply increased in terms of both their tenor and their public visibility. More important, the skirmishes over movie content that erupted into public protest and media coverage reflected an increasingly aggressive sensibility on both sides of the political spectrum. That is, conservatives and liberals openly waged war against various films in an effort to influence cinematic representation and thereby lay claim to its influence. While the two groups tended to protest against the same films for decidedly different reasons—conservatives argued on traditional religious/moral grounds while liberals argued against the negative representations of historically marginalized groups—the simple fact that so many films became lightning rods for public controversy during the 1980s is testament to their perceived importance in defining the culture.

The year 1980 alone saw a number of films that drew various levels of public controversy, including *Windows*, a critically panned thriller about a woman (Talia Shire) who becomes her lesbian neighbor's object of obsession, and *Monty Python's Life of Brian*, a religious parody from the well-known British comedy troupe. However, this chapter will consider three specific case studies of films produced in the early 1980s that were controversial specifically because of their use of screen violence: *Cruising*, directed by William Friedkin; *Dressed to Kill*, directed by Brian De Palma; and *White Dog*, directed by Sam Fuller. These films and their attendant controversies were crucial to the changing nature of Hollywood in the early years of the 1980s because each drew attention to the downside of public controversy in response to screen violence, thus encouraging studios to steer clear of such projects in favor of more conservative and audience-friendly—though not necessarily less violent—action films. In some way, each of these films was aesthetically and ideologically in tune with the previous decade and therefore ran into myriad problems and controversies in marketing and theatrical distribution in the more conservative era of the 1980s.

Because of the manner in which *Cruising, Dressed to Kill,* and *White Dog* drew attention to the relationships among the Hollywood industry, its audiences, and various social groups, each of these films can be defined as a "focusing event," a concept that derives from political science, particularly the study of policy-making and the means through which significant legislative change occurs. It has also been used in the study of mass communication, particularly in terms of agenda setting. Thomas Birkland defines a potential focusing event as "an event that is sudden, relatively rare, can be reasonably defined as harmful or revealing the possibility of potentially greater future harms, inflicts harms or suggests potential harms that are or could be concentrated on a definable geographic area or community of interest, and that is known to policy makers and the public virtually simultaneously" (22). As this definition suggests, focusing events are usually catastrophic happenings such as natural disasters, nuclear accidents, or terrorist attacks that demand attention and some kind of change in existing policy or the creation of new policy. However, focusing events are not "uniform or similar; they occur in a variety of contexts with quite different consequences" (Worrall 323).

Cruising, Dressed to Kill, and *White Dog* functioned as focusing events that forced the major studios to reevaluate the kinds of projects they were funding and distributing. As events, the releases of these three films differ somewhat from Birkland's definition in that they were not necessarily "sudden," as the production of a feature-length motion picture is a long, intensive process, often years in the making. However, they were "rare" in the sense that these films were more in tune with filmmaking of the previous decade than they were of the typical mainstream films being produced in the Reagan era. Also, they were certainly considered "harmful" in two senses: Significant (and vocal) segments of the public viewed them as harmful in terms of their salacious content, which they believed was detrimental to the impressionable minds of viewers, and the studios viewed them as harmful from a public relations standpoint, namely that they would make the studios look bad in the public eye, resulting in a loss of revenue.

Each of the films discussed in this chapter was developed and distributed by a Hollywood studio. Thus, at some point in their gestation, these projects looked viable and profitable to the studios that funded them; otherwise, they never would have made it into production. However, once they were released to the public (or, in the case of *Cruising*, began production), it became clear that these films were not to be well received by certain segments of the public, who made their displeasure apparent through picketing theaters, organizing highly visible public protests, and publishing various forms of printed condemnations, including op-ed columns, leaflets distributed to the public, and letters to the editor.

Ironically, the primary source of protest against these films did not come from conservative factions or politicians associated with Ronald Reagan and the Republican Party but from constituencies typically associated with the Left: gay rights groups (*Cruising*), feminists (*Dressed to Kill*), and the National Association for the Advancement of Colored People (NAACP) (*White Dog*). Thus, it was not just conservatives who were becoming concerned with the portrayals of violence on the silver screen but liberal groups as well. Charles Lyons argues that the protest campaigns waged by these groups "provided ways of testing the extent to which the empowerment they had fought for during the previous two decades had been realized and could be defended" (279). At the same time, conservative groups had their own agenda against such films as they sought to reassert "traditional family values" in the culture. Thus, as in the case of pornography, screen violence in the early 1980s created a rare site in which conservative and liberal activists could pool their collective outrage, even if said outrage emanated from vastly different ideological wells. Liberal groups were troubled by the fact that violence was directed at historically marginalized groups—gays, women, and African Americans, in these cases—while conservatives were more concerned about the intense nature of the bloodshed and, in the case of *Cruising* and *Dressed to Kill*, its association with graphic sexuality. If the political terrain was shifting in the early 1980s toward the Right, there was also a cross-shift in which liberal groups, fearful of losing political power, sought to make their presence known and remind the public of their agenda.

Ultimately, though, what mattered to the studios was that their product was being publicly called out, which not only threatened the industry's assertion that it could properly police itself via the rating system but also risked the loss of box-office dollars and public support. As Metropolitan Theaters CEO Sherill C. Corwin had told Richard Heffner, "If we're going to save our collective asses from the censor, we'd better recognize film violence as one of the things that parents hold most against us" (qtd. in Heffner, "Reminiscences," vol. 5, box 5, 899). Although groups that protested *Cruising, Dressed to Kill,* and *White Dog* were not necessarily representative of the public at large, Hollywood has historically feared the power of various constituencies to shape the terms of the debate and create a negative public aura around the film industry. Thus, the negative activity surrounding these films focused the studios' attention on the potential downside of controversy. Although it was not detrimental to them, it was one extra headache they didn't need, and self-regulating the output of violent films offered a viable option for self-preservation, a long-standing practice dating back to the beginnings of the Hollywood film industry (Jacobs and Maltby).

This was, of course, hardly the first time Hollywood had made significant changes in its operations as a result of focusing event controversies. In fact, most of the major industrial changes in Hollywood have been in direct response to a focusing event. For example, the formation in 1922 of the industry's trade association, the Motion Pictures Producers and Distributors of America, an event that is often viewed as the historical moment when filmmaking officially became an industry, was a direct result of a series of controversies that focused the studios' attention on the connections between the public's perception of filmmakers/stars and their profitability. In the early 1920s, the filmmaking community faced a significant public relations problem in the interrelated issues of censorship at the state and local levels and a series of scandals involving movie stars. This conflation of the public and the private, whereby the rhetoric of progressive reformers framed the perceived immoral content of Hollywood films as a direct extension of the immoral lives of those who made them, cast a tainted shadow on Hollywood's image, thus putting its profitability in jeopardy.

In 1920, there was Mary Pickford's scandalous Reno divorce from her husband, Owen Moore, and her subsequent marriage to Douglas Fairbanks, himself recently divorced, a scant four weeks later. There was also the murder of director William Desmond Taylor and the deaths of two young actors, Olive Thomas and Wallace Reid, both of whom were found to be using narcotics. However, the true focusing event was the scandal involving comedian Roscoe "Fatty" Arbuckle, who at the time was one of the highest paid stars in Hollywood. Arbuckle was accused, though eventually acquitted, of murdering a woman named Virginia Rappe at a party he threw in three adjoining suites at the St. Francis Hotel in San Francisco. The press, sensing a scandal of epic proportions, fed on rumors, half-truths, and, in some cases, outright lies, which resulted in Arbuckle being branded a rapist and murderer long before he set foot in a courtroom. Regardless of his guilt or innocence, the Arbuckle scandal resulted in various reform groups organizing nationwide boycotts, which caused Paramount, to whom he was under contract, to recall all prints of his films and suspend him indefinitely. Not surprisingly, the creation of the MPPDA, which would provide a respected and trusted public face for Hollywood in the form of Will B. Hays, the former postmaster general under President Warren G. Harding, was announced just in time for Arbuckle's second trial. Thus, "the studios turned a potential public relations disaster (the scandals) into an opportunity to consolidate their power and to establish new collusive guidelines to maintain industry profitability" (Lewis, *Hollywood* 93–94).

Something similar happened in the early 1980s as the major studios slowly but surely discarded the kinds of controversial projects that had been so crucial to Hollywood filmmaking a decade earlier. While there was not an overt, concrete change in policy or the creation of a new representative body like the MPPDA, there was a clear shift in focus in Hollywood beginning in 1980, a kind of unstated but obvious self-regulation that resulted in the production of films that differed significantly from those the same studios had championed a decade earlier. Thus, by the mid-1980s, Julie Salamon could write with cautious optimism in the *Wall Street Journal* that there appeared to be a "temporary epidemic of good taste" in Hollywood.

Cruising

William Friedkin's *Cruising* was the first major Hollywood controversy of the new decade. It was met with storms of protest because of the brazen manner in which it combined sexuality and violence, creating a disturbing amalgam of Freud's two unconscious drives of sex and death. The film's setting in the world of gay leather bars provoked multiple controversies: Gay rights groups were incensed because they felt the film unfairly portrayed homosexuality as aberrant and psychotic, while conservative groups were appalled that such subject matter would be at the center of a major Hollywood movie.

As a focusing event, the case of *Cruising* demonstrated the enormous impact a vocal minority group could make on a major studio production, the way in which such controversial films further strained the studios' relationship with exhibitors, and the increasing difficulties they were facing with the Classification and Rating Administration when it came to securing a marketable R rating for extremely violent films. The controversy over the film's rating was central to CARA's increasingly conservative approach to screen violence throughout the 1980s, which made it harder for extremely violent films to receive an R rating, even if they would have several years earlier. Although *Cruising* has been critically reevaluated in the decades since its release (Kermode, "Cruise Control"), it will likely always be remembered as one of the most striking examples of studio-audience disconnect in the Reagan era.

That *Cruising* was destined for controversy was obvious from the start. Philip D'Antoni, producer of *The French Connection,* had secured the film rights to Gerald Walker's source novel back in 1970 but ultimately gave up on the project because he didn't think he could bring it to the screen realistically without it being too horrific and off-putting for most audiences. As he put it, "I felt there was no way of doing it the way I wanted to have it done and be true to the story" (qtd. in Clagett 189).

Nevertheless, director William Friedkin, who had a reputation as one of the most ambitious and arrogant of the New Hollywood directors, took over the project in the late 1970s, confident that he could bring in audiences with the gritty realism and documentary aesthetic that had made him both a critic's darling and a resounding box-office success with *The French Connection* and *The Exorcist.* He had a hit a slump, however, when his next film, *Sorcerer* (1977), went overbudget and bombed at the box office, falling under the enormous shadow of George Lucas's *Star Wars.*[1] *Sorcerer* was an ambitious remake of Henri-Georges Clouzot's existential action-thriller *The Wages of Fear* (*Le salaire de la peur,* 1953), which had won the Palm d'Or at Cannes. Friedkin's desire to remake a popular, widely hailed canonical art-house film—to show, in essence, that he could walk in the footsteps of a masterful French auteur—marked the pinnacle of his confidence in the 1970s, and he fell hard when *Sorcerer* failed both critically and commercially.

Cruising was clearly Friedkin's bid to reassert himself and his vaunted auteur status, even as his star was quickly fading. According to screenwriter Walon Green, who had worked with Friedkin on *Sorcerer* and *The Brink's Job* (1978), Friedkin was intent on pushing boundaries and challenging taboos with *Cruising.* He had seen Pier Paolo Pasolini's *Salò, or The 120 Days of Sodom* (1975) at the 1977 New York Film Festival and had become obsessed with Pasolini's courage in using cinema to explore the most disturbing fringes of sadistic human behavior. Thus, Friedkin wanted to do something similar (Clagett). However, the case of *Cruising* illustrates a filmmaker's fundamental misconception of the extreme nature of his violent subject matter in relation to the willingness of the American public—always a shifting entity—to endure it.

The public relations problems for *Cruising* began long before the film made it to theaters. Friedkin started filming in Greenwich Village in the summer of 1979, and almost immediately the production was beset with protesters. The gay community in New York was rallied by Arthur Bell, a gay rights activist and columnist for the *Village Voice* who, ironically, had written several articles about the murders of gay men in New York that Friedkin had used as part of the film's basis. Bell had read an early draft of the screenplay and was incensed at its narrow and ugly portrayal of homosexual lifestyles. In his July 16, 1979, column in the *Voice*, Bell railed against Friedkin and his film, which was in production at the time:

> [*Cruising*] promises to be the most oppressive, ugly, bigoted look at homosexuality ever presented on the screen, the worst possible nightmare for the most uptight straight and a validation of Anita Bryant's hate campaign. It will negate years of positive movement work and may well send gays running back into the closet and precipitate heavy violence against homosexuals. I implore readers—gay, straight, liberal, radical, atheist, communist or whatever—to give Friedkin and his production crew a terrible time if you spot them in your neighborhood.... And I urge gay men whom Friedkin has signed as extras and bit players in scenes to be shot at backroom bars, piers, bathhouses and Village streets to be aware of the consequences of his project. Owners of gay establishments would do well to tell Friedkin to fuck off when he comes around to film and exploit.

Bell's call to arms was a success. Protesters showed up in large numbers throughout the location shooting in New York City, forcing the production to employ police officers for crowd control. They threw eggs and even bottles, hung banners out their windows protesting the film, and blew whistles and shouted while the cameras were rolling—anything to disrupt the production (Clagett 196). Many of the bars in the Greenwich Village area that had given their permission to be used for locations rescinded at the last minute, and production had to be halted on several occasions because of bomb threats (198). Amazingly enough, all of the protests and disturbances did not result in significant cost overruns, although the noisy demonstrators did complicate postproduction: Nearly 80 percent of the film's dialogue had to be looped, and virtually all of the sound effects had to be recreated.

Not surprisingly, *Cruising* ran into trouble when it came time for CARA to rate the film. United Artists, a member of the Motion Picture Association of America, was handling *Cruising*'s distribution; thus, it could not be released without a rating. If the film were rated X, which by then was largely synonymous in the public mindset with pornography, many theater chains would not show it and most major newspapers would not carry ads for it.

When CARA members first saw the film in late 1979, they did exactly what the studio feared and slapped it with an X rating. Friedkin and producer Jerry Weintraub met with Richard Heffner, chairman of the Rating Board, who told them that they were going to have to cut the film to get an R rating (Segaloff 204). At Heffner's suggestion, Weintraub hired Dr. Aaron

Stern, a New York psychiatrist who had been the head of CARA from 1971 to 1974, as a consultant on how to get the film down to an R rating. To do so meant reducing both the film's violent and sexual content.

First, the graphic violence of the film's opening murder, in which a man is hogtied on a bed and stabbed repeatedly in the back with a large knife, had to be reduced. According to editor Bud Smith, he toned the scene down by completely recutting it:

> I took out some of the more horrifying footage. There was an over-the-shoulder angle of the killer, showing the knife going straight down into the victim's back. Now you see one quick shot showing the knife go into the back. Another shot I had before shows him pull the knife out, and blood squirts into the frame and across the victim's face. I took it out and put in another take, so when he pulls the knife out, you hear the scream and see it from the side angle but you don't see blood squirt into frame. You do see it trickle down his neck but not squirt. (qtd. in Clagett 203)

As the scene now stands, it is still excruciatingly violent, even though blood doesn't "squirt" as much and the number of knife thrusts has been cut down to only three. However, something that is rarely mentioned in the literature on *Cruising* is that Friedkin inserted quasi-subliminal frames of hard-core pornography into this murder sequence as a last-ditch attempt at rebelling against being forced to reduce the violence of the scene.[2] Thus, when the knife is shown penetrating the victim's back, there are a few frames of close-up anal penetration spliced into the shot that are only noticeable when one watches it frame by frame (Friedkin had employed quasi-subliminal imagery in *The Exorcist* and would do it again in *Jade* [1995]). Of course, the visual connection between anal intercourse and murderous stabbing, even on this quasi-subliminal level, only feeds into critiques of the film's homophobia.

Second, there had to be changes made to the sequence known as "precinct night," which takes place at a leather bar in which all the clientele are dressed as police officers. This is one of the film's most lurid sequences, filled wall to wall with overt (though never hard-core) displays of public sexuality. Smith was required to insert a traveling matte in one tracking shot that would cover a man in the background who appeared to be performing fellatio on another man, and three other shots had to be darkened to obscure the sexual activities taking place. While this succeeded in making it impossible to see exactly what was going on, thus satisfying CARA's focus on what is strictly visible, from an atmospheric point of view, the darkening only increases the dirty, salacious, and violent tone of the scene, thus unintentionally heightening the film's negative depiction

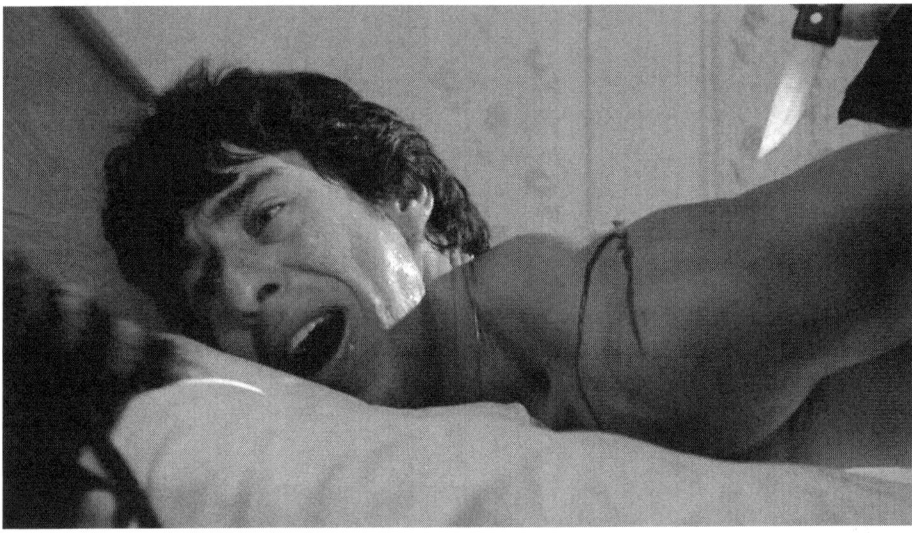

6. The graphic violence of the first knife murder in *Cruising* (1980) had to be toned down in the editing room to avoid an X rating. DVD still.

of gay sexuality by portraying it as something embarrassing and corrupt that can take place only in the darkest of dark corners.

Despite securing an R rating, *Cruising*'s troubles continued as its mid-February 1980 release date drew closer. On February 4, 1980, Friedkin and producer Jerry Weintraub decided to hold a screening for both the gay and straight press. According to Weintraub, this decision was made "under extreme pressure" from media and gay activists. He also noted that exhibitors were getting nervous about the inevitable protests and the possible damage to their theaters that might ensue ("'Cruising' Gets Sole Screening"). Weintraub ended up barring the critic from *Variety* from attending this screening because *Variety* had requested that it be allowed to print a review of the film two days before its release, which hinted at his worries about the impending negative critical reception.

However, before this screening could even take place, on February 1 the nationwide General Cinema Theaters chain announced that it was pulling *Cruising* from the thirty-three screens it had reserved for it. General Cinema had blind-bid on the film back in September 1979, and once executives actually saw it, they decided that the controversy surrounding it would be more trouble than it was worth.[3] Pulling the film violated a legal contract and United Artists threatened to sue, but General Cinema executives defended their decision by noting their corporate policy not to exhibit X-rated movies or, more important, movies that, in their judgment, should be rated X. Thus, the rating of *Cruising* became a matter of dispute, which cast doubt on CARA's ability to discern what the public was willing to accept under the banner of an R rating.

Two weeks later, General Cinema executives took a second look at the film but still refused to exhibit it, dashing United Artists' hopes that they could reach a compromise whereby General Cinema could pull the film from ten screens in Bible Belt areas but show it on the other twenty-three ("'GCC Stands"). Although General Cinema was the only theater chain to actually pull *Cruising* from its screens, several others, including United Artists Theaters, were not satisfied with the R rating CARA had given it and posted signs in their windows declaring that it was, in their opinion, an X-rated film and only those over eighteen would be admitted ("UATC Posts Warning").[4] Although this reduced the number of people who could see the film, thus cutting down on potential profits, this move allowed the theaters to still show the film but defend themselves against community criticism. Such an action is indicative of just how uneasy exhibitors were with such a controversial violent film and how they were willing to sacrifice potential box-office dollars in the short run to maintain their public standing in the long run. At the same time, this flap over the R rating given to *Cruising* was seen as yet another example of how disconnected the Hollywood establishment was from the larger American public, which helps explain why, in the years that followed, CARA became significantly stricter in rating violent movies.

Weintraub and United Artists tried to put the best spin they could on the increasingly negative public relations fiasco. In articles in *Daily Variety* and other publications, both Weintraub and UA executives noted repeatedly that all the press surrounding the film, however negative, was ultimately good for the film's bottom line. As Weintraub put it, "The publicity on this picture is going to make people want to see it, let's face it. . . . You can't buy this kind of publicity" (qtd. in Ginsberg, "General Cinema" 10). In one desperate bid to spin the bad publicity, UA even sent letters to theaters that would be screening the film to "alert" them to all the controversy and encourage them to use it as a selling point (Klain). Theaters, however, were worried about the fallout, and several hired police to protect them from violent demonstrators, an extra cost that UA agreed to foot by allowing the theaters to deduct security costs from weekly house expenses (Ginsberg, "Demonstrations").

When *Cruising* opened wide on more than five hundred screens across the nation on February 15, 1980, it was met by the expected protests, particularly in large cities with significant gay populations like Los Angeles, New York, Chicago, and San Francisco. This had been foreshadowed a month earlier when the National Gay Task Force (the same group that organized to disrupt the filming of *Cruising*) and the National Association of Lesbian and Gay Filmmakers headed a boycott of the thriller *Windows* as well as picketed several theaters in New York City. None of the demonstrations against either *Windows* or *Cruising* turned violent, much to the theater owners' relief, and for a short while it looked like *Cruising* might beat the odds and be a success. As expected, the reviews were uniformly negative, with almost all of them citing the degrading portrait it painted of homosexuality, the intensity of the violence, and the confusing nature of the narrative. As David Ansen put it in his review in *Newsweek*, "What Friedkin's film is about is anybody's guess."

Cruising did exceptionally well during its opening weeks, riding high on the wave of buzz and publicity that piqued audience interest and literally dared them to see something controversial. The film made $5 million in its first five days, and at the end of two weeks it had pulled in $10 million. However, the next two weeks saw it drop off significantly, earning less in fourteen days than it had in its first five (Clagett 207). Still, many who saw the film were put off by it, particularly its violence, once again underscoring how the kinds of graphic violence that were more routinely accepted in the 1970s were no longer tolerable in the Reagan era. As one

7. A sit-in by large numbers of the gay community in Greenwich Village was just one of the extremely public demonstrations staged to protest the production of *Cruising*. This sit-in, which took place on July 27, 1979, was part of a week of sometimes violent demonstrations designed to disrupt the film's production. AP/Wide World Photos.

patron said, "The thing that offended me was the gore. Otherwise, it was kind of monotonous" (qtd. in Pollock).

The film eventually grossed $19.5 million, which made it profitable, but at an enormous cost of bad publicity and increasingly strained relations between Hollywood and the public. *Cruising* became a prime example for many of just how distanced Hollywood filmmakers had become from mainstream audience tastes. The enormous amount of energy that went into making the film acceptable for general theatrical distribution was a drain on studio resources that resulted in little more than the film being cut into near incoherence, thus adding narrative and character problems to the graphic content and further alienating viewers.

Dressed to Kill

The public relations problems caused by *Cruising*'s R rating left a deep scar on the MPAA's credibility in the eyes of both the public and the film industry, and in response it soon thereafter began to take a more proactive stance against violent movies, demanding more cuts to explicit material before awarding R ratings. As Stephen Prince argues, "[The MPAA] assumed its traditional role as mediator and buffer between the industry and the public. If it had not done so with *Cruising*, it would act preemptively to minimize the bloodshed and nastiness of *Dressed to Kill*" (*New Pot of Gold* 365). Brian De Palma's *Dressed to Kill* was another film that mixed sex and violence, although it did so with an edge of hyperrealized style and comic aplomb that was completely lost on its detractors, although not on its audience and many film critics, as it was a commercial and critical hit despite the controversy that surrounded it.

By the time he directed *Dressed to Kill*, De Palma had already made his reputation in Hollywood twice, first with *Greetings* and *Hi, Mom!* (1970), a pair of independently produced, innovative guerrilla films that were admired for their irreverence, and then with a series of clever, often gory horror-thrillers modeled on the work of Alfred Hitchcock: *Sisters*, *Obsession* (1976), *Carrie*, and *The Fury*. The title of Jean Vallely's 1980 *Rolling Stone* article neatly summarizes the discordant understanding of De Palma in the early 1980s: "Brian De Palma: The New Hitchcock or Just Another Rip-Off?" Despite Hitchcock's enormous influence on cinema and the esteem with which he was revered by the critical establishment, De Palma was one of the very few American directors to consciously walk in his footsteps, making films that were overtly Hitchcockian in virtually ever aspect and proudly admitting so in interview after interview. De Palma adopted Hitchcock's flair for extended scenes of suspense, complex tracking shots, and a sense of macabre dark humor. He also shared Hitchcock's penchant for sadism, which he was able to explore in more starkly visual terms than could Hitchcock, who spent most of his career working within the confines of the Production Code. De Palma's films were explicitly sexual and explicitly violent, and his critical reception was frequently mixed, with critics like the *New Yorker*'s Pauline Kael singing his praises, while others like Andrew Sarris viewed him as a slightly clever hack. Nevertheless, De Palma was hell-bent on pushing boundaries, which makes it not particularly surprising that, in the mid-1970s, he had written a complete screenplay for *Cruising* and had intended to direct it. Part of his *Cruising* screenplay involved a sequence where a housewife is murdered, which did not appear in Gerald Walker's source novel. With almost no alteration, this sequence became the basic narrative setup for *Dressed to Kill* (Bouzereau, *De Palma Cut* 57).

Dressed to Kill is essentially a remake of *Psycho*, which is appropriate considering that *Psycho* was Hitchcock's most controversial film, one that threatened to smear his carefully orchestrated public persona, but was a smash hit at the box office and has since come to be regarded as a masterpiece. *Dressed to Kill* was produced and distributed by Filmways Pictures, an independent outfit owned by Samuel Z. Arkoff, best known as the cofounder of American International Pictures, which produced and distributed dozens of science fiction, horror, crime, and biker B-movies in the 1950s, 1960s, and 1970s.[5] *Dressed to Kill* was Filmways' first big-budget production, its bid to compete with the major Hollywood studios; therefore, there was a lot riding on the film financially. This also meant that *Dressed to Kill* was treated as a mainstream Hollywood film, especially since it starred well-regarded actors such as Angie Dickinson, best known for her role on the mid-1970s TV series *Police Woman*, and Michael Caine, who was a highly respected British actor with two Oscar nominations.

The controversies surrounding *Dressed to Kill* began with CARA, which not surprisingly gave the film an X rating. This was not De Palma's first brush with the Rating Board. In fact, his *Greetings* has the distinction of being the first film given an X rating by CARA and, subsequently, the first film whose X rating was appealed by its distributor.[6] Because of the need for *Dressed to Kill* to succeed at the box office, De Palma and his producer, George Litto, did not try to appeal the rating but rather went back and recut the film to accommodate CARA; it took three versions before the board was willing to give it an R rating.[7] This required re-editing the film's three most notorious sequences and redubbing some of the dialogue—for example, replacing the word "cock" with "bulge."

In the opening scene, Angie Dickinson's character, Kate Miller, has a violent nightmare/fantasy in which she is sexually assaulted while showering. This scene was heavily recut to remove several seconds of footage to reduce the voyeuristic close-ups of her pubic hair and also to tone down the violence of her being suddenly attacked from behind. The scene in which Kate is killed in an elevator by a killer wielding a straight razor was also recut, replacing close-ups of the blade slicing her face and neck with long shots from above that minimized the graphic effect of the slashing. The R-rated version of the scene also features several fewer slashes, thus reducing the length of the scene. This was also the case of the shocker "fake" ending (which mirrors the opening scene), in which Liz Blake (Nancy Allen) dreams that someone cuts her throat with a razor. A few frames were trimmed from the actual slicing, as was a close-up of the cut bleeding through her fingers. All in all, the changes amounted to less than a minute of footage, but it was enough to maneuver the film through the gray area between an X rating and an R rating, something that Richard Heffner, then chairman of CARA, admitted was "impossible to define" (qtd. in P. Wood D19). Nevertheless, De Palma was bitter about having to make the changes, largely because he felt that his film was being singled out as a result of the intense criticism heaped on CARA after it gave *Cruising* an R rating. "Why should I suffer for something Billy Friedkin didn't do?" he complained (D19). Thus, the rating fracas over *Dressed to Kill* can be viewed as the first move by CARA to tighten the reins on violent films, which only increased as the teenage slasher genre became increasingly popular throughout the 1980s (see chapter 5 on the horror film).

Like *Cruising*, *Dressed to Kill* was targeted by a vocal group of protesters once it was released in the summer of 1980. In this case, it was anti-pornography feminists, who viewed the film as the mainstreaming

8. Despite having several seconds edited out, the opening sequence of *Dressed to Kill* (1980), in which Kate Miller (Angie Dickinson) has a violent sexual nightmare/fantasy while showering, was a source of controversy and one of the primary targets of feminist critics who argued that the film promoted violence against women. DVD still.

of violent pornography (Prince, *New Pot of Gold* 355). They feared that films of this sort appealed to the basest of male instincts and encouraged violence against women; they read *Dressed to Kill* literally, assuming that, because two very different female characters in the film have violent sexual fantasies, it means that the film asserts that *all* women have such fantasies and, more important, that such fantasies function as wish fulfillment. Their reading of the film as misogynistic is not without merit, although it relies heavily on not looking much beneath the surface, something the protesters assumed the majority of audience members would not do.[8]

Demonstrators assembled in front of theaters in San Francisco, Boston, and Los Angeles. In New York, Women Against Pornography (WAP) organized 100 to 150 picketers at the 57th Street Playhouse, carrying signs denouncing the film as "a racist and sexist lie" and chanting, "Murder isn't sexy, murder isn't funny, but that's how Hollywood makes its money" (Lyons 282). From a rhetorical perspective, it is crucial that the protesters' condemnation of the film was not limited to *Dressed to Kill*, Brian De Palma, or even the studio that financed and distributed it. Rather, it was a condemnation of Hollywood itself, with *Dressed to Kill* being only one example of the depths to which the industry would sink to make a buck. It is precisely this kind of negative publicity, which went well beyond any particular film and tainted the perception of the entire industry, that the studios feared and caused them to back away from such productions in the ensuing years.

The controversy also tainted the role of film critics in the reception of such films. Even though De Palma had his share of dissenters over the years, the critical appraisal of *Dressed to Kill* was largely positive, with many critics lavishing it with near hyperbolic praise. David Denby proclaimed that De Palma had surpassed the cinematic skills of Alfred Hitchcock and also compared the film to the works of Luis Buñuel (Kapsis 205). Pauline Kael, who had been one of De Palma's most openly vocal admirers for years, also compared his work favorably to such masters as Hitchcock, Orson Welles, Jean-Luc Godard, and Roman Polanski but insisted on the ultimate uniqueness of De Palma's vision and highlighted his growth as an artist over the years. "Has any other moviemaker mastered new skills with each picture the way Brian De Palma has?" she asked (*Taking It All In* 35). Steven Schiff of the *Boston Phoenix* declared it was "the best new American film" he'd seen all year (38).

This unqualified praise for what many viewed as a sick, misogynistic, and dangerous film only fired the anger of those who were protesting it. Schiff, for example, found that he was targeted along with the rest of the Hollywood industry: Boston-area protesters urged people to boycott the

9. Members of Women Against Violence Against Women protest the showing of *Dressed to Kill* at the Hollywood Pacific Theatre in Los Angeles. Department of Special Collections, Charles E. Young Research Library, UCLA. Collection 1429 *Los Angeles Times*. Women against Violence protests against Dressed to Kill. CLUS 1429 292848–2 31A.tif.

Boston Phoenix for running Schiff's review, someone spray-painted "Stiff Schiff Porno" on the window of the *Phoenix*'s classified ads office, and he received numerous threatening letters (Schiff 43). This was more of an exception than the rule, though, as the demonstrators were all non-violent and rhetorically framed their movement not as a call for censorship but as a necessary counterbalance to the prevailing critical opinion, which tended to downplay or excuse the film's violence toward women in favor of its aesthetic achievements. According to Dorchen Leidholdt of WAP, "The demonstrations against De Palma's exercise in misogyny and bigotry were intended only to present an opposing voice in the din of critical acclaim that has helped to make *Dressed to Kill* a major box office success" (qtd. in Lyons 283). Thus, WAP and other groups viewed their protests of the film as an educational campaign about a film that they viewed as dangerous.[9]

Of course, the only way to view *Dressed to Kill* as dangerous is to read it literally, which is precisely what its critics did. This was nothing new. De Palma's career had been hounded by accusations of misogyny because many people viewed his films literally and missed their parodic elements. *Dressed to Kill,* with its transsexual serial killer, graphic murder scenes, and steamy shower fantasies that turn suddenly violent, is too easy to find offensive if one sees it all literally. As Kenneth MacKinnon notes, "The movie's imagined appeal to the aesthetic sensibilities of several critics makes it, in the view of its detractors, all the more worthy of combating, since that aesthetic appeal is deemed to have veiled its misogyny" (138).

The film's defenders argue that De Palma's intricate camera work, the mixture of straight and over-the-top performances by the actors, and the manner in which Pino Donaggio's clichéd orchestral score works ironically against the action on-screen show that it is a brilliant send-up of suspense and horror conventions. However, it is not surprising that some reacted against *Dressed to Kill,* because it works *too well.* If De Palma were a shabby, lazy director who made bad movies with violence against women, no one would likely care enough to make a fuss. The problem is that he is too skilled, too perceptive about how viewers' buttons get pushed, and too adept at manipulating their emotions—people get angry because he works them over, but only the ones who can't see the humor in it all—especially their own vulnerability in the darkness of the movie theater.

This is where De Palma excels, and it is the same place in which his spiritual cinematic mentor, Alfred Hitchcock, also excelled. It is at this point, of course, that we should not forget how intensely negative was the response to Hitchcock's *Psycho* when it was first released in 1960. Stanley Kauffman, writing in the *New Republic,* could have been writing about *Dressed to Kill* when he complained that Hitchcock employed "his considerable skill in direction and cutting and in the use of sound and music to shock us past horror-entertainment into resentment" (22).

Despite the troubles *Dressed to Kill* faced, it was a box-office success. When it was released in early August 1980, it was among the top three box-office earners for its first five weeks, hitting number 1 in its first week of wide release. It eventually grossed about $31 million domestically, with rentals of $15 million, which more than doubled its $6.5 million budget, resulting in a handsome profit for Filmways. *Dressed to Kill* was profitable, but it was hardly a major hit; however, it was enough for De Palma to be able to continue making films in this vein for another couple of years.

Although his follow-up to *Dressed to Kill* was *Blow Out* (1981), a political thriller starring box-office star John Travolta that was notably restrained in terms of sex and violence, his next two films were both extremely controversial for their violent content. *Scarface* (1983), a remake written by Oliver Stone of Howard Hawks's 1932 gangster classic, was an epic of violence overload, featuring the infamous bathroom scene in which the title character (Al Pacino) is chained to a curtain rod while his partner is cut to pieces with a chainsaw. Not surprisingly, *Scarface* ran into problems with CARA and had to be recut to avoid an X rating, although De Palma claimed at the time that only a single close-up of an arm that had been cut off in the chainsaw scene was removed (Bouzereau, *De Palma Cut* 66). De Palma ran into the same problem with 1984's *Body Double*, which again veered into Hitchcockian territory (this time riffing on 1954's *Rear Window*) and overt displays of graphic violence against women, including a female character who is killed with an enormous, phallic power drill. This time, however, most critics, even his staunchest defenders, abandoned the film as a cheap exercise in style fraught with violent misogyny, and it sank at the box office.

All this turmoil had an effect on De Palma, as he finally abandoned his fierce resistance to commercial pressures in the mid-1980s by making the mafia comedy *Wise Guys* (1986) and a big-screen update of the classic TV series *The Untouchables* (1987). *The Untouchables* is an unquestionably violent, sometimes brutal film, but one whose violence fits neatly into a traditional narrative framework of good (official hero Eliot Ness, played by Kevin Costner, and his incorruptible band of law enforcement agents) versus evil (sadistic gang kingpin Al Capone, played by Robert De Niro, and his cronies). The recipients of violence, however gruesome, are almost all men, and the violence is comfortably situated within the familiar tenets of the gangster film genre but without any potentially complicating sense of sympathy for the gangster or critique of the source of Ness's moral righteousness (primarily family and country). Even when

Ness kills Capone accomplice Frank Mitty (Billy Drago) in cold blood by shoving him off the courthouse roof instead of simply arresting him, the stark nature of the violence is mitigated by Ness's angry moral righteousness and the cartoonishly unsympathetic nature of the victim, who raises Ness's ire by first mocking the death of his friend and partner Jim Malone ("Your friend died screaming like a stuck Irish pig") and then assuring him that he would "beat the rap." While certainly extreme, Ness's violence is ultimately in the service of law and order and, within the parameters of the film's moral universe, acceptable. Thus, even though De Palma was one of the last of the New Hollywood directors to succumb to the pressures of the retrenched Hollywood industry to change the role of violence in his films, even he wasn't immune.

White Dog

While both *Cruising* and *Dressed to Kill* had difficulties getting through the rating process before being met with virulent and very public protests when they played in theaters, Sam Fuller's *White Dog*, which should have been released theatrically in 1982, never got a theatrical distribution at all. It tells the story of a young actress (Kristy McNichol) who finds an abandoned white German shepherd and eventually learns that it is a "white dog," trained by racists to attack black people. She then works with a black animal trainer (Paul Winfield) in an eventually futile attempt to "cure" the dog by retraining it and erasing its indoctrinated racism.

As a potential storm of controversy brewed around the provocative film, Paramount Pictures decided to cut its losses and shelve it. Although *White Dog* is the least explicitly violent of the three films covered in this chapter, it received the harshest treatment because of the accumulating bad will generated by the films that preceded it. Studio executives had watched all the legal and public relations fiascos the previous films had endured, and by the time *White Dog* was ready for release, most of them were unwilling to go through it all again. Thus, Fuller's film was virtually unseen in the United States for nearly ten years, even though it played successfully in Europe.

Not surprisingly, the project began in the mid-1970s, when Hollywood was a more welcoming place for a socially conscious film about the violence of bigotry. Based on a nonfiction novella by Romain Gary that had first been published as a long story in *Life* magazine, Paramount had originally commissioned the film with the idea that Roman Polanski, hot off *Chinatown*, would direct (other directors attached to the project at various times included Arthur Penn, Don Siegel, and Tony Scott). At the time, Paramount was intensely interested in the project. In an interview, Paramount president Michael Eisner confirmed, "I always thought it was a terrific idea for a movie. I thought it made an interesting statement about how prejudice is taught rather than inherited. But it always ran a high risk of being misunderstood by people" (qtd. in Farber, "Shelf Life" 40).

Eisner was right about the film being at a "high risk of being misunderstood." Even before production began, members of the NAACP, fed by misbegotten rumors that the film would be sensationalist and exploitative, protested, fearing that it might inspire racists to train white dogs of their own. Paramount allowed an NAACP representative to be on set during the production, but this didn't quell their fears. At one point, NAACP national executive director Benjamin Hooks warned the executives at Paramount that the film might be "a 'dangerous' incitement to racism" (qtd. in Farber, "Shelf Life" 40), which was enough to give them the jitters. Hoping to avoid costly re-edits after the production had wrapped, Paramount executives tried to make the film less controversy-provoking, allegedly sending Fuller a ninety-six-page memo of script changes (Callahan). When they saw Fuller's final cut, they were more nervous than ever that the film would provoke controversy and protests. So, in a misguided aim to tone down the film's violence, they re-edited certain sequences and changed dialogue to make it appear that the dog only bit black people rather than killed them. These studio-mandated changes had nothing to do with reducing the graphic representation of violence (in fact, *White Dog* is not a gory film, even in Fuller's original cut, and CARA rated it PG). Rather, it has to do with the *idea* of violence and the fear that it might be imitated, much like the feminist fears that *Dressed to Kill* would encourage violence against women by making it seem enjoyable in a fictional context. The studio executives somehow thought that the idea of virulently racist people training dogs to only hurt black people rather than kill them was somehow less controversial. Ironically, this attempted dilution of the film's provocative content backfired by reducing the intensity of the hate crimes depicted.

White Dog, as conceived by Fuller and co-screenwriter Curtis Hansen, was intended to be "a metaphoric horror story, another nightmarish tale of American madness" (Server 95), with the logical endpoint of that madness being the senseless murder of innocents by a trained animal that doesn't know any better. In effect, the dog is a metaphor for the nature of racism and how it is forcibly passed down from one generation to the next rather than being an inherent element of the human condition. Fuller, a committed liberal filmmaker who had exposed American hypocrisy and racism in numerous films throughout his career, intended the film to be profoundly antiracist. Fuller had a clear history of making films with strong messages about racism and social hypocrisy, and *White Dog* fits neatly into that filmic lineage. He said, "I still don't understand why

Paramount thinks it's touchy; it is strictly an antiracist movie. There is nothing touchy about exposing racists. Nothing at all—except to racists" (qtd. in Osborne, "Rambling Reporter," December 1983, 2). The film's strongest and most disconcertingly complex moment comes with the surprising revelation of the dog's original owner, who turns out to be a decent-looking, grandfatherish character with two small children at his side. As Jonathan Rosenbaum notes, "Unlike the usual clichéd movie iconography, which insists that evil is committed by evil-looking characters . . . Fuller suggests that it can be committed by kindly looking grandfathers as well" (299).

Nevertheless, Fuller and the film's other supporters, including numerous critics and scholars, learned that it didn't really matter what his film was obviously saying; rather, all that was important was that Paramount sensed potential controversy, and in the increasingly conservative atmosphere of the early 1980s, that was to be avoided at all costs. Thus, *White Dog* was shelved. Although Eisner insisted this was done simply because Paramount didn't think it would make any money, Don Simpson, who was head of production at Paramount when *White Dog* was being made, confirmed that the reason the film wasn't distributed was its potentially controversial reception: "After they looked at the picture, the executives felt it was possibly incendiary. There came to be a general feeling that there would not be a good reaction" (qtd. in Farber, "Shelf Life" 41).

Before making the decision to shelve the film, Paramount did test the waters, however tepidly. The film was sneak-previewed in Seattle in early 1982, where it received mixed reactions. That summer, it was again test-screened, this time in Denver, where 75 percent of the audience rated it "good" or "excellent" (Callahan). Based on these responses, Paramount gave the film a limited theatrical run in five theaters in Detroit in November 1982, which resulted in mixed reviews and not much business (Osborne, "Rambling Reporter," November 1983). This was enough justification for Paramount to shelve the $6 million production, but the limited run in Detroit smacks of intended commercial failure used to cover up the studio's real reason for shelving the film. After all, releasing it in only a handful of theaters in Detroit for one week, rather than in larger, more traditionally cinema-oriented cities like Los Angeles or New York, didn't give the film much of a chance to develop word of mouth or positive press.

White Dog was theatrically released throughout Europe in 1982 and 1983, where it was critically acclaimed and made money at the box office. This is not surprising, because Fuller was a highly respected auteur in Europe, particularly in France, while in the United States he was viewed mostly as a relic from a previous era by those who remembered him and was virtually unknown to the generation raised on *Star Wars*.[10] Still, executives at Paramount tried to get as much from the film as they could without stirring up much controversy by licensing it to several pay cable services, including Z Channel, SelecTV, and the Movie Channel. NBC intended to broadcast the film during the February sweeps of 1984, which required Paramount, which was to be paid $2.5 million for two showings, to make the unprecedented move of pulling the film from pay cable only one month into its yearlong run (Graham, "NBC Collars 'White Dog'"). However, the controversy surrounding the film wouldn't die, as NBC abruptly dropped its plans to air it only two days later. Although spokespeople for NBC referred to the film as "well-made" and "anti-racist," the vague statement they presented to explain the sudden move leaves plenty of room to speculate that there was pressure from outside sources not to show the film: "After we notified Paramount of our intentions to buy 'White Dog,' the movie was reviewed in Burbank and New York. A determination was made that it would be inappropriate for us to broadcast it, and we're holding discussions with Paramount about a replacement" (qtd. in Graham, "NBC Pulls 180" 33).

White Dog was eventually given a brief theatrical run in the United States in 1991 in major markets like New York and Chicago, where it was hailed by many critics, including Jonathan Rosenbaum, who declared it the best American movie released so far that year. However, the lingering taint of the controversy that surrounded it in the early 1980s has persisted, and it wasn't until December 2008 that the film was finally released on home video in the United States, and even then Paramount licensed the film to the Criterion Collection, an independent home video distributor, rather than release it under its own banner. Had it been made in the 1970s, *White Dog* might have been seen as a deeply significant film, but it was its great misfortune to have been produced at a time when the commercial and ideological stakes involved in making films with complex violent themes were simply too daunting for Hollywood studios.

Lessons Learned by the Studios

According to Stephen Prince, the fundamental distinction between controversies surrounding screen violence in the classical Hollywood era and the modern (post-1967) era is "the relative degree of emphasis given to referentiality on the one hand, and to style on the other" (*Classical Film Violence* 34). That is, under the Production Code, screen violence was scrutinized more for *what* it represented—a celebration of criminality or an unhealthy fascination with sadism, for example—than *how* it was represented. After the demise of the Production Code, when filmmakers were free to elaborate screen violence in heightened stylistic terms, what

Prince refers to as "stylistic amplitude," violence itself became a category separate from its behavioral referents.

While Prince's argument largely holds true when comparing the classical and modern eras of Hollywood filmmaking, the 1980s poses an interesting discrepancy because the content of violent movies in this era, not just their style, was at the heart of the controversies surrounding *Cruising*, *Dressed to Kill*, and *White Dog*. Scenes of people being stabbed, tortured, and mauled by animals would show up again and again in films throughout the 1980s, but they wouldn't be mired in controversy because the studios eventually learned how to package such instances of violence in a way that made them seem less disturbing to mainstream audiences.

Dressed to Kill, for example, was protested not just because of Brian De Palma's gleefully sadistic depictions of graphic violence but specifically because that violence was perceived as being misogynistic. Many objected to the violence in *Cruising* because of its graphic nature, but many were also disturbed because of its contextual situation within the underworld of gay leather clubs, which fed into the ire of both conservative groups and gay rights activists, if for entirely different reasons. *White Dog* never even got a proper U.S. theatrical distribution because the violence in the film was aimed entirely at African Americans and was thus construed as being racist. Even though the director, Sam Fuller, intended the film to carry an antiracist message, the potentially controversial connection of race and violence was enough for Paramount to shelve the picture. Thus, the contextual mediators of race, gender, and sexuality were central to the controversial nature of these violent films, not just the graphic nature of their aesthetic.

The representations of violence in the films, however gory, was ultimately less important than how they were packaged. These films caused a stir because the violence wasn't packaged for a Reagan-era audience; they were essentially products of the 1970s film culture that came a few years too late. Each of these films became a focusing event for the major Hollywood studios in the early 1980s, directing their attention to the kinds of negative publicity and economic problems that hounded certain kinds of violent films, making them less and less viable products for the studios to fund. The lessons learned from *Cruising*, *Dressed to Kill*, and *White Dog* might be summarized as follows:

First, the New Hollywood directors who came to power in the 1970s were no longer to be trusted with major studio films, particularly ones that dealt with violent subject matter. These filmmakers were still ideologically rooted in an earlier era, which made them problematic from a public relations standpoint. Thus, with only a few exceptions, the studios stopped hiring the New Hollywood directors for major projects, and most of them either slipped into oblivion, struck out on their own independently, or worked their way back into the system by eventually succumbing to Hollywood's mandate for more conventional, conservative, and thus profitable films. For example, William Friedkin tried to blot out the memory of *Cruising* with *Deal of the Century* (1983), an outright comedy about arms dealers starring Chevy Chase. While he tried to recapture the gritty, antiheroic intensity of *The French Connection* in his next film, 1985's *To Live and Die in L.A.*, he had difficulty finding work for the rest of the decade, directing a pilot for a television series called *C.A.T. Squad* and also *Rampage* (1988), a legal thriller that wasn't released theatrically in the United States until 1992. Brian De Palma, on the other hand, continued to make controversial violent films following *Dressed to Kill*, particularly *Scarface* and *Body Double*, both of which willfully thumbed their noses at both the "traditional family values" so coveted by conservatives and the politics of gender representation espoused by leftist social groups. However, in the latter half of the decade, he turned to more studio-acceptable fare, including *Wise Guys*, a mob comedy starring Joe Piscopo and Danny DeVito, and *The Untouchables*, which is particularly telling because it was graphically violent in its depiction of the war waged by federal officer Eliot Ness against Chicago kingpin Al Capone. One of the film's most memorable scenes has Capone unexpectedly bashing someone's head in with a baseball bat at a formal dinner party, after which De Palma uses a lengthy, extreme high-angle crane shot to linger on the ever-growing pool of blood forming around the shattered skull on the table. At the same time, though, the film also asserts with almost parodic conviction the importance of family, honor, and abiding by the law, thus mitigating its graphically violent content.

Second, the studios learned that graphically violent films, particularly those whose violence was tied to challenging or provocative subject matter, were bound to have problems with CARA. This often resulted in films being rated more harshly than the studios wanted, which limited their box-office potential. Warner Bros. learned this lesson with Ridley Scott's *Blade Runner*, a dystopian science fiction film starring Harrison Ford as a man whose job is to hunt down runaway "replicants." The studio thought the film should be rated PG, thus making it more accessible to youth audiences, but CARA stood by its R rating. Universal learned an even harder lesson when dealing with De Palma's *Dressed to Kill* and *Scarface*. While the studios had experimented with releasing X-rated films during the early 1970s, including *Beyond the Valley of the Dolls*, *A Clockwork Orange* (1971), and *Last Tango in Paris* (1972), in the early 1980s it was simply out of the question. Hence, any time a studio-produced or studio-distributed film was rated X by CARA, the filmmakers would have to go back and recut it to obtain an R rating, which was both expensive and time-consuming. Thus, such projects were to be avoided.

Third, intense negative publicity before a film's opening can generate buzz that makes people curious to see a film, but it is usually not enough to sustain the kind of extended theatrical run that results in significant profitability. For example, while *Cruising* had a strong opening largely due to the controversy surrounding it and the attendant curiosity such controversy provokes, its business dropped off sharply afterward. A similar situation occurred with *Dressed to Kill,* which saw its greatest box-office performance the same week that publicly visible protests were at their largest (Lyons); yet, the film went on to become only a modest hit, one whose financial returns were not necessarily worth the negative publicity it had generated.

This leads to the fourth lesson, which is that vocal protesters, even in small groups, can have a significant negative impact on a film's profitability and even keep it from seeing theatrical distribution at all. Although protesters can at first create additional interest in a film, as the cases of *Cruising* and *Dressed to Kill* show, they ultimately create an aura of negativity that is harmful to the studio's public image in the long term. As Charles Lyons argues, "Censorship can be a form of empowerment, a means through which historically marginalized groups can gain a measure of control over the way they are represented in the dominant media" (280). Demonstrations by culturally dominant groups such as the Christian Right tend to result in recognizable acts of censorship, whereas protests by culturally marginalized groups "create an environment that legitimizes suppression and encourages self-censorship" (311). This is precisely what happened when gay rights activists protested *Cruising* and feminists protested *Dressed to Kill.* The immediate results suggest that such demonstrations were failures, in that both films were successful enough at the box office to turn a profit. However, the protests had long-term effects in that the stir was enough to dissuade the studios from funding many films of their ilk for most of the next decade. On the other hand, African American protests against *White Dog,* which never even made it into the public sphere, resulted in that film never being distributed at all, in effect suppressing it from movie audiences. The fact that *White Dog* was scheduled for release in 1982, two years after the trouble stirred around *Cruising* and *Dressed to Kill,* shows how much more willing studios were to avoid controversy as the Reagan decade wore on.

And ultimately, Hollywood learned that, in order for graphic violence to be tolerated by the mainstream public, it needs to be narratively and ideologically packaged in a conservative, unproblematic framework. That is, screen violence in and of itself isn't necessarily a problem; rather, one has to consider *how* it is presented and in *what context.* Screen violence that is deployed in the support or defense of beliefs and values held by the majority is more acceptable, even if it is graphically presented, than screen violence that challenges the audience to question the kinds of traditional values and beliefs that were so crucial to the Reagan-era zeitgeist. Robert Ray argues that the 1970s can be divided into a series of left- and right-cycle films, both of which are internally conservative, with the only difference being the surface radicalism of the left-cycle films. As the studios learned in the early 1980s, even surface radicalism made for an uneasy mix with violence, whereas clear-cut conservatism and traditionalism could contain violence and make it palatable.

As a result of these lessons learned, the studios went into an era of retrenchment, backing away from the kinds of films that were made in the 1970s and focusing on more ideologically conservative, though no less violent, fare that was less likely to stir up protests and bad publicity. One of the obvious choices was the reactionary action film, which we will explore in the next chapter.

3

PURE ACTION, PACKAGED VIOLENCE

THE ROLE OF THE ACTION FILM IN 1980S HOLLYWOOD

PERHAPS THE QUINTESSENTIAL PRODUCT of 1980s Hollywood is the "pure action" movie, whose basic structure and style still dominate many of the most expensive movies produced by Hollywood today. This pure action genre did not simply emerge out of nowhere, nor was it just a reworking of a previously recognized genre or hybridization of multiple genres. Rather, it was the end product of a complex process spawned by controversies over screen violence and driven by a new generation of slick and savvy producers who focused on action spectacle and an ethos of winning at all costs to wipe away the memories of 1970s disillusionment. This was partially a result of increasingly sophisticated cinematic technologies, including the Steadicam, the blood squib, and improved pyrotechnics. But, while the technologies were a driving force, they were only part of the equation. As veteran actor Darren McGavin put it, "Technology has intensified the impact of violence in films. There's a feeling in the industry that the technical possibilities are there, so let's utilize them. The people involved in putting together the film—special effects, makeup, the director—aren't concerned about the political or social connotations. Their concern is: How well does the vest blow out with Technicolor blood? Are the explosions good enough?" (qtd. in Sanoff).

The emphasis on spectacle to the detriment of thematic complexity was central to the primary desires of the Hollywood studios in the 1980s to package screen violence in a way that mainstream audiences would readily accept. The studios understood that audiences wanted violence—this has never been in doubt—and its growing explicitness in the 1970s had set a precedent from which filmmakers could not retreat. Film history has shown repeatedly that depictions of violence tend to escalate over time in terms of their graphic nature and intensity and rarely if ever diminish once a particular level has been reached (see Prince, *Classical Film Violence* 114). However, Hollywood filmmakers were reluctant to wade through the kind of attendant controversies and potentially limited box-office revenues associated with violent movies that touched nerves—the ones like *Dressed to Kill* and *White Dog* that used violence to make social, psychological, and political connections that might be disturbing.

Thus, in an ironic turn, filmmakers made screen violence less controversial by treating it less seriously. The pure action film once again reduced screen violence to a cartoonish level, albeit with a surface of gory verisimilitude that was testament to the lasting influence of the increasing realism of violent films of the 1970s. Yet, after more than a decade of screen exposure, graphic violence had become not just commonplace for American audiences but expected. Even casual moviegoers had come to assume that, when someone was shot on-screen, a bloody squib would rupture to simulate the impact of the bullet, an image that had once been genuinely shocking in and of itself. This was largely true even in PG-rated films, such as Clint Eastwood's *Firefox* (1982), which features a scene in which a scientist is gunned down by a Soviet soldier. The violence in this scene seems particularly gruesome because the contrast of the bloody squibs on the scientist's white lab coat draws absolute attention to them, plus Eastwood frames the shot with the exploding wounds in the foreground and the shooter in the background, thus emphasizing the trauma of bodily damage. This suggests that CARA had also come to see such explicit depictions of violence as customary and accepted—in a word, *normal*. Thus, to move audiences beyond the simplest forms of bodily affect, screen violence had to be not only visually explicit but also placed within a particular context that was geared toward generating an emotional reaction through plot, character, theme, or some combination. This is precisely what pure action films tried *not* to do.

Producers like Joel Silver, Lawrence Gordon, Jerry Bruckheimer, Don Simpson, Mario Kassar, and Andrew Vajna, who were elevated to the level of auteur in the 1980s and became some of the dominant forces within the industry, used the strategy of the pure action genre as one way to package screen violence for profit (very successfully, as it turned out). From an economic standpoint, action films made sense in an increasingly globalized economy in which more than half of a high-budgeted film's box-office take could be expected to come from overseas. Pure action films sold well all over the world because their spectacle translated easily across language and cultural barriers. As actress Meryl Streep quipped, "People don't need to understand English to know something is exploding and to enjoy the spectacle. They don't call it the bottom line for nothing" (qtd. in Prince, *New Pot of Gold* 175).

Meanwhile, audiences could use the pure action films to experience gory thrills vicariously without being disillusioned, disturbed, or threatened. Such films allowed for a sense of detachment, in which the only emotions involved are the primal feelings of fear, excitement, and tension, not to mention the reassurance that the good guys would win in the end, and spectacularly at that. The metaphor of the ride is instructive because it cuts out deep emotional ties and instead emphasizes affect; it makes the viewer's heart pound to see Hollywood action spectacle at its finest, but it doesn't ask much of one's mind, as Martin Scorsese's *Taxi Driver* or Sam Peckinpah's *Straw Dogs* did. The violence can be enjoyed, not questioned. As we will see, even when action films such as *Predator* (1987) contained plot elements with potential sociopolitical ramifications, they were largely ignored by audiences (and many critics) in favor of the film's action dimensions.

As was discussed in the introduction, annual ticket sales had topped out by the 1980s, having been relatively stable at roughly 1 billion for the past twenty years; thus, the studios were not drawing new audience members. However, pure action film producers felt sure that they knew what the audience, particularly the crucial teenage audience, wanted. As Joel Silver, producer of such films as *Lethal Weapon* and *Die Hard*, put it in a 1987 article about Hollywood's growing fascination with adapting comic books into movies, "We're seeing more of a comic-book mentality in the movies today, so it's a national progression. The audience *wants* larger-than-life characters" (qtd. in Gates). And, in discussing the increasing centrality of massive automatic weapons in movies, Silver noted, "Audiences want to see guys with more firepower. However sick it sounds, it's exciting" (qtd. in Karlen and Goldberg). In addition to being "exciting," the violence of the pure action genre was also reassuring. As Sherry Lansing, who became the first woman to head a major studio when she became president of 20th Century-Fox in 1980, put it, "There is so much random violence in the world, and everyone feels very impotent to deal with it. Sylvester Stallone, Charles Bronson, Chuck Norris, Clint Eastwood and Arnold Schwarzenegger take away this sense of impotency. They are mythical figures, bigger than life, who solve all problems. You feel you can't do anything, and then you go to a movie where somebody just takes the law into his hands, righting all wrongs, almost like cowboys used to do" (qtd. in Sanoff).

Violence vs. Action

"Action" had become the keyword for movies by the 1980s because it is just a euphemism for "violence" that doesn't carry a negative charge. It is telling that, when Lawrence Alloway, Toby Mussman, and Robert Smithson put together a retrospective film series at the Museum of Modern Art in the spring of 1969, the title had to be changed from "Violent America: The Movies 1946–1964" to "The American Action Movie: 1946–1964" to placate one of the film companies that was lending its prints (Alloway 7). Apparently, that company didn't want its name associated with "violence," but "action" was acceptable.

This is because "violence" is a harsh, direct word that conveys conflict and damage, trauma and turmoil. In discussing the historical complexity of the term, Raymond Williams notes that, when it is used to refer to "physical force," its most common meaning, it has the connotation of being "unauthorized." That is, whereas terrorists inflict "violence," the police use "force." Thus, to do violence to something, particularly in a social context, is taboo in polite modern society. It is not to be tolerated in any form, and thus it is still hard for many to conceive of it as an acceptable subject for entertainment, which is what Sissela Bok refers to as the "paradox of entertainment violence" (13).

Action, on the other hand, conveys a sense of movement, of velocity, of thrills, but with all the social significance of a roller coaster. It is violence stripped of any meaning or import, which makes it more palatable to the majority of moviegoers because it doesn't force them to confront their own complicity in enjoying violent thrills. It's an unspoken but crucial pact between filmmakers and audiences. Action is a ride—something viewers get on for a brief period of time that allows them to experience vicariously, even relish, the illusion of danger without ever actually being in danger, and then they get off, maybe a little wobbly in the legs and lightheaded, and go home. As Richard Dyer describes it, "To go to an action movie is to sink back in the seat and say, 'show me a good time.' Maybe we also cringe, shield our eyes, convulse our bodies—maybe we are often not so much more sophisticated than those putative Lumière audiences—but mentally we abandon ourselves to the illusion" (20). Critic Stephen Hunter describes a similar reaction to such movies, emphasizing the almost instinctual allure of action and its concomitant universality: "The eye is drawn to action, and if it's skillfully mounted, clearly photographed, gracefully choreographed and vividly edited, it viscerally draws you in. You are responding to the most basic cues—movement and sound, and at some primitive level, your excitement centers are stimulated and you cannot, no matter who you are, deny the urgings of your limbic system" (xxi).

Of course, by the time Dyer wrote his description of action in reference to Jan De Bont's *Speed* (1994) and Hunter wrote his in the preface to a 1995 collection of film reviews, the "action movie" as we currently understand it was a staple of the Hollywood landscape, if not its cornerstone. By the 1990s, action was the most familiar and popular of blockbuster genres, which also include science fiction, fantasy, horror, and comedy.

Yet, those other blockbuster genres have been familiar to audiences since the pre-sound era, whereas the action movie, in its current understanding, is a distinct product of the 1980s, one that was literally created by a cadre of Hollywood producers who struck gold in mining the American audience's desire for screen violence without any overt socially meaningful baggage weighing it down. Producers realized that screen violence, when packaged properly, could sell tickets without stirring controversy. The trick was not to tone down the screen violence but rather to rework it by invoking classical norms in an updated, hyperstylized form. Insulated within reactionary plots, wielded by cartoonish, quip-spouting heroes, and fueled by rock-music soundtracks and eye-boggling special effects, screen violence was made consumer-friendly, even as body counts rose and the verisimilitude of bloody effects was improved.

The Action Film as Genre: The Path to "Pure Action"

Action is a fundamental part of the movies; it is inherent in the name itself. Because of this, for a long time "action movies" were not thought of by either producers or audiences as a separate genre, because their primary defining characteristic—action—was dispersed in varying degrees in almost every genre. In other words, action couldn't be said to be unique to the action movie in the way the iconic elements of the western are associated primarily with that genre.

In its broadest sense, then, up until the 1980s, action as a genre was largely conceived of as a vague umbrella under which a number of other more specifically recognizable genres could be grouped. Thus, in Lawrence Alloway's companion book to the Museum of Modern Art's 1969 film series on American action films from 1946 to 1964, he rarely refers explicitly to "action films" as a category. Instead, he writes at length about "gangster films," "prison films," "war films," "private-detective films," and "Westerns"—all genres with unique characteristics that are unified only by the significant inclusion of violent action.

For most of Hollywood's history, action was linguistically conjoined with adventure to describe a range of films, notably those identified by Alloway, as well as more exotic types such as swashbucklers and jungle adventure films. The term "action-adventure" has a long history in Hollywood marketing, dating back to at least 1927 when *Film Daily* used it to describe a Douglas Fairbanks film called *The Gaucho*. Films bearing the action-adventure label have a number of common characteristics, including spectacular physical action; a narrative emphasis on fights, chases, and explosions; and a combination of state-of-the-art special effects and stuntwork (Neale, *Genre and Hollywood* 52), all of which aptly describe the pure action film as it developed in the 1980s.

However, even though action-adventure films from the 1920s and pure action films from the 1980s have a number of characteristics in common, there is a crucial difference: Pure action films differ from their action-adventure predecessors in the manner in which the action is situated within the film's narrative context. Specifically, the action itself, rather than being one element among many, became dominant; action became the organizing principle of everything in the film, from the plot, to the dialogue, to the casting. Story lines became thinner and often incoherent at times in order to make room for spectacular set pieces, dialogue was reduced to either conveying necessary plot information or throwing out witty quips, and actors who were more renowned for their physicality than their acting prowess (for example, Arnold Schwarzenegger, Sylvester Stallone, Chuck Norris, Dolph Lundgren, Steven Seagal, and Jean-Claude Van Damme) became highly paid international superstars.

Not surprisingly, many critics looked at this development with disdain, seeing it as a blight on the cinematic art, the worst possible combination of populism and profit-seeking. They quickly recognized the subversion of the classical elements of Hollywood filmmaking—plot structure, character motivation, theme—to the demands of on-screen action. For instance, writing about *Missing in Action* (1984), *New York Times* critic Janet Maslin noted, "Unlike 'Uncommon Valor,' another vehement action film about a scheme to rescue missing American soldiers, 'Missing in Action' wastes neither time nor words on veterans' complex feelings about Vietnam, or the war's effects on their families. Instead, it begins as an unabashed shoot-'em-up, with Mr. Norris, as an Army colonel, blasting his way through the jungle" ("Short on Talk"). Similarly, in writing about *Blue Thunder* (1983), Vincent Canby described the action as being "fairly relentless" while the screenplay was "so small it could have been written on the head of a pin," resulting in a film that "isn't especially fulfilling" ("Video Games"). For Canby, as for most mainstream critics, a film couldn't possibly fulfill when it was served up as large portions of action with only minimal side servings of plot, character, dialogue, and theme.

Thus, pure action films are the logical endpoint of what James Monaco has called "the Bruce aesthetic," named after the mechanical shark in *Jaws*. This aesthetic is "visceral—mechanical rather than human," and it results in films that are "machines of entertainment, precisely calculated to achieve their effect" (qtd. in Schatz, "New Hollywood" 19). Rikke Schubart has theorized the shift in the action genre in the mid-1980s in terms of "passion," which "has to do with plot, motive and myth," and "acceleration," which refers to "speed and spectacle, affect and exhilaration" (192). Schubart argues that these two elements used to meet in classic action film plots, in which the action hero was presented as a Christ figure who went through a period of suffering before emerging victorious. Thus, the action hero transforms his suffering into triumph, joining together the twin mythological structures of the "innocent victim" and "lonely avenger," or, in anthropologist René Girard's terms, "the rites of the scapegoat and the rites of the king join in the myth of the action hero" (193). In his suffering and redemption, the action hero was made recognizably human at the same time that his deployment of violence was justified: "The Pain justifies, even demands, vengeance. No one is more justified in using violence than the victim of violence" (196).

Starting with Arnold Schwarzenegger's cyborg antihero of *The Terminator*, though, passion receded from the action film and was almost fully replaced by acceleration: "The heroes of these films have no past as broken idols, they have no need to reenact castration, and they are never in any danger" (Schubart 199). Although remnants of passion remained in post-*Terminator* action films (for example, Martin Riggs's [Mel Gibson] emotional self-torture regarding the death of his wife and his later physical torture by the villains in *Lethal Weapon*), it became less and less crucial to the pleasures the films have to offer. The action hero thus becomes "a narcissistic hero . . . who protects the weak, who on the one hand represents the law and who on the other hand is untouched by the laws of nature and the reality principle—indeed, a paradoxical figure" (201).

This dovetails with the idea of the "hard bodies" of the 1980s action films as collective symbols of America in the Reagan decade—"heroic, aggressive, and determined" (Jeffords 25). To inflict truly damaging violence on these bodies—the kind that for even a moment might suggest potential fallibility—would be a symbolic return to the weakened "soft body" years of the Carter administration. Thus, action heroes were progressively harder and more indestructible, eliminating even a hint of weakness. As we will see in the discussion of the pure action film as conceived in the Don Simpson/Jerry Bruckheimer mold, it was crucial that the new action hero be, at all costs, a "winner."

This loss of passion, of course, results in a loss of character identification, as the audience no longer suffers along with the hero before vicariously experiencing the thrill of his resurrection and vengeance, which is why action spectacle grew bigger, louder, and more violent throughout the 1980s. Thus, by mid-decade, the pure action genre—characterized by increasing spectacle and diminishing emotional and thematic meaning—had become one of the dominant box-office trends.[1]

Red Dawn: The Creation of a Pure Action Film, or How a 1970s Antiwar Film Became a 1980s Action Film

To illustrate this emphasis on the pure action genre in the 1980s and on how a large amount of screen violence could be made palatable to the mass audience by wrapping it in a conservative narrative structure, it is instructive to look at a rather extreme example: *Red Dawn*, which was directed by John Milius and was the first movie to receive a PG-13 rating from CARA (this new rating, a product of changing trends in screen violence in the 1980s, will be discussed in depth in chapter 6). Had it been made ten years earlier at the height of the critical, auteur-driven New Hollywood era, *Red Dawn* would have been an entirely different film in terms of both shape and substance, and its shift from being a psychologically driven, antiwar parable to a rousing, action-oriented anti-Communist fantasy tells us much about the state of the film industry in the 1980s and about how the studios employed screen violence to earn box-office dollars and avoid controversy.

The script was originally written by Kevin Reynolds when he was a student at the University of Southern California's School of Cinema and Television in the late 1970s. Then titled *Ten Soldiers*, it took place in the near future and told the story of a group of young high school students in Colorado who barely escape a surprise invasion of the United States by taking refuge in the mountains, where they eventually develop into guerrilla fighters who resist the foreign invaders. The story had a dark, antiwar edge that did not celebrate the students' heroism so much as it questioned the slippery moral slope on which they stood. The story centered on how the strongest members of the group take control and assert their authority, and one of its overriding thematic threads is how power can be abused.

Peter Bart, who had fostered the original script as a senior vice president for production at MGM/UA, described *Ten Soldiers* as being thematically similar to William Golding's classic novel *Lord of the Flies*, about a group of refined British schoolboys who descend into savagery after being deserted on an island in the middle of a futuristic world war. According to Bart, "The story darkens into a cautionary tale about the brutalization of the innocent" (Bart and Guber 80). Milius had similar memories of the original script, which he also likened to *Lord of the Flies* and described as "very internal" (IGN FilmForce 15). Writer/producer Barry Beckerman, who was the first to option Reynolds's script, saw it as having "the potential to become a taut, tough 'art' picture made on a modest budget that could possibly break out to find a wider audience" (Bart, *Fade Out* 110), which sounds very much like a film that would have been made in the mid-1970s.

That was not the film that was eventually made, however. By the time *Ten Soldiers* finally went into production in 1983 under the new title *Red Dawn*, Milius had significantly retooled the script at the behest of MGM/UA CEO Frank Yablans. Milius's right-wing ideological inclinations and emphasis on action were clearly at odds with the antiwar message in Reynolds's original script.[2] Robert Kolker describes Milius as "a self-proclaimed fascist" whose work "is overblown with portent and violence, full of racism, misogyny, meanness, and vulgarity that go with his ideology" (177). Although routinely grouped with other director-auteurs of the New Hollywood "Film Generation" because he was a student at USC in the same class that produced George Lucas and John Carpenter, Milius was an archconservative, an avid gun collector who stood out among his more liberal associates.[3] His first work in Hollywood in the early 1970s had been associated with the strain of reactionary films that reimagined the western hero as a lone vigilante surrounded by rampant crime in a crumbling American society that was the legacy of the liberal 1960s. He did uncredited screenplay work on *Dirty Harry* and co-wrote its sequel, *Magnum Force* (1973), and that experience with heroic vigilantism is apparent in his work on *Red Dawn*. His biggest directorial success was 1982's *Conan the Barbarian*, which gave Arnold Schwarzenegger his first worldwide exposure as an action star.

Under Milius's direction, *Red Dawn* changed from being a psychologically driven antiwar story to a prime example of the "pure action movie," one that is deeply infused with Reagan-era anti-Communism and celebration of patriotic violence. He kept Reynolds's scenario and even allowed for some suggestions of complexity, such as the depiction of some of the teenage guerrillas turning on each other and the sympathetic portrayal of a Cuban general (Ron O'Neal) who eventually identifies with them. However, the overall message the film proclaims is the mythical, regenerative power of violence—the might of right, so to speak. The band of teenage guerrilla fighters is like a collective vigilante, a lone force fighting against oppressive Communist invaders who round up American citizens, put them in internment camps, and either "re-educate" them or ruthlessly slaughter them. The "criminals" against whom the teens fight are given a new, more globalized face in the invading Soviet, Cuban, and Nicaraguan soldiers, which formed a triumvirate of foreign nations most demonized by the Reagan administration. While the first two nations were viewed as the primary bastions of Communism in the world, Nicaragua was blamed by the Reagan administration for terrorism in Central America. Thus, unlike the films of the 1970s that looked inward to America's own heart to find its villains, *Red Dawn* found the enemy outside, a common trope in pure action films.[4] The vision of bucolic midwestern America overrun with Eastern Bloc and Latin American forces was a potent image at the height of Reagan's re-escalated Cold War standoff with Communist nations—in some ways more visceral, if significantly less likely, than the fear of nuclear holocaust.[5]

Milius made the violence in *Red Dawn* graphic and relentless. According to Peter Bart, this was at the behest of Yablans, who insisted that the movie be more *Rambo* than *Lord of the Flies*: "Milius will shoot Reynolds's script," Yablans said. "He'll just give it a little more energy. After all, *First Blood* grossed a lot more than fucking *Lord of the Flies*" (qtd. in Bart and Guber 80). As Bart put it, Milius "exponentially increased the firepower of the battles, as well as their body count" (80). The guerrilla fighting envisioned by Reynolds as a path to the corruption of the innocent gave way to flag-waving, full-scale battles between the American teenagers and the invading soldiers. In fact, the film's narrative arc can be traced along the line of the teens' increasingly powerful weapons, going from hunting knives, shotguns, and bows and arrows, to AK-47s, landmines, and grenade launchers. Milius wound up making the film so pervasively violent that for a while it was listed in *The Guinness Book of World Records* as the Hollywood film featuring the most acts of violence. At the time of its release, the National Coalition on Television Violence declared it was the most violent film ever made because it averaged 134 acts of violence per hour.

Nevertheless, there were virtually no vocal protests against the film, except for the scathing reviews. Vincent Canby of the *New York Times* described it as "one of those rarely terrible movies that you cannot afford to miss—technically proficient, emotionally infantile and politically nuts, though not, I think, especially dangerous. It's too ludicrous" ("Cockeyed"). Virtually every review about the film commented on its violence but offered an explanation for why it wasn't emotionally disturbing. Bob Thomas of the Associated Press noted that "the battle scenes are neither dramatic nor convincing, merely brutal" ("*Red Dawn*"). While Janet Maslin referred to the film as "alarming," she argued that Milius's over-the-top direction robbed the film's violence of any emotional power: "[Milius] might have turned this into a genuinely stirring war film if he had not also made it so incorrigibly gung-ho. But the effectiveness of its chilling premise . . . is dissipated by wildly excessive directorial fervor at every turn" ("World War III"). Vincent Canby was the most direct in connecting the lack of impact in the film's violence to the way it was packaged aesthetically and thematically: "The violence in 'Red Dawn' is mostly so impersonal and conventional—so obviously the work of special effects artists—that the movie seems less violent even than Mr. Milius' earlier comic-strip of a film, 'Conan the Barbarian'" ("Cockeyed").

Red Dawn is an instructive example of how screen violence in the 1980s could be pumped up in terms of quantity and gruesomeness (despite Canby's assertions, much of the violence in the film *is* quite realistic, at least physically) yet not have the divisive, controversy-provoking impact on audiences that so many violent films of the 1970s had. First, the film's violence is directed against recognized foreign antagonists rather than women, minorities, homosexuals, and other marginalized groups within the United States, which, as we have seen, led to numerous protests and controversies with films like *Dressed to Kill* and *White Dog*. By directing the film's violence against foreign bodies, the era's social unease was displaced from socially sensitive internal targets to an easily demonized external target that few people were willing to defend.

Thus, the violence in *Red Dawn* was packaged as one aspect of a conservative fantasy that played on and then placated Cold War audience fears by imagining an awful, just barely plausible scenario and then supplying an easy solution. The trauma of invasion is easily remedied by the subsequent rise of American determination via the teenage rebels. As Canby put it, the violence in *Red Dawn* "makes small and comprehensible a war that many experts believe would be the last. It doesn't exactly defuse healthy anxiety. It ignores it by substituting for a vision of the possible holocaust a contemporary cowboys-and-Indians yarn" ("Cockeyed"). Further, the film simultaneously refutes and underscores American power, thus assuaging guilt: By making the United States the victim of invasion, the film shows that the nation is always vulnerable; thus, we must continue to maintain a vigorous watch. On the other hand, the film shows that even such an invasion would not be enough to kill the American spirit, which here becomes all-encompassing by appropriating the fighting style associated with U.S. enemies, namely the Vietcong and Latin American and Middle Eastern terrorists.

According to Peter Bart, the conservative ideology in *Red Dawn* was not just a by-product of the times in which it was made but rather a purposeful strategy enacted by the studio:

> The official line of the studios is that ideology doesn't figure in the filmmaking process. That makes "Red Dawn" an infamous exception. The people who made the movie cynically distorted its original anti-war theme. Mid-'80s America, to their thinking, was shifting sharply to the right, and "Red Dawn" was intended to capitalize on this movement. Indeed, the then-CEO of MGM/UA [Frank Yablans], which financed the picture, actually recruited Alexander Haig, Ronald Reagan's "I-am-in-control" top aide, to consult with the film's director and inculcate the appropriate ideological tint. ("'Red Dawn'")

The studio was so intent on making the film a right-leaning fantasy of regenerative violence that it even made the famously conservative Milius a bit uneasy. Bart noted that as production moved ahead, Milius became "alarmed" about the direction the film was headed. "Wandering into my office one day, he confided his concern that he was being railroaded into what he described as 'a flag-waving, jingoistic movie.' Milius said his intent was to make a movie about the 'futility of war,' adding, 'I have a nervous feeling that Yablans and Haig are jabbering away on their hot line about a different movie'" ("'Red Dawn'").

Regardless of how involved Milius was in Yablans's strategy, it ultimately paid off in that it was only film critics, a lone television watchdog group, and the Soviet press who were appalled enough by the reactionary violence of *Red Dawn* to generate any press reports. There were no protests of any kind when the film was released at the end of the summer of 1984, and it had a healthy box-office take of $38 million, which, according to Milius, made it the film that "saved MGM that year" (IGN FilmForce 15).[6]

Since then, *Red Dawn* has gained a substantial following on home video and cable television, making it a film with a significant legacy, particularly because the viewers most attracted to it were adolescent boys who now consider it to be part of their childhood experience. While not as markedly associated with gung-ho Reaganite filmmaking as *Rambo: First Blood Part II* (1985), *Red Dawn* has seeped into the popular culture mindset as an example of either fervently patriotic or frighteningly reactionary entertainment, depending on one's point of view. Thus, the film cropped up in the news in 2003 when the U.S. troops assigned to tracking down Saddam Hussein after the successful toppling of his government in Iraq named their mission "Operation Red Dawn." According to army captain Geoffrey McMurray, the officer responsible for choosing the name, "Operation Red Dawn was so fitting because it was a patriotic, pro-American movie" (qtd. in Soriano). Captain McMurray also noted that he thought "all of us in the military have seen *Red Dawn*," and his first encounter with the film was when he was ten years old.

Producers in Control: Don Simpson and Jerry Bruckheimer

While *Red Dawn* is one of the more extreme examples of how screen violence was conservatively packaged in action films of the 1980s, the decade was replete with scores of ideologically and aesthetically similar films that were, like *Red Dawn*, popular with audiences and largely scorned by critics. However, one cannot conceive of this shift in screen violence and its role in the increasingly popular pure action genre without considering the changing role of the producer.

The model for this producer control of the pure action genre can be traced to Albert R. "Cubby" Broccoli's James Bond franchise and Gene Roddenberry's *Star Trek* television series (Welsh). Until his death in 1996, Broccoli oversaw the production of every "official" James Bond film, starting with 1963's *Dr. No.*[7] Although those sixteen films featured almost as many directors and four different actors who embodied the British secret agent (Sean Connery, George Lazenby, Roger Moore, and Timothy Dalton), "the influence of Broccoli as the producer of these entertainments remained constant" (164). Similarly, James M. Welsh argues for the centrality of Roddenberry to the *Star Trek* universe not only because he created the original television show in the late 1960s but because he was largely responsible for being able to bridge the media gap from television to feature films in the 1980s.

Thus, as the director was central to understanding filmmaking in general, and screen violence in particular, in the late 1960s and throughout the 1970s, the 1980s turned into the decade of the producer, in which young, ambitious Hollywood producers assumed control from the faltering wunderkinds of the New Hollywood and asserted a new vision of what mainstream filmmaking should be. While the Film School Generation directors remained mired in the "world of revolution," as Jack Valenti had put it, many producers were more in tune with what the majority of American audiences wanted in the Reagan era, and they delivered a string of box-office hits that were defined largely by their escapist screen violence and increasing centrality of action spectacle at the expense of character, narrative, and theme. In the genre of pure action, producers ran the show.

Chief among these producers was the team of Don Simpson and Jerry Bruckheimer, who were known collectively within the industry as "the boys." By the time they were in their early forties, they had produced some of the most commercially successful high-concept Hollywood movies of the era, including *Flashdance* (1983), *Beverly Hills Cop, Top Gun,* and *Beverly Hills Cop II* (1987), the last three of which were the highest or second-highest grossing movies of their respective years, making Simpson and Bruckheimer the most powerful producers in Hollywood. In terms of hit-making in the 1980s, they were virtually without peer (only Steven Spielberg could be said to be more consistently successful at the box office), as their movies generated $2.27 billion by the end of the decade (Prince, *New Pot of Gold* 209). As John N. Krier, president of National Exhibitor Relations Co., put it, "They're hitting the pulse of the theater audience like no one else" (qtd. in R. Grover).

Not only did their films rake in dollars at the box office, but they established a tone and style that was later emulated by the rest of the industry. Thus, Simpson and Bruckheimer were cinematically influential—pioneers, in their own way—helping to develop and make popular a visually slick, narratively simple, fast-paced, feel-good, high-concept formula that many likened to feature-length music videos. The movies they made were fundamentally different from the majority of those that had been made ten years earlier, and they were central to the shift in tone and style between the 1970s and 1980s. As head of production for Paramount Pictures in the early 1980s, Don Simpson had been prescient in his understanding of the larger cultural shifts that were taking place and what audiences wanted. In 1981, he butted heads with Paramount president and chief operating officer Michael Eisner over Sam Fuller's *White Dog*, which Eisner insisted would be the next *Jaws* (Fleming 33). But Simpson clearly saw the writing on the wall that, as the previous chapter made clear, *White Dog* was a film of a different era, and he wanted to focus his attention on *An Officer and a Gentleman* (1982), which Eisner derided as "a little romantic movie" (33). In the end, *White Dog* provoked so much pre-release controversy that it ended up on the shelf, while *An Officer and a Gentleman* went on to earn $55 million and become the fourth highest-grossing film of 1982, cementing Richard Gere's movie star status in the process.

Like any good partnership, Simpson and Bruckheimer complemented each other's strengths and weaknesses; they often described themselves as two sides of the same brain. Simpson, who began as a production assistant at Paramount in 1975 and moved his way up to production chief in less than ten years, was the story side of the Simpson/Bruckheimer collective brain. He was well known in the industry for digging up great ideas, and he worked tirelessly with writers to fashion them into high-concept screenplays. Bruckheimer, who had worked as a still photographer and director of commercials, focused on the visuals. He made sure that, if anything, Simpson/Bruckheimer films looked good. They were polished, efficient, and immensely enjoyable eye candy.

From a business standpoint, Simpson and Bruckheimer not only knew how to develop films that drew audiences to the theaters but also took an active role in how their movies were sold. Early on, they were attuned to Hollywood's emphasis on ancillary markets (Schatz, "New Hollywood"), as the rock music–fueled soundtracks for their films sold in the millions (the soundtrack for *Flashdance* sold an astounding 17 million [R. Grover]). They were even able to convince Paramount to create a merchandising unit after the studio failed to take full advantage of the leg-warmer and bomber jacket fashion fads inspired by *Flashdance* and *Top Gun*, respectively (R. Grover; Kent 208).

More than anything, though, Simpson and Bruckheimer were the models of the new producer as auteur, a label they not only accepted but actively coveted. "For better or worse, Jerry and I have been the authors of our movies," Simpson declared (qtd. in Taylor 145). In the 1970s, producers were understood within the industry as being back-office men who dealt with money and schedules but had little real impact on the look and feel of the films they produced. Simpson described such producers as exactly what he didn't want to be: "Unfortunately, most producers today call themselves producers but what they really do is stay in their offices and make phone calls. That's why producers have gotten a bad name. They're not filmmakers. They're deal-makers. And they're not developers. They don't know anything about script. They are businessmen" (qtd. in Litwak 145).

Simpson and Bruckheimer were anything but back-office money managers. Rather, they actively thought of themselves as and acted like filmmakers, asserting control of their productions at virtually every phase. They were "control freaks," a term that was in vogue in the 1980s business world (Taylor 135). Simpson described their approach: "We're not only hands-on, we're feet-on. We don't take a passive role in any shape or form" (qtd. in Prince, *New Pot of Gold* 209). This was true at every stage of a Simpson/Bruckheimer film's development. Before cameras rolled, Simpson would work with the screenwriters, sometimes going through dozens of drafts before he approved, and he and Bruckheimer made all the major casting decisions. They were also constantly on the set of their films—if not directing the film itself, then directing the director—and they were centrally involved in their films' marketing and promotion, usually giving more prime interviews than the film's director. John Taylor likens Simpson and Bruckheimer to the studio heads of the fabled Hollywood Studio Era: "They were the most prominent examples of a group of individuals who took control of the film-making process away from the directors and placed it back in the hands of the producers. Simpson and Bruckheimer came to run their operation the way Selznick and Thalberg and the other studio heads had run their studios. They exercised total control" (141).

By mid-decade, the advertising for their films began to reflect their authorial presence, thus visually marking them as Simpson/Bruckheimer products. For example, the advertising one-sheet for *Top Gun* prominently features "A Don Simpson/Jerry Bruckheimer Production" near the top of the design, just above the names of stars Tom Cruise and Kelly McGillis, thus textually giving them nearly the same luminous star power. The complete absence of the director's name anywhere on the poster except in the credits at the very bottom also clearly reinforces Simpson and

Bruckheimer as the film's "authors." *Top Gun*'s tag line, "Up there with the best of the best," which runs across the very top of the poster, refers to the aspirations of the young ace navy pilot played by Cruise, but it might as well have been written to describe Simpson and Bruckheimer.

Similarly, the advertising one-sheet for *Days of Thunder* (1990), another vehicle for Tom Cruise that many rightly likened to *Top Gun* on a racetrack, prominently features Simpson and Bruckheimer's authorial agency by placing "A Don Simpson/Jerry Bruckheimer Production" directly above the film's title but relegating the director's name to the list of credits at the bottom. Granted, the word "Cruise" at the top of the poster textually dominates everything on it, thus reflecting the rising enormity of Tom Cruise's star power, but the close placement of Simpson and Bruckheimer's names to the title makes it look as though they are conjoined, almost possessive.

The textual placement of Simpson and Bruckheimer's names and the absence of the director's on the advertising posters for their films visually reflects how they maintained their authorial power by controlling the director, treating him as if he were just another member of the crew. Not surprisingly, the one commercially unsuccessful Simpson/Bruckheimer production during the 1980s was 1984's *Thief of Hearts*, which is the only one to have been made by someone who both wrote the script and directed the film, thus suggesting a higher level of directorial power in shaping the finished product.

In order to maintain control, Simpson and Bruckheimer chose again and again to work with young, visually gifted directors who had started out directing commercials and music videos but were just breaking into feature films. These directors were skilled, efficient, and talented but relatively powerless within the industry; thus, Simpson and Bruckheimer could exert a consistent level of control over them to ensure that the movie turned out the way they wanted it. Simpson and Bruckheimer did not regard the director as an artist with a unique, personal vision—that might get in the way of their own. The directors they chose to work with included Adrian Lyne, a British commercial director whose only feature film was the 1980 teen drama *Foxes* before he directed *Flashdance*; Martin Brest, who had been a promising film student at New York University and had directed two feature films by the late 1970s but hadn't worked in almost five years when Simpson and Bruckheimer tapped him to direct *Beverly Hills Cop*; and Tony Scott, who directed *Top Gun, Beverly Hills Cop II*, and *Days of Thunder*.

Scott is a particularly interesting case because he represents the two things that Simpson and Bruckheimer seemed to cherish most in a director: visual acumen and a lack of power. Scott, brother of director Ridley

Scott (*Alien*, 1979; *Blade Runner*), had directed thousands of TV commercials in the 1970s, but his only feature film was the visually gorgeous but critically slammed modern-day vampire tale *The Hunger* (1983), which critics saw as a vapid exercise in style and audiences largely avoided. Thus, Scott had proved his aesthetic sensibilities, but the disaster of *The Hunger* was almost enough to push him out of the business, making him a perfect choice to play by Simpson and Bruckheimer's rules.

By the end of the 1980s, Don Simpson and Jerry Bruckheimer had been so successful that Paramount Pictures offered them an unheard-of deal: $300 million for developing, producing, distributing, and marketing five Simpson/Bruckheimer movies over the next ten years that did not require studio script approval. In effect, they were given free reign to produce whatever they wanted at the studio's expense; that's how badly Paramount wanted to keep them on its lot. And, even though the deal eventually fell through less than a year later, at the time it was announced, it marked "a new pinnacle of producer power" (Kent 190).

"Losers Are Boring": Violence for the Sake of Winning

While Don Simpson and Jerry Bruckheimer had a substantial effect on the look and style of pure action movies in the 1980s, their most effective contribution to Hollywood filmmaking and the one that most clearly tied them to the excesses of the decade was thematic. They reinvigorated the action genre by shifting the thematic focus away from specific external goals to the aggrandizement of one central character who won in the end, not for some larger purpose, but for the simple sake of winning. As Simpson put it, "By and large life is separated. There are people who are successful and who win. They have moments of pain but they are winners. Then there are losers. Jerry and I side with the winners. We aren't interested in losers. They're boring—to us" (qtd. in Taylor 144). Such an attitude immediately separates Simpson and Bruckheimer's films thematically from the New Hollywood films of the 1970s, which were obsessed with depicting "losers." These would include the embittered, increasingly psychotic Travis Bickle (Robert De Niro) in Martin Scorsese's *Taxi Driver*; the cynical private detective Jake Gittes (Jack Nicholson), who is unable to save anyone, much less himself, at the end of Roman Polanski's *Chinatown*; and the motorcycle-riding outsiders (Dennis Hopper and Peter Fonda) of Dennis Hopper's *Easy Rider*, who fail to "find America" and wind up dead by the side of the road. These are precisely the kinds of characters Simpson and Bruckheimer were not interested in; rather, they wanted to depict, in Bruckheimer's words, "the inner strength of the character and the conviction to better themselves, to attain their own personal goals" (144).

A good example is Axel Foley, the fast-mouthed, rule-breaking Detroit police detective played by Eddie Murphy in *Beverly Hills Cop* and *Beverly Hills Cop II*. In the first film, Foley travels to Beverly Hills in order to find out who killed his best friend, Mikey Tandino (James Russo). Although he uncovers a drug smuggling operation masked by an art gallery, Foley's desire to defeat the villains has literally nothing to do with their criminality and everything to do with his desire for personal vengeance. This is reenacted in the sequel when he returns to Beverly Hills to find out who shot down Andrew Bogomil (Ronny Cox), the police lieutenant-turned-captain he befriended in the first film. Thus, everything he does in both films is framed by his individual need to find out who hurt a friend and exact the proper punishment. Although Foley is a police officer and thus a public servant, his goals are entirely personal. Victory at the end is victory for Axel Foley and no one else.

A similar principle is at work in many pure action films of the 1980s, as the hero pursues villains less to protect society than to assert his own personal superiority. *Predator* is another good example, as the entire film literally boils down to a mano-a-mano standoff between Major "Dutch" Schaeffer, played by Arnold Schwarzenegger, and the alien predator who has hunted and killed his platoon of soldiers one by one. The ethos of the genre can be summed up by the tag line of another Schwarzenegger film, *Commando* (1985): "Somewhere . . . somehow . . . someone's gonna pay!"

Thus, winning in and of itself becomes the end goal, which reflects not only the bull-market mentality of the Reagan era in general but the attitude of the producers themselves. It's no small surprise that Simpson and Bruckheimer considered themselves to be their own primary audience; as they said in many interviews, they made movies that they as moviegoers would want to see. John Taylor describes this attitude as an appetite—the willingness to do literally anything to achieve a goal because one is voraciously hungry for victory. This appetite tended to define Simpson and Bruckheimer's central characters as well, and audiences gorged on this big-screen fantasy of Reagan-era power after a decade of defeat and cynicism. Alan Nadel argues that the equation between winning and legitimacy endemic to Reagan-era films made them structurally more like games than classical narratives, in which "the players are, theoretically, equal and interchangeable" and "each act responds to the immediate situation, with the only objective being to win" (122). Furthermore, "since a game has no justification beyond its own arbitrary existence as the source of equally arbitrary roles, efficacy is the only ethic, and anyone who invokes other restraints, either internal or external, is simply a bad player" (122).[8] This helps explain the insistent emphasis in *Beverly Hills Cop* and *Beverly Hills Cop II* on renegade rule-breaking, as Axel Foley can achieve his goal of personal vengeance only by subverting the rigid codes and "by-the-book" procedures of the Beverly Hills police detectives, who are "bad players" because they have ethics outside of Foley's efficacy. Several of these Beverly Hills police detectives, namely Sergeant Taggart (John Ashton) and his partner, Detective Billy Rosewood (Judge Reinhold), endear themselves to Axel and the audience only after they break the rules, thus displaying their "appetite" for victory.

This attitude also distinguishes pure action movies from one of their cinematic precursors, the western, which presents the prototypical narrative and reactionary structure for justified violence. These two genres share in common the same idea of regenerative violence, in which the protagonist is ultimately redeemed through the justifiable use of force (Cawelti; Wright). Beyond this, though, they diverge completely in their use of violence. Whereas John G. Cawelti defines the western hero as being "fundamentally committed to the townspeople" (73), the modern action hero is fundamentally committed to himself, and any social usefulness he provides is largely incidental. When Maverick shoots down attacking Soviet fighters in *Top Gun*, the meaning of the violence is more personal than nationalistic; he has overcome his own self-doubt, and the externalization of that inner victory is the defeat of his enemies.

The modern action hero is also not reluctant to use violence in the way the western hero was; just as most James Bond movies begin with an action sequence to set the tone and prime the audience, many pure action movies kick off immediately with action, showing their heroes to be men of violence who are not afraid to use force when needed. In fact, they often use force first, as if it were the only option. In the opening sequence of *Cobra* (1986), which reteamed Sylvester Stallone with *Rambo* director George P. Cosmatos, Stallone's character, a hardened renegade police officer named Marion "Cobra" Cobrietti, is called in to take care of a shotgun-wielding psychopath who has taken over a local supermarket. When the villain demands that he be given television cameras in order to proclaim his vision of a "New Order," Cobra simply declares, "I don't talk to psychos." Then, fulfilling his role as "judge, jury, and executioner," as a nosy reporter puts it, Cobra takes down the villain by throwing a knife into his chest and pumping half a dozen rounds into him. The film unequivocally states that this is not only the proper course of action but the only one available.

This stands in direct contrast to the traditional western hero, who was bound by a set of morals and values that are largely lacking in the modern action hero, particularly those in the Simpson/Bruckheimer mold. The western hero would certainly employ violence, but usually as a last resort and only for the sake of the community he was protecting. The pure action heroes are outwardly aggressive and determined, and their primary objective (solving the case, defeating the Soviets, taking out a terrorist, and the like) is less important than their victory in attaining it. At one point in *Cobra*, Stallone's character declares, "This is where the law stops . . . and I start," which essentially defines the pure action hero: completely outside the law, both social and moral, and all the better for it.

This divide between the western hero and the new action hero may account for why the western genre seemed so antiquated in the 1980s and all but disappeared from theaters entirely.[9] As Roger Ebert notes:

> One of the many ways in which the Western has become old-fashioned is that the characters have values, and act on them. Modern action movies have replaced values with team loyalty; the characters do what they do because they want to win and they want the other side to lose. The underlying text of most classic Westerns is from the Bible: "What does it profit a man if he gains the whole world, but loses his soul?" The underlying text of most modern action movies is from Vince Lombardi: "Winning isn't everything; it's the only thing." (rev. of *Open Range*)

It is somewhat ironic, then, that President Reagan, the "premiere masculine archetype of the 1980s" (Jeffords 11), got so much mileage out of portraying himself as a president in the mold of the traditional cowboy, even though he clearly disdained any hints of the vulnerability or moral uncertainty that characterized western heroes. Some of the most memorable images of Reagan during his presidency are not of him in the Oval Office behind a desk but rather on his ranch chopping wood or riding a horse. When *Time* magazine declared him "Man of the Year" for 1980, the picture they ran on the front cover was not of Reagan in a suit and tie but rather in a work shirt and jeans with a large western belt buckle. Yet, Reagan as president was much more closely aligned with the heroes of pure action films of the 1980s than with the traditional western heroes he sought to emulate, at least on the surface. When replying to the threat of a congressional tax hike, Reagan did not quote Gary Cooper or Henry Fonda in some western but rather Clint Eastwood in *Sudden Impact* (1983): "Go ahead, make my day." At a press conference in 1985 after the release of thirty-nine hostages in Lebanon, Reagan remarked that it might have been a better idea to go in blasting rather than working it out diplomatically: "Boy," he said, "I saw *Rambo* last night. Now I know what to do the next time this happens" (qtd. in Rogin 7). Like a pure action hero, Reagan's idealized national ethos was one of victory at all costs, something that was embodied in everything from the Cold War, to the stock market, to the movie screens.

Simpson and Bruckheimer explained the appeal of their films in relation to two interconnected themes that perfectly embodied the need to win in the Reagan era: "the Emotion of Triumph" and "the Romance of Professionalism" (Taylor 143). These themes require victory for emotional fulfillment; the emotional high their movies strove to hit necessitates that a character who excels in his or her given profession triumph in the end, overcoming obstacles that are ultimately less important as obstacles than they are as signifiers of the path to victory. No longer is it acceptable for simple survival to be the goal, as in the spate of disaster movies that filled theaters in the 1970s. A character like Rocky Balboa (Sylvester Stallone) cannot stand tall at the end of the film just because he went all sixteen rounds as he did in *Rocky* (1976); instead, he has to not only knock out his opponent but be crowned World Champion for his efforts, as he was in both *Rocky II* (1979) and *Rocky III* (1983). This ethos was taken to the international stage in *Rocky IV* (1985), in which the Philadelphia pugilist's defeat of hardened Soviet super-boxer Ivan Drago (Dolph Lundgren) was an audience-rousing symbolic victory of the Cold War.

Because Simpson and Bruckheimer tended to produce mostly action movies, violence was the key tool in achieving victory—the heroes had to unequivocally blow the villains out of the sky or gun them down. The incessant focus on winning and the concomitant "emotion of triumph" and "romance of professionalism" were not limited only to Simpson and Bruckheimer's films but spread across pure action films of the 1980s that were associated with other well-known producers such as Joel Silver, Lawrence Gordon, and Mario Kassar and Andrew Vajna. This resulted in the development of several key characteristics of the pure action film that allowed producers to comfortably package violence for mass consumption because the end product conformed to the same set of aggressive, optimistic, and victory-seeking values for which audiences were hungry. These include simplifying and demonizing an external enemy, displacing the impact of violence through comedy, and subverting classical narrative coherence to action spectacle.

Simplifying and demonizing the enemy. Victory in the pure action genre requires that someone be vanquished, and filmmakers produced a stream of villains that the heroes could violently conquer in grand fashion, leaving absolutely no question in the end as to who was the winner and who was the loser. However, because the "emotion of triumph" emerges from the simple act of winning rather than from the particularities of what was accomplished, there was little requirement for complexity in the villains. In fact, in most pure action movies, they are interchangeable at best, signifying their menace in the broadest and simplest terms without any subtext or complication. In other words, it didn't matter who the villains were or what they wanted, only that they could readily and easily be identified as bad people who were going to lose in the end. In this respect, it was crucial that the villains not be sympathetic in any way, lest their humanity add a hint of ambiguity to the hero's eventual victory. They were nothing more, to use *Cobra*'s terminology, than a "disease" for which the only "cure" was death.

Thus, it is easy to see why the villains in pure action movies were usually borrowed from newspaper headlines and then ideologically simplified through exaggeration, much as Reagan himself did in vilifying the Soviet Union as nothing more than an "evil empire." This way, filmmakers could speak to the American audience's anxieties as a nation by reducing what was perceived as a global threat into a manageable group of cinematic villains who could be systematically and violently defeated by American "winners." Unlike many of the films of the 1970s, which used screen violence to contribute to audience anxiety rather than to placate it, the violence of the 1980s pure action film was perceived as unthreatening not only because of its increasingly cartoonish exaggerations but because it was being directed toward obvious, irredeemable common enemies. These could be terrorists (*Night Hawks,* 1981; *Die Hard*), drug runners (*Beverly Hills Cop*; *Lethal Weapon*), organized crime lords (*Tango & Cash,* 1989), or even a cult of vicious ax-wielding serial killers (*Cobra*), but they had to be clearly villainous and, preferably, foreign.

Not surprisingly, then, many of the villains of Reagan-era action movies were, if not Soviets themselves, then Communists or members of other Eastern Bloc nations. The members of Reagan's "evil empire" presented a common enemy so obvious that filmmakers couldn't resist incorporating them, even when it meant going to somewhat ridiculous narrative extremes. For example, the inclusion of Soviets working together with the Vietcong in *Rambo: First Blood Part II* is a stretch at best, patently incredulous at worst. But, it allowed the filmmakers to simultaneously defeat the demons of the past (Vietnam) and the demons of the present (the Soviet Union), not to mention the kind of choking government bureaucracy that Reagan claimed to be against, all through the superior agency of one man, John Rambo (Sylvester Stallone), who, in redeeming himself through regenerative violence, symbolically redeemed the entire nation. As Stephen Prince puts it, "As a charged national symbol . . . Rambo enacts his country's symbolic transformation in the Reagan years from disengagement and false consciousness to the triumphant application of military force" (*New Pot of Gold* 317).

The vilification and simplification of the Soviet enemy is well represented in *Top Gun,* in which the Soviet pilots are always shot inside the tight cockpits of their jets through a slightly distorted fish-eye lens and from a menacing low angle that accentuates their mirrored, faceless black helmets. While the humanity of the American pilots always emerges from behind their heavy equipment, guaranteeing especially that we get to see the face of star Tom Cruise even during the most hectic of action sequences, the Soviets are completely dehumanized, turned into little more than black-clad automatons. Thus, when Maverick and the other American pilots blow them out of the sky, the emotional charge that accompanies the violence isn't complicated with notions of the loss of human life. Rather, the violence is sanitized through simplicity, the fiery explosion merely marking yet another victory, as in a video game.

Some pure action movies extended outside the Soviet Union and other Communist countries to find their villains, but the same simplifying effect was always in command. For example, in *Predator*, Arnold Schwarzenegger's Major "Dutch" Schaeffer is flown into an unnamed South American country to lead a rescue mission to reclaim some high-profile hostages from a band of guerrillas hidden deep in the jungle. The rescue operation doesn't exactly go according to plan, but it does allow the movie to engage in plenty of explosive pyrotechnics and ruthless gunning-down of the South American guerrillas, who are never given any ideological impetus for their actions; rather, they're just foreign game pieces to be knocked down by the American soldiers. The film eventually reveals that the so-called rescue mission was actually a setup to trick Dutch and his men into being little more than assassins, which plays as a stark reminder of the Reagan era's legacy of violent, covert noodling south of the border. But, any sustained critique of such activity is roughly on par with the fantasy bureaucratic stonewalling to hide POWs in *Rambo* and is quickly subsumed by the movie's action-oriented obligations.

Displacing violence through comedy. The enjoyment of comedy and violence has been bound up since the beginnings of cinema. Peter Kramer argues that the mechanics of comic violence are timeless because they reduce "everything social and psychological to the physicality of objects and human bodies" (104). Thus, slapstick comedies by Max Sennet or Looney Tunes comic shorts with Bugs and Daffy can contain graphically destructive moments of violence against people and objects with literally no effect on the audience other than the generation of laughs. It's a form of reductionism, whereby actions that would have serious, even lethal, consequences in real life are made silly and enjoyable through the context in which they are presented.

In a sense, filmmakers did something similar with pure action movies in the 1980s, although the intertwining of comedy and violence was not as overt as it is in slapstick, where the two are virtually inseparable. Pure action filmmakers did not try to make the violence itself directly funny, because that is a tricky procedure that often results in dividing the audience instead of bringing it together.[10] Rather, juxtaposed moments of comedy were used to displace the impact of screen violence, making it seem "fun" rather than serious. Comedy thus became a central strategy in the pure action genre, usually necessitating either comic bantering between heroes (for example, Mel Gibson and Danny Glover's odd couple in the *Lethal Weapon* films, Sylvester Stallone and Kurt Russell's competitive cops in *Tango & Cash*) or a comedian in the lead role (such as Eddie Murphy in *Beverly Hills Cop*). As Leo Charney argues, "Humor provides a safety valve against the violence of violence," and the success of pure action films lies precisely in "their structural ability to make appalling levels of violence seem light and larky" (59).

Central to this strategy, particularly in terms of comedy acting as a "release valve" to deflate the violence of violence, was the emergence of the "quip," the funny, unexpected pun or comment made by an action hero in response to a moment of screen violence. Thus, in *Predator*, after Arnold Schwarzenegger hurls an enormous knife, pinning an enemy soldier through the heart into a wall, he quips with a grin, "Stick around." In *The Running Man* (1987), after strangling an opponent named Sub-Zero, Schwarzenegger remarks, "What a pain in the neck," and later taunts the host of the game-show-to-the-death by declaring, "Here's your Sub-Zero, now plain zero." When a terrorist threatens to blow up a supermarket in *Cobra*, Stallone's cool reply is, "Go ahead—I don't shop here." In effect, the quip functions as a signifier of action hero status, as can be seen in *Beverly Hills Cop II* when the overweight, usually reluctant Sergeant Taggart finally steps up to the plate by shooting down one of the main villains, played by Brigitte Nielson, which gives him the power to deliver a quip: "*Women.*"

It was Schwarzenegger, however, who perfected the art of the bad-punning quip in his films. Like Hitchcock's cameo appearances, they became an expected ingredient that played with the division between screen and audience, temporarily rupturing the fabric of suspended disbelief. Such silly, ridiculously out-of-place lines of dialogue became exceedingly common, and they worked effectively as release valves, an on-screen wink to the audience not to take any of this too seriously. At the same time, the quip feeds into the "winner" mentality that was so crucial to the acceptance of violence in action movies. Because quips almost always follow an act of violence in which the hero dispatches a villain, they function also as a taunt, a verbal assault following the physical assault to further degrade the enemy and underscore the hero's victorious status.

Another form of displacing violence with comedy in pure action films was not contained within single lines of sarcastic dialogue but rather permeated the entire tone of the film. This can only be referred to as "attitude," and the single best example is *Beverly Hills Cop.* Seizing on the smart-ass, streetwise persona created by Eddie Murphy in *48 Hrs.* (1982), an unexpected hit two years earlier, *Beverly Hills Cop* catapulted Murphy into superstardom by organizing the entire film around his character's unflappable attitude of cocky self-assurance. In fact, one could argue that the film is about nothing but attitude. It has to be: Short in the narrative department, filled with caricatures, and largely lacking in any real surprises, all it has is attitude. Its blend of comedy and violence was trendsetting, but its engine was fueled by Murphy's comic-book self-assurance and laid-back attitude. Even more so than Tom Cruise's Maverick in *Top Gun,* another character whose attitude forms an often comic context for the film's violence, Axel Foley never flinches, never quits, and is always primed with a witty quip or a surefire comeback—he's the comedian as supercop (or is he the supercop as comedian?). The two meld together because both his humor and his violence spring from the same well of confidence, which allows him to do anything and everything he needs to do to win in the end. Several years later, Bruce Willis mined that same attitude in *Die Hard,* resulting in the immortal "Yipee-kay-eh, motherfucker" line he delivers to Hans Gruber (Alan Rickman), the movie's villain.

In all of these cases, whether the comedy is about quips or attitude or both, its central effect is to reduce screen violence to a game at best, a joke at worst—ultimately and most important, nothing for audiences get upset about.

Narrative rupture. Producer Joel Silver, nicknamed "The Selznick of Schlock" in an article in *Premiere* magazine, coined the term "whammo" to describe the action spectacle—a car chase, a shoot-out, an explosion—that should occur at least every ten minutes in an action movie to keep the audience interested. Naturally, this often results in some form of narrative rupture in that many action sequences do little to forward the plot. Rather, they exist for their own sake.

This is not, however, the same kind of attention-drawing, self-reflexive narrative rupture that characterizes, for example, the theatrical works of Bertolt Brecht, American avant-garde films by Maya Deren, or French New Wave films by Jean-Luc Godard. Rupture in those films is much more severe, often completely distorting time and space as a means to jolt the audience out of the traditional flow of the narrative and force them to reflect on the artificiality of what they're watching. Moments of narrative rupture in pure action films, on the other hand, maintain enough of a connection to the main narrative that the audience can integrate them into the flow of the story, even as they often do nothing to promote that flow. Like the song-and-dance sequences in a musical, these rupturing action sequences provide pleasures that paper over the divide between them and the rest of the film. As Elizabeth Cowie argues, because such ruptures are motivated generically—that is, in a pure action film, the audience *expects* to see moments of pure action, whether such moments are narratively intrinsic or not—the text is nevertheless "unified" in the audience's mind, although not necessarily in the terms of classical Hollywood narrative's insistence on cause and effect (183).[11]

A perfect example of this is found in the opening sequence of *Beverly Hills Cop,* in which Axel Foley has gone undercover to bust an operation dealing in stolen goods. The scheme fails and results in a chase through a Detroit ghetto in which an eighteen-wheeler crashes down the street, smashing into cars while being chased by a string of wailing police cruisers, most of which end up crashing into each other. This sequence serves absolutely no narrative purpose other than to provide an opening "whammo." It doesn't even successfully establish the tough character of Axel Foley, because he spends the entire sequence in the back of the truck just hanging on.

Sometimes, though, just the opposite happens: An otherwise unmotivated action sequence ruptures the narrative in order to allow the hero to assert himself in some significant way. This sort of narrative rupture is clearly embodied in *Top Gun,* in which Maverick must overcome the nagging self-doubts created by the accidental death of his co-pilot, Goose (Anthony Edwards), in order to rise to the narratively convenient challenge of facing down several Soviet aggressors. There is never any real doubt that Maverick will be up to the task, and the delayed gratification only intensifies the emotional impact of the victory. Of course, what is central here is that the victory only has meaning in relation to Maverick's character. The scant narrative attention given to explaining the need to face the Soviet planes shows that the challenge of defeating them exists only for Maverick to conquer and therefore prove himself a winner. It is in no way related to any other aspect of the movie's narrative, and it arrives conveniently with no build-up or other connection to plot or character.

Yet, audiences never thought to question such a strategy, because it reinforced Maverick as a winner, a big-screen reflection of how they wanted to see themselves. Thus, by employing such strategies—simplified foreign villains, comedy, and narrative rupture—Hollywood pure action films of the 1980s were able to satiate the audience's desire for screen violence without overtly threatening their ability to sink back into the theater seat and enjoy the spectacle.

The pure action film is perhaps the quintessential genre of the 1980s. Its emphasis on winning as the only ethic, its highly stylized form and streamlined narrative, and its control by high-concept producers who understood how to package screen violence in the right ideological contexts made it a unique product of the Reagan era, one whose impact on the film industry is still being felt today. No other set of films was able to address so consistently and effectively the desire for uncomplicated screen violence, thus rectifying the controversies that ignited the beginning of the decade and establishing, at least for the time being, the dominance of market-minded producers over artistically driven directors.

Even more important, the aesthetic qualities and ideological tendencies of screen violence in the pure action genre did not stay contained within that genre but rather slipped out and affected other genres and film cycles as well. In the next chapter, we will look at another of the most important developments in violent cinema of the 1980s, the Vietnam film, and how some of these films revived the specter of Vietnam and the violence associated with that war in order to reinforce the dominant conservative ideology of the Reagan era while other films critiqued and questioned it.

4

FIGHTING OUTWARD, LOOKING INWARD

VIOLENCE IN THE 1980S VIETNAM FILM

IT IS NOT WITHOUT SOME irony that the 1980s, the decade in which screen violence was being packaged more and more for easy mainstream consumption, marked the first sustained period in which U.S. filmmakers dealt openly with the memory of the Vietnam War. However, the studios' depiction of Vietnam was far from consistent or harmonized. Such stridently different Hollywood films as *Rambo: First Blood Part II* and *Platoon* powerfully suggest the disparity with which Hollywood filmmakers approached the topic. Unlike the pure action genre, which was covered in the previous chapter, Vietnam films in the 1980s constituted a cycle of deeply conflicted films, some of which staunchly reinforced the mainstream conservative ethos of the era, while others questioned the very nature of American identity.

Much has been written over the years about Hollywood's representations of Vietnam, especially since the cycle of Vietnam films peaked in the late 1980s, but little has focused primarily on the depictions of violence in these films. My contention is that the use of violence in Reagan-era Vietnam films—specifically, at whom the violence is directed—is central to understanding their ideological approach to the war and its implications. The complicated social, psychological, and moral issues raised by depictions of violence in these films also offer a crucial and telling example of the inherently difficult nature of the major studios' desire to package violence—whether fantastical or realistic—for the pleasures of mass consumption in the 1980s.

Vietnam in Hollywood

The Vietnam War was a multi-decade, often undefined and misunderstood military conflict that produced deep strains of divisiveness throughout the United States. Long after the U.S. military had removed all troops from Vietnam in 1975, negative sentiments lingered on both sides of the political divide, with some bemoaning the United States' unprecedented loss of the war, while others were angry that the country had gotten involved in the first place, especially since the popular perception was that the government had consistently lied to the public about the situation in Southeast Asia. Regardless of one's political or ideological stripe, the very word "Vietnam" conjured for Americans painful, negative memories of national loss and identity crisis.

Given the difficult and divisive emotional, ideological, and political baggage associated with Vietnam, it is not surprising that the major Hollywood studios were not eager to represent the war and its aftermath on-screen. In fact, they effectively avoided it altogether. Aside from John Wayne's then-popular but ultimately ridiculed *The Green Berets* (1968), a jingoistic and defensive attempt to adapt the successful formula that had fueled so many World War II films to the situation in Vietnam, there were no Hollywood films about the war set in-country until 1978, five years after all U.S. combat units had left the country. That year saw the release of two independently produced but major-studio-distributed films about the war in Vietnam: *The Boys in Company C* (distributed by Columbia), which prefigured the boot-camp-to-Vietnam narrative arc used by Stanley Kubrick in *Full Metal Jacket* (1987), and *Go Tell the Spartans* (distributed by Avco Embassy), which is set in 1964 when the U.S. military was still in its advisory role and makes explicit historical connections with the failed French Indochina War (1946–54). Of course, it was also in 1978 that Universal released Michael Cimino's controversial and Oscar-winning mythopoetic epic *The Deer Hunter*, a major studio production that, despite its resounding emotional impact, was not an accurate representation of the experiences of combat troops.

The following year saw the release of Francis Ford Coppola's *Apocalypse Now*, a notoriously expensive and troubled film that had actually begun production back in 1976 and was still technically "unfinished" according to Coppola when it premiered at the Cannes Film Festival, where it shared the festival's top prize with Volker Schlöndorff's *The Tin Drum* (*Die Blechtrommel*). Despite being set entirely in Vietnam, *Apocalypse Now* further entrenched Hollywood's distance from the war by restaging Joseph Conrad's novel *Heart of Darkness* in Southeast Asia and thus treating the war in largely symbolic terms. There are moments throughout the film that speak directly to the surreal absurdity of Vietnam—particularly Lieutenant Kilgore's (Robert Duvall) attack on a village to secure a point for surfing and the scene in which Sergeant Willard (Martin Sheen) finds himself among confused troops guarding a bridge who respond to his question about who's in charge with "Ain't you, man?"—but the film's driving intent is the exploration of the darkest recesses of human nature, not the historical Vietnam War.

Those exceptions aside, films that mentioned Vietnam in the 1970s (and these were virtually all independent, low-budget productions) did so from the perspective of veterans, who were usually depicted as psychologically damaged and unstable, if not criminal and dangerous. For example, there was a rash of exploitation motorcycle movies released in the late 1960s and early 1970s that simply replaced familial dysfunction with the trauma of combat to explain the gang members' antisocial and violent tendencies (Adair). Such films include *Angels from Hell* (1968), in which a Vietnam veteran returns to reclaim leader status in his old biker gang; *Satan's Sadists* (1969), in which a Vietnam veteran is terrorized by a biker gang and uses his combat training to defend himself; and *Chrome and Hot Leather* (1971), which features four Green Beret instructors banding together to avenge their leader's fiancée, who was murdered by a Hell's Angel.

When major studio films touched on the violence of the Vietnam War, they tended to do so indirectly in films such as *Soldier Blue* (Avco Embassy) and *Ulzana's Raid* (Universal), which used the western genre (specifically the U.S. military's treatment of Native Americans) as an allegory for the situation in Southeast Asia. Working far below the radar, Robert Altman was able to make the stridently anti-military farce *M*A*S*H* at a major studio (20th Century-Fox). *M*A*S*H*'s groundbreaking mixture of comedy and gruesomely realistic depictions of the results of battlefield violence was mitigated by the fact that it was ostensibly set during the Korean War, although audiences and critics understood it primarily as a film about Vietnam.[1] By the mid-1970s, major studios were producing or distributing films that depicted returning veterans with varying degrees of sympathy, including *Welcome Home, Soldier Boys* (20th Century-Fox, 1972), *Taxi Driver* (Columbia), *Heroes* (Universal, 1977), and *Coming Home* (United Artists, 1978). This focus on returning veterans allowed filmmakers to deal with pertinent social issues related to the war (a popular trend in the New American Cinema) without having to directly represent the violence of the war itself.

Julian Smith argues that Hollywood took so long to cope with Vietnam on-screen because "Vietnam's disorienting effect on our society, the indeterminate nature of that war we couldn't seem to win or abandon, was reflected in our filmmakers' inability to find an appropriate format for presenting the war to a mass audience" (22). This sentiment is also echoed by Gilbert Adair, who, writing about Vietnam films from the vantage point of the late 1970s, notes, "In general the subject matter proved too complex, too multilayered to be comfortably confined within the closed plot structures—a beginning, middle and end in that order—that were natural to the American cinema" (10).

The decade of the 1980s, then, is notable for Hollywood's finally being able to find the "appropriate format" for depicting the complexities of Vietnam, especially the war's violence, which didn't fit comfortably in the previously set molds established by the classical Hollywood war films of World War II, which Thomas Schatz has called "Hollywood's military Ur-narrative" ("New War" 75). The cycle of theatrical Vietnam films was part of a larger movement in American culture in the 1980s to finally come to grips with the war, which also included art installations like the Washington Project for the Arts' "War and Memory: In the Aftermath of Vietnam"; the establishment of numerous Vietnam War memorials around the country, most notably the one in Washington, D.C.; the 1983 PBS documentary *Vietnam: A Television History*; and television shows such as CBS's *China Beach* (1988–91). The road was long and difficult, evinced by the fact that most of the films made about Vietnam in the 1980s had their genesis in scripts that had been kicking around Hollywood for a decade or more, lacking only a producer and studio willing to take on the potentially incendiary material.

The cycle of Vietnam films produced by Hollywood studios in the 1980s finally came about because, instead of waiting for some kind of mythical consensus on the war, the studios found *multiple* formats that would cater to the divided perspectives on Vietnam—realistic combat films (for example, 1987's *Hamburger Hill*), behind-the-lines escape films (1988's *Bat 21*), reactionary revenge films (*Rambo: First Blood Part II*), morality tales (1989's *Casualties of War*), romantic melodrama (1984's *Purple Hearts*), and even comedies (1987's *Good Morning, Vietnam*). As Linda Dittmar and Gene Michaud argue, the American cultural reengagement with Vietnam and its veterans in the 1980s was done on terms that were "still being negotiated across a vast expanse of cultural and political activities" (1). This chapter will focus on how the use of screen violence in Hollywood films about Vietnam reflected that "vast expanse" of political turmoil raging beneath the seemingly monolithic surface of the Reagan era.

Inward and Outward Violence

Vietnam films in the 1980s are usually organized into one of two categories: reactionary revenge films and realistic combat films, the former being exemplified by *Rambo: First Blood Part II* and the second by *Platoon* (Studlar and Desser). However, it is also useful to look at these 1980s Vietnam films specifically in terms of how violence was directed in them because such a perspective allows us to focus on how depictions of screen violence shape meaning in conjunction with broad genre and narrative characteristics. In looking at the violence of Vietnam films, we have to consider not only the obvious—at whom the violence is directed—but also what the enactment of that violence says about the aggressor. We must consider the narrative and thematic justifications of the violence; its presentation as either morally acceptable or unacceptable and how it either functions as a signifier of power and heroism (as in the pure action genre) or undercuts national authority; and, most important, how the film's violence and its meaning reflect the various perspectives on the Vietnam War. The key to each of these films' positioning as either nationalistic or oppositional is coded in its violence.

From this perspective, then, we can categorize 1980s Vietnam films as "outwardly violent" or "inwardly violent," with the former generally aligning with right-wing political sentiments about justifiable force and American superiority (both militarily and morally) and the latter generally aligning with leftist critiques of power, masculinity, and U.S. imperialism. The fact that both cycles of films found substantial success at the U.S. box office at roughly the same time is indicative of how divided the nation still was on the subject of Vietnam in the 1980s.

In the category of outwardly violent films, the violence is directed at a foreign enemy and/or the corrupt, and therefore un-American, bureaucracy that caused the United States to lose the war. The violence itself thus creates a stark dichotomy between "us" and "them." The key is that the enemy is someone who is not truly "American," even if he wears a suit and claims to represent the U.S. government, but especially if he is visibly foreign and represents a conflicting political ideology—namely Communism, the great evil of the Reagan era. The underlying message of these films is that "We can still win the war," which aligns them most clearly with the country's conservative focus on reinvigorating American spirit, morality, and faith in U.S. power—the "New Morning" in America promised by the Reagan administration. The outwardly violent category is populated primarily by Vietnam revenge films like *Missing in Action* and *Rambo: First Blood Part II,* although it also includes *Hamburger Hill,* a realistic combat film about a ten-day assault on a North Vietnamese position.

In the category of inwardly violent films, the violence tends to be directed at the U.S. military and even American culture and identity as a way of exploring how a superpower like the United States could fail to defeat an insurgent army popularly understood as being composed primarily of peasants and farmers, which suggests both military and moral weakness. In this category, the true enemy is ourselves, which not only makes these films morally and ideologically disturbing but also stands them in stark contrast to the prevailing attitudes of U.S. culture and Hollywood in the Reagan era. This category includes the majority of realistic combat films of the latter half of the 1980s, including *Platoon, Full Metal Jacket*, and *Casualties of War*, but also includes *First Blood* (1982), a film whose ideological separation from its more-popular sequel is too frequently understated.

Outward Violence: We Can Still Win the War

If the outwardly violent Vietnam film tends to take the form of a reactionary revenge narrative, then *Missing in Action* is the prototype. In its response to the lingering specter of loss in Vietnam, *Missing in Action* establishes an absolute and unquestionable reliance on outward violence as a means of correcting the mistakes of the past.

Chuck Norris, a former world karate champion who had already parlayed his martial arts skills into a successful B-movie career in the late 1970s, stars as Special Forces colonel James Braddock, who was held as a prisoner of war for seven years by the Vietcong before escaping (an event that is chronicled in the film's prequel, 1985's *Missing in Action 2: The Beginning*, which was shot simultaneously and was originally intended to be released first). Braddock begrudgingly returns to Vietnam in 1984 (one year after his escape) to take part in talks between the American and Vietnamese governments about the lingering rumors of American prisoners of war being held in Vietnam. Knowing that the hearings will produce no real progress in finding the POWs (the United States is represented by a button-down senator who appears to be more interested in his own appearance than in getting to any actual truth), Braddock strikes out on his own and conducts a secret mission into the Vietnamese jungles to reclaim the lost American soldiers. Thus, *Missing in Action* establishes a clear dichotomy of diplomacy versus action, and the superiority of the latter and pointlessness of the former is unequivocally confirmed when the film concludes with Braddock not only rescuing the prisoners (and killing dozens of Vietcong in the process) but bursting in on the final day of the hearing with the prisoners by his side. The ethos of violent military action trumping weak diplomacy is codified in the film's final image: a close-up freeze-frame of Braddock and one of the rescued POWs.

The story line in *Missing in Action* is similar to *Uncommon Valor* (1983), which is about a millionaire (Robert Stack) and a retired military officer (Gene Hackman) who recruit a group of Vietnam veterans to return to Vietnam and rescue their two sons, who have been held as prisoners of war for a decade. Thus, the idea of returning to Vietnam and rescuing POWs was already established, but *Missing in Action* extends the logic of such a scenario by replacing a personal mission with a more nationalistic agenda that is intended to right wrongs and offer a belated opportunity for American victory by reclaiming its lost men. It also presents a revitalized American military hero who stands in contrast to the compromised antiheroes of the 1970s. Rather than going either insane (*Taxi Driver*) or soft (*Coming Home*), as Vietnam veterans tended to do in films of the previous decade, Braddock (and later Rambo) reasserts his violent prowess and, by proxy, the United States'.

This is clearly the primary emphasis in *Missing in Action*'s theatrical trailer, which ends with an image of Braddock exploding out of a river in slow motion with an M-60 pointed directly at the audience as the narrator intones, "America had no more heroes . . . until now!" Within the film itself, this image is iconic in the way it distills what the first wave of 1980s Vietnam action films were all about. The scene begins with Braddock driving a boat that is shot out of the water by a Vietcong grenade attack. The boat explodes in a fiery ball, hurling Braddock into the river. The film then cuts to a shot of three Vietcong soldiers laughing heartily, after which Braddock explodes out of the water and guns them down. In broadly symbolic terms, it is not hard to read the laughing Vietcong as stand-ins for any foreign enemies who delighted in U.S. defeat and Braddock as the newly reenergized America under Reagan, ready to reassert global dominance through sheer force of will.

The violence that Braddock inflicts throughout *Missing in Action* is powerful and uncompromised, and despite being constantly in mortal danger, his body never bears any marks of damage or injury. Even when

10. The image of Colonel James Braddock (Chuck Norris) exploding out of the water in *Missing in Action* (1984) is emblematic of the film's emphasis on a reenergized America under Reagan, ready to reassert global dominance through sheer force of will. DVD still.

a Vietcong assassin shoots a rocket-propelled grenade into Braddock's Bangkok hotel room, he shows no physical signs of trauma whatsoever. However, several civilians below are severely wounded, including a young child who is carried away by his shrieking mother and father and a young man who must cover his bloody face with his hands. When Braddock emerges into the street and sees the results of the violence intended for him, he appears to contemplate the ramifications. However, within the logic of the film, this violence only valorizes Braddock's indestructibility and emphasizes the weak bodies of the foreign others around him, as well as supplies him with further righteous indignation that he uses against his would-be assassin. When he later kills this villain, Braddock tells him, "You shouldn't have hurt those people in Bangkok," just before forcing an ax blade into the villain's chest.

While critics at the time saw *Missing in Action* as a routine action vehicle (Janet Maslin of the *New York Times* called it a "simple, bullet-ridden, crowd-pleasing action movie" ["Screen"]), Norris saw the film as a genuine way to honor those who had fought and died in Vietnam, especially his brother, Wieland Norris, who was killed in action in 1970. According to Norris, when producer Lance Hool first brought him the script for *Missing in Action,* he immediately saw it as a "vehicle through which [he] could honor not only Wieland, but also the more than two thousand American soldiers who had not been accounted for in that horrific war" (Norris 144). Although Hool and Norris had a hard time interesting anyone in Hollywood in the early 1980s, they finally secured financing from the Cannon Group Inc., which was just beginning its run of successful low-budget action movies.[2]

Although many had been skeptical about the potential for a movie about the rescue of imprisoned American soldiers to be a box-office success, *Missing in Action* proved that U.S. audiences had a growing appetite for revisiting Vietnam as long as they returned victorious. Although not a smash success, the film was one of the top 50 hits of 1984, earning $22 million at the box office (*Box Office Mojo*). More important, though, the film spoke to the audiences who saw it, igniting in them an excitement for American heroism in Vietnam. When Norris went to a public screening of the film in Westwood, California, "the audience literally stood to their feet in a standing ovation following the climactic scene" (Norris 145). The film also tapped into its audience's desire to demonize a foreign enemy. According to Maslin, when she saw the film at the Rivoli Theater in New York City, the "audience also showed enthusiasm for the film's attitude toward Vietnamese soldiers and officials, who are depicted as no less unequivocally shifty, villainous and deceitful as their stereotyped Japanese counterparts were in B-movies about World War II" ("Screen").

Similarly themed but substantially more successful at the box office was *Rambo: First Blood Part II*, which was released the following year. A sequel to the successful *First Blood* (which will be discussed in more depth later in this chapter), *Rambo* tells the story of Vietnam veteran and one-man army John Rambo (Sylvester Stallone) returning to Southeast Asia on a mission to discover the whereabouts of American soldiers still missing from the war. He is brought into the covert operation by Colonel Samuel Trautman (Richard Crenna), his former commanding officer and the one man Rambo trusts. The operation itself is run by Murdock (Charles Napier), a shifty special operations bureaucrat who has no intention of actually finding POWs; rather, his sole interest lies in the political gain of satisfying lingering questions from government officials and soldiers' families. Although the mission is intended to fail from the start, Rambo does indeed find a camp full of American POWs in Vietnam, and when Murdock aborts the mission and deserts him, Rambo must take it upon himself to rescue the prisoners, in the process fighting not only dozens of Vietcong but also members of the Soviet army who support them. Thus, the film fully conflates two U.S. enemies and solidifies the Reagan-era fear that the Soviet Union was growing in power and influence.

Despite an audience-limiting R rating, *Rambo: First Blood Part II* was an immediate success when it was released theatrically in May 1985. It earned more than $32 million in its first six days (a total bested at the time only by *Return of the Jedi* and *Indiana Jones and the Temple of Doom*) and went on to earn more than $150 million at the domestic box office, making it the second highest-grossing film of the year behind the time-travel comedy *Back to the Future* and just ahead of Stallone's other Cold War triumph, *Rocky IV*, in which America's favorite pugilist defeats Ivan Drago (Dolph Lundgren), the symbolic pride of the Soviet empire.

More important, though, *Rambo* transcended mere box-office success and became part of the cultural lexicon, the name itself coming to stand for any person who used violence as a means to an end. The name "Rambo" also entered into common usage to refer allusively to everything from patriotism, to militaristic fantasy, to a generally gung-ho attitude.[3] It was invoked throughout the media in both the United States and abroad in hundreds of newspaper and magazine articles and TV news reports, especially when the topic at hand had anything to do with Communism, foreign affairs, or the military. For example, when Congress debated a $12.6 billion foreign aid bill in the summer of 1985, mere months after the film's initial theatrical release, the name "Rambo" was used by lawmakers at least a dozen times (Roberts), and military recruiting officers began hanging posters of Rambo on their office walls.[4] The spread of "Rambo" throughout the culture was also aided by the aggressive marketing of ancillary products in the wake of the film's smash success, including action figures, toy guns, candy bars, video games, clothing, and a spin-off animated television series. Most of these products were aimed at children who were too young to see the R-rated film without an adult guardian and as a result endured substantial criticism from various social advocacy groups and toy manufacturer watchdogs. However, the very fact that a violent, R-rated action film was being marketed to children and adolescents through toys and candy is indicative of how accepting much of the culture was of violent entertainment in the Reagan era as long as it hewed to a particular ideological line.

Critics immediately seized on *Rambo*'s political implications, despite director George P. Cosmatos's insistence that he was not making a political film but merely an escapist action movie. Similarly, Stallone, who co-wrote the screenplay and was instrumental in shaping the film's editing, brushed off the idea that *Rambo* was intentionally political, saying he worked purely by "intuition" and "emotions" (Grenier). Whether genuine or not, Cosmatos's and Stallone's assertions that *Rambo* was intended to be apolitical were flatly contradicted by the film's press agents, who encouraged journalists and critics to "see it as a sociological feat—one of a small, gutsy band of films that dare to break a long silence and probe the Vietnam war's troubled aftermath" (Sterritt, "'Rambo'"). Critics did recognize the film's relationship to the United States' painful memories of Vietnam, but most saw it as simple-minded, if not wantonly dangerous. Vincent Canby noted *Rambo*'s underlying agenda, saying that it "does nothing less than rewrite history. Though the movie doesn't say so, it's designed to win the war that officially ended 10 years ago in humiliating defeat" ("Sylvester Stallone"). Writing in the *Washington Post*, Paul Attanasio called it "a crudely effective right-wing rabble-rouser, the artistic equivalent of carpet bombing—you don't know whether to cheer or run for cover." He then went on to compare it, not to stirring World War II–era American war films, but rather to "the Nazi and proto-Nazi cinema of the '20s and '30s. It has all the elements: the Aryan hero; the warrior concubine—Rambo's Vietnamese guide, played by Julia Nickson; the inspirational shots of tall mountains; the emphasis on primal virtues; the mute, expressionless killer; the ideology of an Army undercut by the government back home."

Rambo is no doubt a crude film, but it is also a strikingly effective one; there's good reason why reactionary conservatives embraced it and antiwar liberals found it so repugnant. The film's violence is sharp and relentless and aimed explicitly outward, which is why it was seized so immediately as a prototype for a new kind of American patriotism, one that centered on strength, willpower, and the absolute destruction of the enemies that had caused the United States to doubt itself in the wake of Vietnam. In this sense, John Rambo is less a character than a brute symbol for a particular American fantasy vision of itself that found strong roots in the Reagan era. All bulging muscles and studied silence, Rambo cuts a bloody swath through three broad areas of villainy: memories of defeat in Vietnam (symbolized by the rescue of the American POWs), the then-current threat posed by the Soviet Union (symbolically defeated by Rambo along with its minions, the Vietcong); and spineless, conniving politicians who had no faith in the American fighting man and thus enabled the country's defeat in Vietnam (personified by Murdock, who Trautman describes in the film as "a stinkin' bureaucrat trying to cover his own ass").

Rambo dispatches the explicitly foreign villains with righteous intensity, relying primarily on modern updates of primordial weapons like a high-powered compound bow and a twelve-inch hunting knife. Technology in the film is associated with bureaucracy and weakness; thus, Rambo is explicitly anti-technological. Early on he cuts away the heavy tracking equipment he is supposed to take into the field with him and later machine-guns Murdock's wall of computers and monitors in the film's longest episode of sustained gunfire. The film's most famous sequence replicates a similar sequence from *First Blood* in which Rambo utilizes his guerrilla tactics to pick off his enemies one by one. He uses snares, traps, and silent sneak attacks to strangle, stab, or shoot an arrow into the Vietcong and Soviet soldiers. The violence is close and intimate, which underscores the personal nature of Rambo's, and by proxy the country's, vengeance. According to *Rambo*'s editors, Mark Goldblatt and Mark Helfrich, each of these killings was wildly cheered by audiences, suggesting that *Rambo*'s outwardly directed violence struck a real emotional chord.

The film's two primary individual villains are given particularly spectacular deaths in scenes that evoke the classic showdown in that most quintessential of American genres, the western. Rambo dispatches the Vietcong captain Vinh (George Kee Cheung) with an explosive-tipped arrow after they face off near a waterfall, with Captain Vinh's panicky revolver shots missing the preternaturally calm Rambo despite his standing on a rock in full view (in no other scene in the film does Rambo appear more superhuman; the bullets might as well bounce off his chest). Later in the film, Rambo takes out the Soviet lieutenant colonel Pudovsky (Steven Berkoff, who had recently played the heavy in both the 1983 James Bond film *Octopussy* and 1984's *Beverly Hills Cop*) by luring Pudovsky's helicopter in close by feigning unconsciousness in his own downed helicopter and then suddenly rising and destroying the Soviet airship with a rocket launcher. Thus, both primary villains die explosive, fiery deaths that were clearly calculated to tap into the "triumph of emotion" so popular in the pure action films of the decade.

The uncomplicated demonizing of the Vietcong and the Soviets clearly marks *Rambo* as an outwardly violent Vietnam film, but the emotional and later physical violence directed by Rambo against Murdock, a high-ranking member of the U.S. government, would seem to suggest that *Rambo* is, at least partially, also an inwardly violent film. However, unlike the truly inwardly violent Vietnam films, *Rambo* does not position Murdock as a genuine representative of the United States. Rather, he is a snake who is trying to manipulate the American system to his own end and, in the process, undermine the good intentions of "real" Americans like Rambo and Colonel Trautman.[5] Murdock explicitly says as much when he tells Trautman, "Wasn't my war [referring to Vietnam], Colonel. I'm just here to clean up the mess." In refusing to claim any stake in Vietnam and its aftermath (in fact, he even lies about serving a tour of duty in Southeast Asia in 1966), Murdock cements his non-American status because, in *Rambo*'s worldview, having a stake in "winning" the Vietnam war is *the* linchpin of American identity. Furthermore, Murdock is associated with the politicians whom many blamed for the loss in Vietnam when Trautman connects Murdock's phony mission to find POWs with the war itself: "It was a lie, wasn't it? Just like the whole damn war!"

The film's true Americans—Rambo and Trautman—not only are unable to forget the pain of the U.S.'s military defeat in Vietnam but actively desire to rescue the country through belated military victory. When Trautman tries to assure Rambo that "the old Vietnam is dead," Rambo replies, "I'm alive, it's still alive." The film's most famous line, though, comes early in the film after Rambo reluctantly agrees to return to Vietnam to search for the POWs. "Do we get to win this time?" he asks Trautman, to which the colonel replies, "This time it's up to you." The idea of "winning" Vietnam ten years after the U.S. withdrawal from Saigon was the seed from which grew a new national fantasy in which history could be rewritten, even fictionally. When Rambo asks Trautman, "Why now? Why me?" when approached about the mission, his words can also be read in terms of the film itself. Why this film and why now? The answer is supplied by Stallone himself: "The American people have waited too long to find a way of expressing patriotism. *Rambo* has triggered off repressed emotions which have been out of fashion for far too long" (Wills).

This repressed sense of patriotism and desire to win the Vietnam War, at least symbolically, was also at the heart of *Hamburger Hill*, the only mainstream Hollywood film that depicted the war itself in outwardly violent terms. The other combat films produced during the 1980s, which will be discussed later in this chapter, tended to focus on the inward violence of American defeat by showing how war corrupts and debases humanity and turns Americans against each other. *Hamburger Hill*, on the other hand, wears its ideological view of war quite clearly in its marketing tag line: "War at its worst. Men at their best." In other words, much like the war films produced by Hollywood during World War II, *Hamburger Hill* presents the gritty violence of warfare as a means by which men come together and forge lasting bonds that transcend politics and ideology.

Like the other Vietnam combat films of the 1980s, *Hamburger Hill* has a significant stake in authenticity. The film's screenwriter, James Carabatsos, served with the First Air Cavalry Division (1968–69) in Vietnam and had friends who fought in the battle depicted in the film: a ten-day struggle in May 1969 in which three battalions of the 101st Airborne fought the Twenty-eighth North Vietnamese Regiment to secure a mountain in the Ashau Valley generally marked on maps as Hill 937 (its actual name was Dong Ap Bia; see Davenport). For critics of the war, the taking of Hill 937 was representative of the U.S. military's strategic mismanagement: The battle cost hundreds of American lives, yet the hill was abandoned a month after it was secured. Similar to Lewis Milestone's *Pork Chop Hill* (1959), a Korean War film on which *Hamburger Hill* is clearly modeled, the later abandoning of the hill is never explicitly mentioned. If it had been, the film would have played more like other inwardly violent Vietnam combat films, with the blood and gore of the battlefield being contextualized within the ultimately pointless nature of the military endeavor. Instead, *Hamburger Hill* focuses primarily on the experiences of the American soldiers and their solidarity in the face of a common enemy.

Like many war films, *Hamburger Hill* features a microcosm of soldiers who represent different racial, ethnic, and socioeconomic backgrounds that are overcome via their bond as soldiers. Racial issues are particularly heated among the men, but even the black/white divide, which was so sharp during this period in American history, is bridged by the common goal of winning the battle. At one point, two soldiers get into a fight over a callous comment made by one about the other's girlfriend, and when their commanding officer intervenes, he barks at them, "Shake hands, men. We're Airborne. We don't start fights. We finish 'em." That, in essence, summarizes the ideological approach to war evinced by *Hamburger Hill*. The causes of the war are immaterial to the call of duty.

More so than other Vietnam combat films of the 1980s, *Hamburger Hill* is graphically violent in terms of how it presents the visual details of the damage done to human bodies by bullets and shrapnel. The film begins in the middle of a skirmish already in progress, and within the first two minutes there is an explosion followed by a shot of an American soldier falling directly into the foreground, giving the viewer a close-up shot of his disemboweled torso, the long blades of grass around him literally framing his exposed intestines. The second half of the film falls into a pattern that alternates bloody battle scenes on the hill with moments of repose below in which the soldiers are allowed to express themselves as characters, which makes their deaths even more troubling. The battle sequences present death in graphic terms, for both the U.S. soldiers and the North Vietnamese. In fact, *Hamburger Hill* is one of the few Vietnam films to give substantial screen time to the North Vietnamese, albeit only to better establish them as the enemy. There are shots of the North Vietnamese soldiers hiding inside bunkers during U.S. airstrikes, and many of them are shown in close-up when they are killed. In the film's most graphically violent shot, a North Vietnamese soldier's entire head is eviscerated by close machine-gun fire. Such imagery differs significantly from other Vietnam films of the 1980s, which tend to depict the North Vietnamese enemy as shadowy figures lurking in the darkness of the jungle or as minimized figures in extreme long shots. By emphasizing the presence of the North Vietnamese, *Hamburger Hill* presents a clear, verifiable enemy at which violence can be directed.

Critics picked up on the distinctions between *Hamburger Hill* and the other Vietnam combat films, noting its downplaying of political ideology in favor of gruesome combat realism. Left-wing critics and pundits recognized that the focus on such "realism" is itself ideological and accused producer Marcia Nasatir of "being an Ollie North–loving reactionary, a right-wing Republican" whose film "glorifies war" (Michelson). Ironically, Nasatir, who was considered liberal and antiwar, had been directly involved in the production of the explicitly antiwar film *Coming Home*, which was made at United Artists while she was vice president.

The violence in *Hamburger Hill* is intended to make its own statement, but like violence in many Hollywood films, it downplays its own social and political roots. *Hamburger Hill* ends on what might be termed an ambiguous note, as the U.S. soldiers, having finally achieved their goal, stand at the top of Hill 937 with looks of slight bewilderment: Mission accomplished, but now what? This coda is left deliberately vague, and as a result it does little to undermine the film's larger message about the unifying effect of war, especially against a discernible enemy.

Inward Violence: The Enemy Is in Us

Given the enormous financial success and resonating cultural effects of *Rambo: First Blood Part II*, the ultimate outwardly violent Vietnam film, it is not surprising that its predecessor, *First Blood*, is frequently ignored, conflated with its sequel, or discussed merely in terms of its having introduced the character of John Rambo. However, *First Blood* and *Rambo* are stridently different films, arguably with more differences than similarities. This is true not only of their divergent depictions of Rambo himself but also of the ideological implications of his violence. While *Rambo* enacts its violence outwardly through the demonization of the Communist Vietcong and Soviet soldiers and a corrupt government bureaucrat whose underhanded dealings helped facilitate American defeat, *First Blood* directs its violence decidedly inward by depicting a misunderstood Vietnam veteran waging war against a bucolic small town—the very thing he was once fighting to protect. Thus, between these two films that are so often lumped together, we can chart a direct shift in the ideological representation of Vietnam's aftermath, from the damaged vet of 1970s films to the avenging heroes of the 1980s.

The general American cultural understanding of John Rambo stems primarily from *Rambo: First Blood Part II*, not *First Blood*, because in the sequel Rambo is more direct, uncomplicated, and undeniably cartoonish in his superhuman prowess; he's a one-dimensional action figure, not a multidimensional human character. The John Rambo of *First Blood* is a thoroughly different creature: an ambivalent, confused, and reckless misfit whose misguided retaliation places him much more in line with the brutal antiheroes of 1970s violent cinema than in the sword-rattling superheroes that started to dominate American action films in the 1980s.

Throughout *First Blood*, Rambo is referred to as being "crazy," a "psycho," and a "maniac." Although these sentiments come from the mouths of the film's less sympathetic characters, they are not far off the mark, despite Rambo's having been significantly toned down from the character in David Morrell's 1972 source novel, who J. Hoberman describes as "a Frankenstein's monster [who] kills the entire posse that chases him up into the hills, returns to burn down Main Street, and is finally terminated by the very Green Beret officer who trained him" (57). Stallone was intently aware of this during the film's editing: "When we looked at the footage we got back from the labs we were scared to death. This Rambo character looked nihilistic, almost psychopathic. The random violence. But we worked it over in the editing room until it felt right" (qtd. in Grenier). However, all the editing in the world couldn't erase the ambivalence of a central character who not only is clearly unhinged but eventually goes on an out-of-control rampage that most would associate with terrorism.

After wandering into the small town of Hope, Oregon, Rambo is harassed and quickly shuttled out of town by local sheriff Will Teasel (Brian Dennehy), who informs him, "We don't want guys like you in this town."[6] When Rambo attempts to return after being dropped off outside the town limits, Teasel arrests him on trumped-up charges of vagrancy, resisting arrest, and carrying a concealed weapon (a twelve-inch hunting knife). Rambo is then systematically beaten and tormented by the police, particularly the gruff and sadistic Art Gault (Jack Starrett), which taps into his post-traumatic stress tendencies and causes him to lash out against his captors and escape. Rambo disappears into the surrounding woods, which leads Teasel to call in a massive manhunt utilizing not only his own department and the state police but also the National Guard. Thus, the decorated "war hero" becomes a hunted criminal, underscoring the film's emphasis on the negative treatment of American soldiers returning from Vietnam.

In stark contrast with the violence to come, the opening of *First Blood* is gentle, very nearly pastoral, as it depicts Rambo walking down a rural road and smiling at the small collection of houses he discovers at the base of a hill, complete with children laughing and playing, birds singing, and dogs barking. In 1982, Stallone was still associated primarily with the lovable pugilist Rocky Balboa, whom he had portrayed in two films at that point, and he plays Rambo as a sweet-natured, slightly goofy guy in the Rocky mold (as he searches for a photograph, he self-deprecatingly jokes about "all this junk" in his pockets). However, Rambo's demeanor instantly changes when he learns that the friend and former platoon mate he has been trying to find had died of cancer earlier that year as a result of his tour in Vietnam: "All that orange stuff they spread around—cut him down to *nothing*," says his still grieving mother. Jerry Goldsmith's musical score shifts immediately from gentle and upbeat to somber as Rambo's face falls, and it is soon thereafter that he first encounters Teasel. Thus, Rambo's stoic demeanor throughout the film is less a signifier of masculine prowess than it is the self-enacted shell of emotional defeat; having learned that the last member of his platoon in Vietnam has died ("Got himself killed in 'Nam, didn't even know it," Rambo later says), he is figuratively and literally alone in the world.

Throughout *First Blood*, the film's violence is constantly directed inward at America itself, whose representation by both Rambo the war hero and the community that rejects him suggests the still-conflicted nature of the country in the early 1980s, despite the Reagan administration's attempt to rejuvenate the national mood. The violence enacted by Rambo is directed at his "enemies," except his enemies are not the easily demonized foreign agents of Communist countries but rather the very Americans he was supposedly protecting from the ravages of Communism during his horrific tours of duty. To emphasize this, the film directly equates the police with the Vietcong during Rambo's incarceration at the police station. Rambo's instinctual decision to fight back and escape is established by cutting rapidly between his first-person view of a police officer brandishing a straight razor with the intent to shave him (although this intention comes with a vaguely disguised threat that Rambo might "cut [his] own neck") and a Vietcong officer brandishing the same object as a weapon of torture. The surface intention of this back-and-forth montage is psychological—to show what triggers Rambo's reaction—but it also works ideologically to conflate the violence of Rambo's past and present enemies, thus further confounding any simplistic divide between "us" and "them."

First Blood goes to great lengths in its opening passages to establish the ordinary, everyday, quaint qualities of Hope as a representative small American town where everyone knows everyone else. Teasel is certainly a bully, and Gault is a sadist, but not all the police officers are one-note villains. For example, the younger deputy Mitch (David Caruso) is clearly disgusted by Gault's cruel treatment of Rambo, at one point leaving the room because he cannot watch Rambo being battered with a high-pressure water hose. Rambo's other antagonists are drawn directly from the local population, including a man named Orval (John McLiam), whose dogs are used to track Rambo in the woods, and the various members of the National Guard. However, as Rambo says at one point, "There are no friendly civilians," which can be read as either an indictment of the American population's mistreatment of returning Vietnam veterans or an indication of Rambo's mentally unhinged paranoia. Either way, the violence that results from this "private war" between Rambo and the civilian world has nothing to do with external enemies and everything to do with the fear that America was tearing itself apart from within.

Much of the writing about the violence in *First Blood* refers to the violence enacted by Rambo against his pursuers, which makes it easy to forget how much violence is directed first against him. After all, the title of the film (taken directly from David Morrell's source novel) refers to Rambo's contention that the police "drew first blood" against him—that, in effect, they started it. For the film's first twenty minutes, Rambo is the unwilling recipient of violence, enduring mistreatment by the various police officers, which includes being hit in the back of the legs with a nightstick, being battered with the high-pressure water hose, and then being forcibly restrained while an officer threatens to shave his face "dry" with a straight razor. He is also the victim of verbal violence, with Teasel and the others systematically dehumanizing him with taunts and harsh pejoratives, which dovetails directly with Rambo's exhausted speech at the end referring to the treatment of returning vets who were spit on and called "baby killers." When Mitch first sees the scars on Rambo's chest back at the police station and asks, "What the hell's he been into?," Gault's reply of "Who gives a shit?" is representative of a particularly demeaning

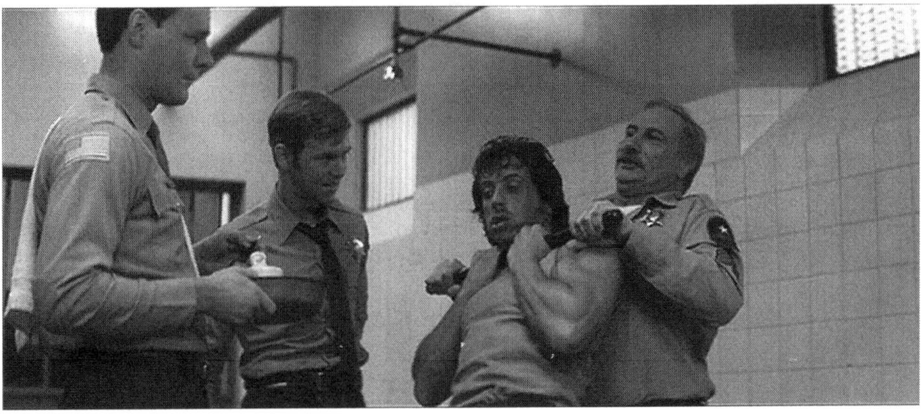

11. The violence enacted by the police officers against John Rambo (Sylvester Stallone) in *First Blood* (1982) stands in for the physical and emotional violence inflicted by the American population on returning Vietnam veterans. DVD still.

attitude toward vets. In effect, then, the violence enacted by Teasel, Gault, and the others stands in for the physical and emotional violence inflicted by the American population on returning Vietnam veterans.

In contrast to the aggressive, sadistic violence enacted against him, for much of the film all of Rambo's violence is strictly defensive. Although in the novel he kills numerous people, in the film he is only indirectly responsible for one death: He hurls a rock at a helicopter from which Gault is wantonly shooting at him against orders, causing the officer to fall out. Rambo's feelings about this incident are purposefully ambiguous. Immediately after Gault is killed, Rambo scrambles across the rocks at the bottom of the ravine, hoists up Gault's bloody corpse, and stares into his lifeless eyes with a look of intense derangement that is accompanied by the same musical motif that played when Rambo was experiencing post-traumatic-stress-induced flashbacks at the police station. Soon thereafter, however, Rambo steps out into the open, despite rifles being trained on him, and insists that he doesn't want to see anyone else hurt. More people are hurt, however, as the police respond to Rambo's semi-surrender by firing upon him, once again suggesting that he is more defensive victim than active aggressor, at least in the film's first half. Rambo later maims half a dozen officers in the woods with sneak attacks and barbed traps as they attempt to track him. His use of homemade weapons and traps aligns him with the Vietcong, his previous enemy, although his conscious choice not to kill the officers when he could have (a point he makes explicit as he holds his knife to Teasel's throat) suggests that he is not the "animal" or "machine" they want to see him as.

The violence in *First Blood* becomes much more complicated at the film's climax when Rambo finally becomes the outright aggressor in returning to Hope for no other purpose than to wage a one-man war against the town itself. In the process he blows up a gas station, a lot full of cars, and the local gun shop and shoots up the police station with an M-60 stolen from a National Guard truck. This violence is wanton and ultimately pointless except as the expression of Rambo's uninhibited rage, which again emphasizes its inward direction. The violence enacted against the small town, the pastoral signifier of everything good and worthy in American culture, is an expression of years of frustration felt by returning veterans who felt that their sacrifices were not only dismissed but actively disparaged. Lacking an identifiable external enemy, Rambo's violence must be directed inward against his own countrymen and their inability and/or refusal to understand him.

Inwardly directed violence is also central to the so-called realistic combat films that came to dominate representations of Vietnam in the late 1980s, particularly Oliver Stone's *Platoon*, Stanley Kubrick's *Full Metal Jacket*, and Brian De Palma's *Casualties of War*. Each of these films is set in Vietnam during the height of the war, and each lays claim to some form of verifiable reality: the semi-autobiographical *Platoon* was based on writer/director Stone's own experiences serving in Vietnam in 1967–68; *Full Metal Jacket* was based on war correspondent Gustav Hasford's novel *The Short Timers* and was weighted with the barking presence of R. Lee Ermey, a marine staff sergeant who served one and a half tours of duty in Vietnam; and *Casualties of War*, which is about an actual war crime, was adapted by Vietnam veteran and playwright David Rabe from an article published in the *New Yorker* in October 1969 by war correspondent Daniel Lang. These combat films, while maintaining the same emphasis on gritty verisimilitude as *Hamburger Hill*, convey a message diametrically opposed to that outwardly violent film. If *Hamburger Hill*'s tag line was "War at its worst. Men at their best," then these inwardly violent films collectively suggest that when war is at its worst, men are at their worst, too.

The first of these films, and in many ways the most representative, is *Platoon*. The story concerns a young, idealistic private named Chris Taylor (Charlie Sheen) who shucks off his middle-class background by dropping out of college against his parents' will and signing up for the infantry. Taylor is assigned to a platoon operating near the Cambodian border during the war's "stalemate period" from 1967 to 1968. His grueling experiences in the jungle incorporate in one way or another virtually every well-known negative facet of the Vietnam War: jungle skirmishes, drug use, soldiers "fragging" their officers, atrocities committed against civilians, and even the practice of U.S. soldiers cutting off the ears of dead Vietcong as souvenirs. Throughout these experiences, Chris is torn between two "fathers": Sergeant Barnes (Tom Berenger), a scarred brute who has let the violence of warfare turn him into a savage, and Sergeant Elias (Willem Dafoe), who has maintained his humanity despite three years in the jungle. At the end of the film, Taylor offers a final thought in voice-over narration that serves as both the film's coda and a fitting description of all the inwardly violent Vietnam films: "I think now, looking back, we did not fight the enemy, we fought ourselves. And the enemy was in us."

The immediate emphasis in *Platoon* is on realism. It was billed in its advertisements and described by critics and journalists almost exclusively in terms of its realistic depictions—not only of the Vietnam War but of war in general. The film's theatrical trailer, which begins with a photograph of Oliver Stone and his platoon in Vietnam while a narrator tells us that Stone received a Bronze Star for gallantry during his service as a combat infantryman ten years before winning an Oscar for writing *Midnight Express* (1978), ends with the narrator intoning, "The first real casualty of war is innocence. The first real movie about the war in Vietnam is *Platoon*." While not denying that other films had been made about the Vietnam War, this trailer asserts that *Platoon* is the first legitimate film because it was written and directed by a recognized Hollywood talent who had experienced the war firsthand (not surprisingly, such an assertion denies credibility to the dozens of low-budget, independently produced feature films and documentaries made about the war since the late 1960s). Newspaper and magazine articles stressed again and again not only Stone's Vietnam experience but the fact that he had hired marine captain Dale Dye as a military advisor and put his actors through an unrelenting two-week boot camp to show them firsthand what the experience was like and to wear them out so they appeared on film more like haggard soldiers than Hollywood actors playing war. According to Stone, "I wanted to make it real. War movies look phony to me. Most of the guys look too clean. I wanted the look of a man who doesn't sleep, doesn't eat well, doesn't shower. You gotta get that in the actors. So we beat 'em down. After two weeks they looked mean and tired, and they hated me" (qtd. in Base).

The emphasis on realism in *Platoon* extended to its depictions of violence, which were calculated to contradict the typical expectations of war movie violence. Film critic Roger Ebert noted this in the first paragraph of his review:

> It was François Truffaut who said that it's not possible to make an anti-war movie, because all war movies, with their energy and

> sense of adventure, end up making combat look like fun. If Truffaut had lived to see *Platoon*, the best film of 1986, he might have wanted to modify his opinion. Here is a movie that regards combat from ground level, from the infantryman's point of view, and it does not make war look like fun.

Because the majority of the film takes place in the jungle, with only a few respites in the relative safety of base camp, *Platoon* is an unrelentingly violent film. There are numerous skirmishes, ambushes, and all-out firefights, including a near-apocalyptic final fight based on an actual battle on New Year's Day in 1968 in which five hundred men were killed when two regiments of the North Vietnamese army attacked the base at which Stone was stationed (Davenport 269). Even when guns aren't being fired or grenades exploding on-screen, there is always the lingering threat that violence could break out at any moment. This perpetual state of violence or its potential was Stone's primary goal in making the film: to depict the grim horrors of warfare—both physically and spiritually. *Platoon* is filled with broken and bleeding bodies torn apart by shrapnel and bullets, but it is even more memorably full of broken souls, characters who are beaten down by their role as soldiers and turn monstrous as a result.

The violence in *Platoon* is ostensibly directed at the enemy—the Vietcong. However, the enemy combatants are depicted in fragmented, shadowy terms; rarely are they seen clearly, and when they are, it is only for a split-second. It is telling that the film's climactic battle takes place at night, so that the violence is rendered even more chaotic and spatially disoriented by the darkness, reaching surreal levels close to the waning moments of *Apocalypse Now*. Similarly, it is rare in *Platoon* that there is a clear objective. Unlike the outwardly violent *Hamburger Hill*, which staked its depictions of violence to a clear military objective that could be attained, the war violence of *Platoon* is scattered, incoherent, and fractured.

The clearest military objective in the film appears near the midway point when the platoon is ordered into a Vietnamese village that is suspected of holding artillery and food for the North Vietnamese army and of harboring Vietcong sympathizers. This is the film's most intense and disturbing sequence, as it ignites memories of atrocities like the My Lai massacre in depicting American soldiers brutalizing and, in some instances, killing the villagers, whose relationship to the Vietcong is never clearly established. The violence is directed at the villagers in particularly brutal ways, such as when Bunny (Kevin Dillon) smashes in a one-legged man's head with the butt of his rifle and Sergeant Barnes shoots a hysterical woman point-blank in the head and then threatens to do the same to her young daughter unless the woman's husband admits to being VC.

However, the source of the violence is not a military objective but rather the soldiers' internal rage after the killing of several of their comrades. The rage runs deeper, though, as it taps into months (and for some, years) of frustration emanating from the impossibility of fighting an unknowable enemy in an alien country and the concomitant fear that ruled the days and nights of infantrymen in the jungle. Taylor is not immune to such emotions, and in this sequence he comes close to losing it altogether, screaming at the villagers and even shooting at their feet to make them "dance." "I'm sick of this fuckin' shit!" he yells, and when someone tries to tell him that the villagers are just scared, he retorts angrily, "Oh, *they're* scared?," implying that it is, in fact, he who truly bears the brunt of omnipresent fear.

The violence is at its most intense when Barnes and Elias come to blows over Barnes's treatment of the villagers, thus solidifying *Platoon*'s thematic focus on the internal rather than external enemy: Even when battling the Vietcong, the soldiers are really battling themselves. Barnes and Elias represent two sides of the combat soldier, and the fact that the village is soon burned to the ground and Barnes eventually tries to murder Elias in the jungle makes it clear which half is victorious. The final nail is driven home in the film's concluding sequence, which finds Taylor with the choice of calling a medic to help Barnes, who has been wounded in battle, or killing him. He chooses the latter, and the unexpectedly sudden burst of gunfire from his AK-47 (a weapon he pulled off

12. Filled with the anger and frustration of battling an often invisible enemy, Sergeant Barnes (Tom Berenger) threatens to shoot a child unless a villager admits to being Vietcong in *Platoon* (1986). DVD still.

a dead North Vietnamese soldier) is *Platoon*'s last depiction of violence. Thus, a mainstream American war film ends with one American soldier murdering another.

Platoon's theme of the enemy within is carried on in several other Vietnam combat films, most notably *Full Metal Jacket*, which extends director Stanley Kubrick's fascination with the mechanics of dehumanization, and *Casualties of War*, in which Brian De Palma uses Vietnam as a backdrop for a story about the nature of moral choice. Although Kubrick denied consciously imparting an explicit prowar or antiwar stance in *Full Metal Jacket*, its counterhegemonic critique of American military power, particularly through violent displays of indoctrinated racism and sexism, is overwhelming. What makes *Full Metal Jacket* a tricky film ideologically is that it clearly begins as an inwardly violent film but then switches abruptly to what appears to be an externally violent film. However, Kubrick is actually expanding the inward violence of the first half into the externally violent arena of the war zone, thus suggesting that they are one and the same; that is, to exact violence against another is to enact violence against one's self—one's own humanity. This is the thematic link that connects the two halves of *Full Metal Jacket*, which to some critics played like completely different films.

The film begins at a U.S. Marine Corps training camp on Parris Island, South Carolina, where fresh recruits are battered into shape by the fiercely commanding Gunnery Sergeant Hartman (R. Lee Ermey). The process by which the "maggots," as Hartman calls them, are turned into marines hinges entirely on sadistic physical and psychological violence. Hartman trains the men by tearing them down verbally and then retraining them to be indiscriminate killers—to make them "born again hard." Much of the psychological violence in the form of verbal abuse is distinctly sexual, with Hartman berating the recruits' masculinity by calling them "faggots," accusing them of exaggerated homosexual practices, and replacing any sense of normal sexuality with a required fetishization of their rifles, which they must christen with a female name and sleep with at night. Hartman also peppers his insults with ethnic slurs, although under the guise of a perverse kind of inclusion: "There is no bigotry here," he barks. "I do not look down on niggers, kikes, wops, or greasers. Here you are all equally worthless."

The lesson that Hartman imparts, which Kubrick gives us in fragmented scenes that supply little sense of any world outside the barracks and training grounds, is that marines kill and die and that is all. He instills in them a killer instinct, telling them explicitly that if they do not kill, they will become "dead marines." The violence he directs against them, then, is ostensibly to prepare them to be externally violent—to kill the enemy without question or remorse. Any moral context is purposefully negated, illustrated by Hartman's straight-faced usage of Charles Whitman, who shot and killed twelve people from the observation tower at the University of Texas at Austin in 1966, and Lee Harvey Oswald, who was accused of assassinating President John F. Kennedy in 1963, as examples of "what a motivated marine and his rifle can do." These twisted examples of military proficiency with a firearm are offered without irony or comment because, for the recruits to become soldiers, they must kill without discrimination.

Unlike traditional war films that begin in combat training and then follow the new recruits into the field, *Full Metal Jacket* does not depict growing cohesion and solidarity among the men but rather dehumanization and fragmentation. There is no sense that the young men under Hartman's tutelage cohere into a unified fighting force. Near the end of the film's first half, Kubrick gives us a shot of the newly trained marines rushing toward the camera in slow motion with their grimacing "war faces" and drawn rifles, but the effect is one of chaotic violence, not the controlled sense of unity so valued in depictions of American fighting men. The only time Kubrick depicts the trainees coming together harmoniously is to enact vicious, late-night punishment on the hopelessly inadequate recruit nicknamed Private Gomer Pyle (Vincent D'Onofrio), whose constant screw-ups have caused Hartman to begin punishing the rest of the recruits. The men gather together in what is clearly a preplanned endeavor, pin Pyle to the bed and gag him, and then one by one successively beat his unprotected stomach with handcrafted mallets made by wrapping a hard bar of soap in the end of a towel. It is a brutal, unrelenting scene of inwardly directed violence—the recruits beating one of their own. Kubrick emphasizes the physical agony felt by Pyle as a result of his fellow recruits savagely hazing him but also the emotional agony of Private Joker (Matthew Modine), the squad leader Hartman has put in charge of whipping Pyle into shape. Joker is the film's point of identification, and this scene represents a significant moral choice for him, which he answers by allowing his anger and frustration to take over (much like what happens to the soldiers in the village sequence in *Platoon*) as he pounds on Pyle more times than anyone else.

This first half of *Full Metal Jacket* concludes by taking inwardly directed violence to its logical conclusion, as Pyle, clearly driven insane by his mistreatment at the hands of both Hartman and the other recruits, kills Hartman with his rifle and then turns it on himself. Thus, the first forty-five minutes of the film paint a brutal portrait of the process by which young men can be dehumanized into racist, misogynistic killers and then suggest that such a process ultimately must turn inward.

Without a clearly defined enemy or notion of what they are fighting for (throughout basic training, the war is rarely if ever mentioned explicitly), the soldiers' enforced killer instincts must be directed somewhere, a sentiment earlier reflected in *First Blood*'s depiction of Rambo's violent instincts turning against a representative small-town American community. As *Platoon* ended with one U.S. soldier killing another, so ends the first half of *Full Metal Jacket.*

The second half of the film, which takes place in Da Nang, Vietnam, an undetermined amount of time after basic training, appears at first to take on the qualities of an externally violent Vietnam film. But, like in *Platoon,* even when the violence is directed outward at an enemy, its wellspring of moral confusion marks it as implicitly inward. This section of the film takes place immediately before and after the 1968 Tet Offensive, in which the North Vietnamese army staged a series of unexpected attacks on crucial U.S. military positions. Each of the preceding Vietnam combat films discussed in this chapter were placed in a specific temporal context (a title card in *Platoon* establishes the year in which it begins, and *Hamburger Hill* counts off its passage of time with title cards giving us each date), but *Full Metal Jacket* was the first combat film to be set during a major historical event. Setting a significant portion of the film during what is often viewed as the turning point in the war when many lost hope that the United States could prevail in Vietnam immediately sets the stage for failure.

Private Joker, now working as a combat correspondent for *Stars and Stripes,* ends up in the ravaged Hue City with a platoon commanded by Sergeant Cowboy (Arliss Howard), with whom he was in basic training. Although there are two battles with North Vietnamese soldiers during this part of the film, the majority of screen time concerns the platoon being pinned down by a lone sniper who shoots several soldiers and continues riddling them with non-lethal shots in order to draw the rest of the men into the open. Unlike the rapid, chaotic violence in the opening half of the film or the battles with North Vietnamese soldiers, Kubrick draws out time as the soldiers are being shot by the sniper, depicting each bullet hit in slow motion that emphasizes not only the gruesome damage done to the human body by a bullet but also the ruthless pain and agony being inflicted.

Under Cowboy's leadership, the rest of the platoon decides to fall back rather than risk more fatalities to save their comrades. This direct order is countered by Animal Mother (Adam Baldwin), a hulk of a soldier whose bulging muscles, gung-ho attitude, and massive M-60 mark him as an explicit parody of Rambo, Braddock, and their action-movie ilk. However, unlike Rambo, Animal Mother's savage bloodlust is complicated by his commitment to his fellow soldiers. At one point, when he and the other members of his platoon are standing around two of their fallen comrades, his only words are, “Better you than me.” Yet earlier, another soldier said about him, “Under fire Animal Mother is one of the finest human beings around.” Thus, Animal Mother’s humanity is reliant on his being in the midst of violence, which is the very lesson that was imparted to the trainees in the film’s opening half. He is, then, the ultimate soldier, not because he is good at what he does but because it is the only thing he can do.

Full Metal Jacket concludes with the eventual killing of the sniper, who unexpectedly turns out to be a thin, frail, extremely young woman. Joker puts the wounded girl out of her misery against Animal Mother’s stated desire that she should “rot” and “be left for the motherlovin’ rats.” Throughout the film, Joker has played the divide between humanity and savagery, his helmet painted with the phrase “Born to kill” contrasted by the peace button he refuses to remove from his flak jacket. In this sense, Joker is a bit too obvious a conceit for Kubrick’s humanistic agenda, especially when he tells a commanding officer that his helmet and pin are meant to suggest “the duality of man” in the Jungian sense. The self-conscious irony of Joker’s stance toward the violence of Vietnam—he professes a desire to kill yet is clearly a pacifist—suggests the confused nature of the war machine itself, which breaks down when confronted with a lone, undetectable sniper. One could even view the sniper sequence as a metonym for the war itself, with the heavily armored U.S. soldiers uselessly unloading thousands of bullets toward an invisible enemy that is cutting them down one by one. Again, the depiction of war here is chaotic and uncontrolled, with little unity among the men and only a fragmented idea of anything resembling a true military objective.

The decision to find the sniper and kill her is depicted not as a military objective but a personal one, just as the destruction of the village in *Platoon* was fueled by a personal vendetta. “Let’s get some payback,” Animal Mother says, which would seem to code the killing of the sniper as a perfect example of external violence: a clear enemy eliminated through violent force. Yet, the underlying emphasis of the scene is not triumph, even though Rafter Man (Kevyn Major Howard), the soldier who initially shoots her, celebrates his kill. Rather, Kubrick emphasizes the dehumanization of violence for both the soldiers who enacted it and the victim, who is depicted in lingering extreme high-angle shots suffering and begging with her last breaths to be shot. This is clearly a moment of moral revelation for Joker, whose sarcastic and ironic commentary throughout the film about killing comes face to face with the real deal. It is ugly and it is brutal, and what the viewer is left with is not a sense of righteous vengeance but rather of sickening absurdity.

Kubrick then tacks on the final irony, as the soldiers march through the hellishly burning city singing the theme to *The Mickey Mouse Club.* Crucially, the first line we distinctly hear them singing is "We play fair, we work hard, and we're in harmony," which plays as ironic commentary on the decidedly unharmonious nature of the U.S. military and the war in general. Although the soldiers do not kill each other in the second half of *Full Metal Jacket,* their actions in battle do not carry the heroic charge of an externally violent film but rather the sinking feeling that what has truly been killed is their own humanity.

Brian De Palma also emphasizes the death of humanity in *Casualties of War,* which is a distinctly different combat film in that its sole focus is a specific war crime: a squad of U.S. soldiers on a reconnaissance mission kidnap a Vietnamese girl (Thuy Thu Le), systematically rape her, and then kill her to cover up their crime. However, the film is thematically similar to *Full Metal Jacket* in that it uses violence to suggest the duality of humankind, not through the conflicted feelings of a single character like Joker but rather through the conflict between two characters who represent distinctly different responses to war: Private Eriksson (Michael J. Fox), who repeatedly refuses to engage in the crime and commits himself to exposing it to military authorities, and Sergeant Tony Meserve (Sean Penn), his commanding officer, who hatches the idea in the first place. Like Chris Taylor in *Platoon,* Eriksson is new to Vietnam, while Meserve has been in-country for a long time and is hardened because of it. Like Sergeant Barnes in *Platoon,* his moral compass has become so twisted that he is unable to distinguish right from wrong.

Similar to other inwardly violent combat films, the violence in *Casualties of War* is often directed at an external enemy, but the morally disfigured nature of that violence suggests that its true direction is inward. While there are several conventional battle sequences, the majority of the film's violence is directed at either the kidnapped Vietnamese girl or Eriksson. Meserve repeatedly insists that the girl is a "VC prisoner," which helps him justify the crime to himself and the other members of the squad but also plays on the difficulty U.S. soldiers had in determining the "real enemy." The completely amoral nature of the sexual and physical violence inflicted on the girl makes it virtually unwatchable, even though De Palma carefully keeps the majority of it offscreen, suggesting its intensity and duration via sound and slow dissolves. The rape sequence feels unbearable, although we see only small glimpses of it in often out-of-focus long shots, which is all the more impressive given the criticism De Palma had sustained for making sexual violence sensual and alluring in *Dressed to Kill* and *Body Double.* The physical suffering of the girl is matched by the understanding that, as in *Full Metal Jacket,* the soldiers are violating their own humanity at the same time. This is especially true of Private Herbert Hatcher (John C. Reilly), who is depicted as mentally slow and therefore more susceptible to pressure and intimidation, and Private Antonio Diaz (John Leguizamo), who at first tells Eriksson that he will refuse to rape the girl but ultimately caves because he's afraid of being verbally tormented. Eriksson spends most of the film being harassed by his fellow soldiers, and once they are back in base camp, he becomes a physical target when they try to kill him to keep him quiet. Thus, like in *Platoon*, the violence in *Casualties of War* cannot be contained with the simple "us versus them" dichotomy of the externally violent Vietnam films but rather explodes within, turning soldiers against each other.

The film's title, then, which is taken directly from Daniel Lang's 1969 *New Yorker* article, is purposefully ambiguous: Who are the casualties of war? That question haunts all the inwardly violent Vietnam films, as the answer they repeatedly return to is ourselves.

In stark contrast to the pure action film of the 1980s, films about Vietnam and its aftermath represented a contested site in which Hollywood productions attempted to make sense of a controversial war that still divided the nation. The violence of these films demonstrates the nature of that conflict, with some films directing their violence outward at a clear-cut enemy, while others directed it inward, suggesting that the true enemy was not some identifiable target "out there" but rather our conflicted selves.

This cycle of Vietnam films was brief, with the majority of productions being released commercially between 1985 and 1989. By 1988, there were already grumblings that no one wanted to see another Vietnam film, which is reflected in their declining box-office popularity. *Platoon* was the third highest-grossing film of 1986 with $138 million in domestic revenues, putting it just behind the pure action adrenaline of *Top Gun* and the Australian-in-New York comedy *Crocodile Dundee.* In 1987, *Full Metal Jacket* was in the top 25 with $46 million, while Barry Levinson's war comedy *Good Morning, Vietnam,* starring Robin Williams, was the fourth highest-grossing film of that year with $124 million. However, in 1988, *Hamburger Hill* couldn't crack the top 50 at the U.S. box office, nor could *Casualties of War* the following year. *Born on the Fourth of July* (1989), which continued Oliver Stone's exploration of the "death of innocence" in Vietnam by telling the story of real-life Vietnam veteran Ron Kovic, made $70 million at the box office in 1989, but that success was primarily due to the star power of Tom Cruise, who was seeking to reinvent himself as a serious actor by subverting his iconic status as the very face of the pure action hero by playing an embittered paraplegic. After that, there were few if any Hollywood productions that took place in Vietnam or were in any way about the war. Stone ventured into Vietnam one final time in 1993 for *Heaven and Earth,* based on the memoirs of a Vietnamese woman and her experiences during and after the war, but it was a flop at the box office and did not receive the critical attention of his previous films.

Throughout the 1990s there were films such as *Jacob's Ladder* (1990) and *Forrest Gump* (1994) that had sequences *set* in Vietnam during the war, but the films themselves were not *about* Vietnam, which suggests that depictions of the war had become comfortable enough that they could be integrated seamlessly into other narratives without the perceived need to comment explicitly on the war itself. The very presence of these Vietnam films, no matter how disturbing they may have been, made the violence of that war part of the Hollywood landscape, thus incorporating it into some form of familiarity. In this sense, despite their conflicted approaches to the war, the legacy of the Hollywood Vietnam war films of the 1980s is much like the legacy of violent films throughout the Reagan decade: They helped to pave the path by which screen violence was made palatable for the mass audience.

5

DISAVOWING HORROR

INDEPENDENT PRODUCTION, FANDOM, AND THE FETISHIZING OF MAKEUP SPECIAL EFFECTS

BECAUSE IT IS THE INHERENT nature of the horror genre to transgress boundaries and challenge visual taboos, it is of little surprise that horror films have been at the center of social and political controversy throughout the history of cinema and were thus seen as especially problematic for the major studios during the 1980s. From the early cycle of 1930s horror films from Universal Studios, such as *Dracula* and *Frankenstein*, to low-budget independent shockers like *Maniac* (1980), to Oscar-nominated, mainstream blockbusters like *The Exorcist*, horror films have constantly been enmeshed in controversy, most often because of what they show us. As Mark Kermode argues, "Even the most narratively reactionary, moralistic horror movies feed upon the ecstatic shock of speaking the unspeakable, showing the unwatchable" ("Horror" 155). Horror films are, at their base, about violence: "Taken as a whole, the entire genre is an unsystematic, unresolved exploration of violence in virtually all its forms and guises" (Waller 260).

This has especially been the case since the late 1960s and 1970s, which saw the rapid development of increasingly graphic visual representations of monstrosity and bodily carnage. Whereas previously the details of violence in horror films had been largely hinted at and suggested just outside the cinematic frame, modern horror films have moved them front and center, turning decapitations, disembowelments, stabbings, burnings, maulings, and other assorted visual atrocities into one of the genre's chief draws. Although there were antecedents in cinema history that predated the gory work of Herschel Gordon Lewis, Mario Bava, George A. Romero, and other filmmakers who pioneered the "splatter film,"[1] gore became the central organizing principle of horror films starting in the 1960s, reaching its apotheosis in the late 1970s and early 1980s. At this point, explicit violence and the horror genre were virtually inseparable in the popular imagination, and as a result gore became one of the genre's chief selling points, much to the consternation of the mainstream film industry.

Nevertheless, horror was an extremely popular and profitable genre in the 1980s, which makes it an excellent case study for examining the ways in which the margins of any culture industry sometimes intrude on the center. Regardless of how hard the Hollywood studios have tried to maintain control over various forms of representation throughout film history, there have always been alternate voices at the margins that not only thrive on what the mainstream industry refuses to produce but ultimately influence and affect the cinema as a whole. The major studios had to find ways to avoid being overtly associated with the presumably transgressive violence of the horror genre, particularly as it developed in the 1980s with a brash mixture of graphic displays of gore mixed with often cartoonish humor and blunt sexuality, while still benefiting financially. Just as, during the classical era, "the organized film industry denigrated exploitation films, creating barriers to their distribution and exhibition[, and] . . . also depended on the contrast of exploitation to construct its own image as a responsible business" (Schaefer 14), the mainstream studios in the 1980s had an ambivalent relationship to horror films: On the one hand they brought negative publicity and were open targets for public criticism, but on the other hand they appealed to a significant demographic and were highly profitable. Thus, in the horror genre we can see how the margins sometimes collapse into the center and vice versa.

This chapter will explore the role played by the horror genre in the 1980s. Specifically, it will look at how the major studios, in trying to maintain a more conservative public image, tried to disavow their involvement with horror films. This resulted in horror becoming largely the province of smaller, independent production companies that struggled against the barriers imposed by the dominant film culture, particularly as embodied in the Motion Picture Association of America's Classification and Rating Administration. Since they couldn't achieve mainstream success, horror producers became more insular, catering primarily to their very specific fan base, whose fervent adoration of this disreputable genre found a voice in *Fangoria* magazine. *Fangoria* made the horror genre more gruesome by focusing on the most graphically violent aspects of its films while simultaneously denying this screen violence any true impact by fetishizing the makeup effects technologies used to create it. Thus, while horror movies in general and *Fangoria* in particular offered an apparent alternative to the general conservatism of Hollywood cinema in the 1980s, they also played a role in constructing the mainstream industry's "ideology of entertainment" by denying the real-world impact of graphic violence—making it, for lack of a better word, *fun.*

This disassociation of horror violence from reality helped to separate the horror genre from real-world anxieties during the 1980s, which is precisely the work Andrew Britton attributes to the Reaganite "ideology of entertainment," which encourages the viewer to see each film as a commodity to be consumed rather than as a text to be read. In fact, in writing about the role of entertainment in the 1980s, Britton may as well have been writing about the horror genre:

> The construction of the otherness of entertainment is inseparable from its solipsism: the active mobilization of the ideology of entertainment absolutely requires the active presentation of its conventions. The spectator is invited to become aware of those conventions and to think of them as defining a hermetic, autonomous world which has no bearing and no tendency and which relates to other social practices only by being different from them. (5)

Few genres are more reliant on conventions and a self-aware audience than the horror genre, which Britton notes in his less-than-ideal experience watching *Hell Night* (1981) with a predominantly teenage audience: "It became obvious at a very early stage that every spectator knew exactly what the film was going to do at every point" (2). This knowledge extends directly to the role played by explicit violence in 1980s horror films and the manner in which *Fangoria* tamed it by making it familiar, funny, and understandable as a form of "movie magic." In other words, *Fangoria* "produce[d] a certain kind of complicity with the spectator, a knowing sense of familiarity with the terms of the discourse" (5). Thus, although the blood and guts of horror had a facade of subversiveness, enough that the studios generally steered clear of the genre, it ultimately played a conservative role, drawing the violence of horror away from the socially inflected resonance that largely defined horror films in the 1970s such as *The Last House on the Left* (1972), *The Texas Chainsaw Massacre* (1973), *The Exorcist*, and *The Hills Have Eyes* (1977) and infusing the genre with "the ideology of entertainment."

Disavowing Horror in the 1980s

It is certainly ironic that the envelope-pushing visual sensibility of the horror genre was reaching a peak in U.S. filmmaking at precisely the same time that the major studios were trying to maintain a more conservative public image. Horror film production spiked early in the decade of the 1980s, going from only thirty-five films in 1979, to seventy in 1980, and ninety-three in 1981. The *Washington Post* declared that the fall of 1980 would be remembered as "the season when horror movies, those unspeakable celluloid things, cracked out of their pods en mase [*sic*] to gorge anew on the wallets of American filmgoers," although it also predicted that "like the predestined perpetrators of their own fevered tales, they too will return to restless graves, there to spawn a new cycle of cinemagraphical excess. So it's a hello-goodbye to the biggest glut of nightmare movies in film history" (C. Williams). This prediction proved to be partially correct: There was a glut of horror product in the early 1980s, so much so that Roger Corman, who had specialized in producing low-budget independent horror and science fiction since the 1950s, canceled a horror production due to market saturation in 1980 (C. Williams). And, because there were more horror films than the industry could handle for distribution, production dropped off sharply for the next five years. However, it spiked again in the later 1980s to a new high of 105 films in 1987 (Prince, *New Pot of Gold* 298).

How, then, was it possible that an industry that was trying so hard to align itself with what it perceived to be a more conservative public could allow the production, on such a large scale, of films that are intended primarily to offend, enrage, and otherwise subvert polite sensibilities? The answer lies in simple disavowal. Despite the proliferation of increasingly gory horror films in the 1980s, the major studios attempted to keep a far enough distance from them to create the outward appearance that they were not involved in their production. In general, the major Hollywood studios simply did not produce or distribute most of the horror films of the 1980s, particularly after the early part of the decade. As John Veitch, then president of the Columbia Pictures production unit, said, because of the increasing condemnation of horror movies from both critics and members of the public, "we're all being a bit more selective" (qtd. in S. Grover). Instead, the studios allowed independent production and distribution companies to handle the bulk of production and distribution of horror films, but not without policing them. CARA's increasing restrictions on overt displays of gory violence helped to assure the public that it was keeping the content of independently produced horror films in check, much to the chagrin of horror producers who understood their audience's desire for outlandish bloodshed. Thus, the various battles over horror films being denied a marketable R rating and, as a result, having to cut much of their visceral gore helped, rather than hindered, the industry in appearing to be responsible. Horror films couldn't be stamped out completely, but they could be managed.

Independent Production

Of the roughly seven hundred horror films produced in the United States between 1980 and 1989—not counting horror-inspired comedies like *Haunted Honeymoon* (1986) and *Beetlejuice* (1988)—the largest U.S. studios had a hand in the production of fewer than eighty of them. Paramount, Universal, 20th Century-Fox, Warner Bros., MGM/UA, Columbia/Tri-Star, Orion, and Disney accounted for roughly 12 percent of horror film production in the United States during the 1980s, even though horror was one of the decade's most popular and profitable genres (Prince, *New Pot of Gold*).

This strategy of avoiding the production and distribution of horror films because of the controversies involved and the censorship problems they routinely faced had long been employed by the major studios. During the horror film's brief emergence in the early 1930s as a significant Hollywood genre, the "Big Five" Hollywood studios (20th Century-Fox, Paramount, Metro-Goldwyn-Mayer, Warner Bros., and RKO) accounted for less than a third of overall horror film distribution; with its *Frankenstein, Dracula, Mummy,* and *Invisible Man* cycles, a single minor studio, Universal, distributed nearly as many horror films as all five majors combined. The studios had good reason to shy away from horror films, because they frequently raised the ire of local censorship boards, which were still quite powerful in the early 1930s. The Studio Relations Committee, which at the time was the industry's enforcer of the recently minted Production Code, vastly underestimated the response that horror films like *Frankenstein* would have, and as a result the film met with costly demands from regional and foreign censorship boards and, in at least a few cases, outright bans. As a result, the industry began to police the horror film with much more fervor, eliminating virtually all hints of violence, both visual and aural, with the ultimate result being the genre devolving in the 1940s and 1950s into outright parody like *Abbott and Costello Meet Frankenstein* (1948) and "safe adolescent programming" like *Frankenstein Meets the Wolf Man* (1943) and *House of Dracula* (1945) (Prince, *Classical Film Violence* 85).

The horror genre saw a significant resurgence following the controversial success of the imported Hammer films in the late 1950s and Alfred Hitchcock's *Psycho* in 1960, and many critics view the 1970s as a high point of the genre, with non-studio-produced films such as Tobe Hooper's *The Texas Chainsaw Massacre,* Wes Craven's *The Hills Have Eyes,* and George A. Romero's *Dawn of the Dead* (1978) standing as exemplars of both low-budget creativity and social relevance. The genre also generated two massive blockbusters in the 1970s with *The Exorcist* and *Jaws* and was reignited on a different scale with the unexpected box-office success of the independently produced *Halloween* (1978), which earned more than $50 million on a budget of only $400,000. As a result, the major studios found it difficult to resist the allure of low budgets and high profits, and many of them hopped aboard the horror bandwagon in the late 1970s and early 1980s. However, when the major studios delved into violent horror in the early 1980s, they attempted to offset their involvement in such a disreputable genre by giving their productions an air of prestige. This meant that studio horror films were usually associated with a popular literary figure such as Stephen King (for example, Warner Bros.' *Creepshow,* 1982; Universal's *Firestarter,* 1984; Paramount's *Pet Semetary,* 1988) or was made by a respected auteur (for example, Warner Bros.' *The Shining,* 1980, directed by Stanley Kubrick; Universal's *Cat People,* 1982, directed by Paul Schrader; MGM/UA's *Poltergeist,* 1982, produced by Steven Spielberg; Orion's *The Believers,* 1987, directed by John Schlesinger).

Columbia Pictures, which, according to head of production John Veitch, was being "more selective" in choosing its projects, is a good example of the studios' wariness of horror films by the middle of the 1980s. While Columbia began the decade by producing a pair of notorious early slasher films, *When a Stranger Calls* (1979) and *Happy Birthday to Me* (1981), the studio quickly adopted a policy of producing more "highbrow" horror films, including *Christine* (1983), a film about a possessed car that was based on a novel by Stephen King and directed by *Halloween*'s John Carpenter; *The Bride* (1985), an expensive remake of *The Bride of Frankenstein* (1935) fueled by the star power of Sting, frontman for the British pop group the Police, and Jennifer Beals, who was hot off her leading role in *Flashdance*; and *Fright Night* (1985), a well-made vampire horror-comedy that explicitly mocked the critically derided slasher movie cycle by having Roddy McDowell, playing a washed-up horror movie actor, bemoan the current state of affairs in horror filmmaking by saying, "The kids today don't have the patience for vampires. They want to see some mad slasher running around and chopping off heads."[2] The only real exception was Columbia's release of *The New Kids* (1985), a teenage revenge melodrama directed by Sean S. Cunningham (*Friday the 13th,* 1980), which was poorly reviewed and quickly disappeared from theaters.

When major studios did finance and/or distribute horror films, their publicity departments often made every effort to disassociate these films from that genre. For example, Universal's remake of *The Thing* (1982), directed by John Carpenter, was promoted as a blend of science fiction and fantasy, thus playing down the film's overwhelmingly horrific tones. Another remake of a horror classic produced by Universal in 1982, Paul

Schrader's *Cat People,* was advertised as "an erotic suspense story interwoven with a contemporary love theme," a description that clearly left out any hint of the graphic gore the film contains, including a character (Ed Begley Jr.) having his arm ripped out of its socket by a giant cat, complete with snapping tendons and spurting arterial blood. The theatrical trailer for *Cat People* plays almost entirely on the film's erotic elements (the film is even subtitled "An Erotic Fantasy"), and its soundtrack is dominated by David Bowie's pop anthem "Cat People (Putting Out the Fire)," which reduces the brief glimpses of horror imagery to little more than music-video-style quick-cut flashes.[3] The disavowal of graphic screen violence in studio-produced horror is also evidenced by the marketing of Warner Bros.' *Creepshow,* directed by George A. Romero, who had scored a major independent hit in 1978 with his graphically violent *Dawn of the Dead.* Although the film contains more than its share of gory images inspired by EC horror comic books, a spokesman for Warner Bros. made a point of noting that the gore was "held to a minimum" and that colored lights and filters reduced its shock value (Sterritt, "Hollywood Horror Film").

By generally not being involved in the production of low-budget horror films—the kind that were typically the most graphically violent and were viewed as having the least artistic merit—the major studios were able to project a sense of "quality," illustrating to the public that they were above such mindless (and, in some people's minds, dangerous) dreck. As David Sterritt put it, "Clearly, the makers of such 'class' productions [as *Cat People* and *The Thing*] want to put a lot of distance between themselves and the unrelieved mayhem that has lately passed for horrific entertainment" ("Hollywood Horror Film"). The effectiveness with which the studios created and maintained this "quality" public image for themselves can be seen in Janet Maslin's comments on the slasher genre in an article in the *New York Times*:

> The slice-'em-up genre, which now occupies the honored position last held by occult-oriented thrillers, has produced almost nothing of any merit, with the exceptions of such acknowledged critical successes as "Halloween." It has also failed to produce much in the way of imitation from the major studios, perhaps because it's easier for the majors to distribute independently-made, low-budget thrillers—as Paramount did with "Friday the 13th"—than to make their own films as cheaply. Also, this is a genre in which quality is virtually beside the point, so the studios have no reason to improve on it. ("Tired Blood")

The notion that studios would not want to be associated with such films because they are the product of a formula that can't be "improved" because "quality is virtually beside the point" is indicative of how well the studios had publicized themselves as the producers of quality entertainment.

This is not to say that the studios produced only "quality" horror films during the 1980s. Quite the opposite, the studios were involved with the production and distribution of some of the most notorious slasher films of that decade, which received the brunt of public criticism about the role of violence in horror. Because slasher films are "drenched in taboo and encroaching vigorously on the pornographic," they lie "by and large beyond the purview of the respectable (middle-aged, middle-class) audience" (Clover 22). Critics derided such films as "dead teenager," "slash-and-chop," "teenie-kill," or "slice-'em-up" movies, thus effectively reducing everything about them to the moments of graphic violence in which the characters meet their end. That mainstream critics responded in this manner is not at all surprising, because slasher films address the spectator's body directly by engaging in the sensationalistic display of creative forms of murder; thus, they are viewed as lowbrow. This directness marks them as being part of a low genre of filmmaking, whereas indirect horror films, those that generate thrills through more subtle cinematic means such as lighting, camerawork, and sound, are often thought of as being, if not highbrow, then at least more artistically worthy. As Gregory A. Waller notes, "The equation of explicitly violent horror with pornographic gore is often based on the assumption that truly effective horror is always indirect and suggestive" (260).

However, the equation of slasher films with pornography was often not extreme enough for the genre's critics. Slasher films weren't understood as just violent films; they were violence itself. Thus, they were, in essence, exactly the kind of potentially controversial violent films from which the major studios wanted to keep their distance, particularly because of the way in which they intertwined sex and violent death in an even cruder form than *Dressed to Kill* and *Cruising* had, at least on the immediate surface.[4] Unfortunately, due to their low budgets and high popularity with teenage audiences, slasher movies were quite profitable, and some of the majors risked being associated with them. In particular, Paramount paid $1.5 million for the domestic distribution rights to *Friday the 13th*, an independent production written, produced, and directed by Sean S. Cunningham, best known for producing *The Last House on the Left*. Paramount was then financially involved in the subsequent production of seven *Friday the 13th* sequels released between 1981 and 1988.

Being directly involved in such productions put the studios at risk of overt public criticism, which is exactly what happened to Paramount when the release of *Friday the 13th* set off a round of condemnations led by the well-known Chicago-based film critics Roger Ebert and Gene Siskel,

13. The lowbrow and gory nature of slasher films made them difficult for major studios to distribute, a lesson Paramount Pictures learned after a vocal campaign led by *Chicago Tribune* critic Gene Siskel against *Friday the 13th* (1980). Nevertheless, their immense popularity with teenagers and high profit margins made them difficult to resist. DVD still.

whose syndicated PBS show, *Sneak Previews*, gave them a national televised forum from which they could deride slasher films and those who produced them. Siskel and Ebert saw slasher films in general as "a disturbing new trend in today's movies" that hated women and were artistically bankrupt. Although Ebert did not write a review of *Friday the 13th* in the *Chicago Sun-Times*, when Siskel reviewed it for the *Chicago Tribune* on May 12, 1980, the weekend after it opened, he made no effort to contain his vitriol. Not only did he refer to writer/director Cunningham as "one of the most despicable creatures ever to infest the movie business," he used the opening paragraph to give away the film's ending in the hopes that it would dissuade viewers from seeing it. More important, though, Siskel directed his anger over the film's violence at its distributor, Paramount, and Paramount's chairman, Charles Bluhdorn. Siskel noted his "surprise" that "a major, publicly held film company would handle a movie as bloody as this," and he included Bluhdorn's corporate address in the review with the admonition that viewers should write him and complain about the film. Siskel also took umbrage at the MPAA and its rating board, accusing it of giving the film an R rating rather than a deserved X rating because "Paramount pays part of the salary of the MPAA people who determine the ratings, and this is clearly a case where a big studio gets a less-restrictive rating than is proper."

Ebert joined Siskel in his pronounced contempt for the genre when they dedicated an entire episode of *Sneak Previews* on October 23, 1980, to condemning *Friday the 13th* and other similar films. It is important to note, however, that Siskel and Ebert were not conservative bluenoses who had no appreciation for the horror genre at all. In particular, Ebert had been a vocal champion of *Dawn of the Dead* and *The Last House on the Left*, the latter of which most mainstream critics (Siskel included) found loathsome. During the slasher episode of *Sneak Previews*, both Ebert and Siskel praised *Halloween* as an example of how a horror thriller could be done with artistry and respect for its female characters. However, their contempt for most slasher films and their accusations of overt misogyny in such films formed the core of their message, which they took onto other television programs with much larger viewerships than *Sneak Previews* had, including NBC's *Today* and *The Phil Donahue Show.*

Despite its high public profile, the Siskel and Ebert campaign against slasher films didn't have much of an economic effect, as *Friday the 13th* and its immediate sequels and imitators were significant box-office hits.[5] However, their efforts did result in other critics and journalists joining the campaign and many newspapers and magazines refusing to review such films anymore (Kapsis 165) or carry their advertising.[6] Paramount's public image took a significant hit when Siskel wrote an open letter to the studio's executives, attacking them "for having gotten behind such a blatantly violent and exploitative film" (McCarty 146). Siskel also urged the readers of the *Chicago Tribune* to boycott *all* Paramount films in protest of *Friday the 13th*, thus further entangling Paramount's public image with a single, violent horror film that it hadn't even produced but merely distributed.

As it turned out, the wave of horror film production in the early 1980s declined substantially by 1983, leaving the major studios little incentive to risk their image by being involved with them. Thus, the studios left the majority of horror film production to smaller, independent studios and distributors like Empire Pictures, New World Pictures, Film Ventures, Analysis Film Releasing, and New Line. These companies, which were less concerned with their public image than the major studios and their multinational conglomerate owners, thrived on producing low-budget movies that could turn tidy profits when marketed to the youth audiences with whom they were associated.

CARA's Tougher Stand on Horror Violence

With the growing sophistication of makeup special effects, horror films in the 1980s had the potential to be more realistically gruesome than ever. Particularly after the release of *Friday the 13th*, graphic screen violence in the horror genre became a constantly escalating game of one-upmanship, with each film in the genre trying to top the previous one in terms of cleverly presented gruesomeness. Lacking marquee stars, big budgets, and complex plotlines, horror films turned to gore as their chief draw, and it became the thing that people came to see.

There was a major obstacle, though: CARA. Because the vast majority of newspapers and radio stations wouldn't accept advertising for films with an X rating and many theaters wouldn't book such films, producers were forced by economic concerns to ensure that they could get an R rating. And, while CARA had been allowing greater and greater levels of graphic screen violence into R-rated films throughout the 1970s, in the 1980s it began to consciously tighten the restrictions on allowable screen gore, particularly in horror films. This move was led by CARA chairman Richard Heffner, who felt compelled to reverse the precedents set by his predecessor, Dr. Aaron Stern, who tended to focus primarily on displays of sexuality and nudity with little concern for depictions of violence. In fact, prior to Heffner's tenure at CARA, no film had gone into theatrical release with an X rating specifically for screen violence, although several, including *The Wild Bunch*, had to be trimmed to avoid the rating. Gerard Jones of the *New York Times* branded Heffner "The Man Who Gave an 'X' Rating to Violence" after Heffner insisted that the Sonny Chiba martial arts film *The Street Fighter* (*Gekitotsu! Satsujin ken*, 1974), which was produced in Japan and distributed in the United States by the then independent distributor New Line Cinema, carry the restrictive rating because of its graphic violence, which includes scenes of Chiba gouging his opponent's eyes, tearing flesh from others' bodies, and, in one instance, tearing off a man's genitals with his bare hands.

Heffner was quite open about what he perceived to be the need for CARA to take violence seriously when considering what rating would be most appropriate for a particular film. For example, in 1978, Independent Artists Corp., a small U.S. distributor, acquired the rights to *Las Garras de Lorelei*, a 1974 Spanish horror film that was retitled *When the Screaming Stops*, and submitted it for a rating. CARA rated it X for violence, and when Miles Nelson, president of Independent Artists, appealed the rating before the MPAA Appeals Board, Heffner boldly refuted Nelson's argument that *When the Screaming Stops* should be rated R as is because earlier R-rated horror films like *The Texas Chainsaw Massacre* were just as violent. In Heffner's prepared statement at the appeals hearing, he said:

> I have read Mr. Nelson's letter. And while his use of *Texas Chainsaw Massacre* and *Night of the Living Dead* as precedents for an R rating may seem understandable, the fact is that his concern about precedent is precisely our own. For in recent years the rating

> system's approach to gore and violence has thoroughly reversed the trend of those earlier ratings. And we don't want some other filmmaker to come in tomorrow and say that R for *When the Screaming Stops*—as it is right now—is a new precedent and indicates that we are back to the same old stand. (Heffner, "Reminiscences," October 5, 1978, box 1, 1)

Heffner later concluded by saying, "This Appeals Board has time and again over the past few years upheld us in finally making gore and violence loom large in film classification. And there is no indication at all that American parents are clamoring for us—or for you—to reverse that posture" (2). This final statement is particularly telling because, as noted in the introduction, the Appeals Board, unlike the CARA Rating Board, is composed of a dozen members drawn from the studios, the National Association of Theater Owners, and the Producers Guild of America (Vaughn)—in essence, the major constituent parts of the mainstream U.S. film industry. Thus, their willingness to support CARA in harsher ratings for violent films is indicative of the industry's overall desire to skew movies and the violence in them toward the mainstream. Not surprisingly, Nelson lost the appeal and ultimately had to trim *When the Screaming Stops* in order to secure an R rating.

Thus, the threat of a film receiving an X rating for violence was very real and loomed large in the minds of producers as they set about the task of incorporating maximum bloodshed into their films without incurring a rating that would effectively exclude them from the theatrical marketplace. This was a significant problem for horror film producers because the gore itself had become one of their major selling points; in essence, CARA was forcing them to remove much of the appeal of their films if they were to be awarded a market-friendly R rating. Not surprisingly, this was at roughly the same time that the major studios began to abandon the horror genre completely after a few productions in the early 1980s, meaning that it was the independent producers who suffered the most.

With both the application of the Production Code Seal of Approval from 1930 to the mid-1960s and the classification system from 1968 to the present, the MPAA has a long history of treating different genre films differently. Because of its disreputable status, the horror genre has always been scrutinized more carefully in terms of its content and subsequently suffered more threats of censorship than any other genre. According to Stephen Prince, in the classical era, "violence in . . . Hollywood film was less the issue than the behaviors to which it was attached and the moral example that these films provided" (*Classical Film Violence* 33). Thus, violence in westerns and combat films could be more explicit and there could be more of it because "it was typically presented as a kind of righteous violence, carried out by heroes of strong moral purpose" (33). Violence in the horror genre is typically anything but "righteous" and is usually described as "gratuitous," "excessive," or "sadistic," marking it as socially unacceptable in polite circles. When Universal Pictures introduced its cycle of classic horror films in the 1930s, the Production Code Administration was fairly lenient regarding their depictions of cruelty and suffering, although regional censor boards were not so flexible. This resulted in the PCA having to clamp down much harder on horror violence by mid-decade, to the point that the agency was requiring filmmakers to remove virtually every horrific element—visual and aural—from their films. Prince argues that this suppression of depictions of violence and related horrific imagery and sounds had a significant effect on the genre:

> The genre . . . would eventually devolve into safe adolescent programming (e.g., *Frankenstein Meets the Wolf Man, House of Frankenstein, House of Dracula*). This devolution is usually attributed to an exhaustion of the genre's classical monsters and narrative formulae. But it also stems at least in part from the suppression of violence, instigated by the reactions of regional censors to the horror pictures and the PCA's increased scrutiny of the genre. (85)

Exactly fifty years later, history essentially repeated itself, except this time it was CARA withholding R ratings instead of the PCA refusing a Seal of Approval, which, despite the significant industrial changes in Hollywood between the 1930s and the 1980s, was essentially the same thing: a needed brand whose absence carried untenable economic consequences. CARA's limits on screen violence in an R-rated film had already been tested numerous times throughout the 1970s. For example, to secure an R rating, Sam Peckinpah had to make a number of trims to *The Wild Bunch,* including the climactic moment when the Mexican general Mapache slits the throat of Angel, one of the members of the bunch.[7] Martin Scorsese also had to make concessions to get *Taxi Driver* an R rating, but rather than remove gore, he chose to visually darken the final shoot-out to tone down the graphic bloodshed. Even *The Street Fighter* (1974), which was the first film to be released theatrically with an X rating for violence, was eventually withdrawn, re-edited, and released with an R rating (Jones).

In the horror genre, filmmakers were routinely required to snip a few seconds or more from graphically violent sequences before their films were given an R rating (in some cases, entire scenes had to be cut). Brian De Palma had to make several concessions on *Dressed to Kill,* particularly the razor slashing of Angie Dickinson in the elevator, although the cuts did little to alleviate the controversy that engulfed that film.

Wes Craven's numerous experiences with rating horror films have led him to the belief that CARA's decisions regarding horror violence is often not predicated on any specifics of what is shown and therefore can be cut out of a scene but rather on the intensity of the scene, making it virtually impossible for filmmakers to know what to cut out to make it more acceptable (Craven). According to Heffner, a similar sentiment was expressed quite directly by Jack Valenti in a 1981 interview with Robert Butler in the *Kansas City Star*: "The problem with screen violence isn't how graphic it is, but how gratuitous it is. Violence can be dramatically valid, after all, but there are different kinds of violence" (Heffner, "RDH Pre–Oral History Memorandum 1981," box 1, 15). Of course, such thinking goes against the tenor of the genre itself, whose purpose is to shock, frighten, and enthrall with ghastly images—to cross comfortable binaries and show the unshowable. While horror violence is certainly "dramatically valid" from a fundamental narrative point of view (after all, without the threat of bodily harm, where is the horror?), it is all too easy to view such violence as "gratuitous" because of the disreputable nature of the genre itself, which was the overriding sentiment of CARA when rating horror films throughout the decade.

Thus, during the 1980s, CARA functioned effectively to curb the excessive tendencies of the horror genre, reining it in and making it a more docile, though still disreputable, creature. The tendency in such situations, especially for the filmmaker whose film is being rated, is to cry "Censor!," but this is too simplistic and reactionary. CARA functioned in the same vein as the PCA did during the Studio Era: "The agency was a braking mechanism—not an industry censor—designed to inhibit, but not expunge, depictions of violence and brutality" (Prince, *Classical Film Violence* 83). That is, it was not the goal of CARA to work against filmmakers but to work with them to make their products conform better to general cultural expectations of what was allowable on-screen and thus protect the industry as a whole from the kinds of economically dangerous controversy that attended films like *Dressed to Kill* and *Cruising.* Most filmmakers and distributors were willing to work within this system because it offered them some financial protection, guaranteeing that they would have access to advertising and distribution, although there were a few non-MPAA outliers who were willing to risk releasing a horror film unrated.

Horror films released without a rating included George A. Romero's *Dawn of the Dead* and *Day of the Dead* (1985), William Lustig's *Maniac,* Stuart Gordon's *Re-Animator* (1985), and Sam Raimi's *The Evil Dead* (1982) and *Evil Dead II* (1987). Instead of a rating, the advertising for these films carried general warnings about the nature of the films' content, often with an age restriction. The poster for *The Evil Dead* noted at the bottom, "The producers recommend that no one under 17 be allowed to see *The Evil Dead*," while the poster for *Dawn of the Dead* was more specific and restrictive: "There is no explicit sex in this picture. However, there are scenes of violence which may be considered shocking. No one under 17 will be admitted."

All of these unrated horror films were distributed by independent companies that were not affiliated with the MPAA and therefore did not have to submit to the rating system, although they had the option to do so and usually did. Unfortunately, when they did, independents often found that they were the victims of an unspoken and long-criticized tendency of CARA to treat studio films and independent films differently, with more latitude being given to the former. According to Stephen Farber, who was a member of CARA for six months in 1970, "The board [CARA] is almost always much harsher in demanding cuts from independent film-makers who are in less of a position to fight them" (*Ratings Game* 62).

This was especially true of CARA's treatment of horror films in the 1980s, as the studio-produced films were frequently allowed a surprising amount of latitude in their graphic content, whereas independently produced films were often required to make extensive cuts. Even though CARA was taking a stronger stand on rating screen violence in all films, there was both an underlying assumption that audiences would be more accepting of it if it were part of a "quality" film directed by a respected filmmaker with name recognition and also overt pressure from the major studios to ensure that their product received a market-friendly rating. For example, in the next chapter we will see how the horror film *Poltergeist*, which was directed by Tobe Hooper, who was still best known for having helmed *The Texas Chainsaw Massacre*, but was co-written and produced by Steven Spielberg, arguably the most powerful filmmaker in Hollywood, was eventually rated PG against the Rating Board's insistence that it be rated R because it was a big-budget studio film whose failure at the box office could affect the industry as a whole.

Producers and distributors of films not associated with one of the major studios frequently cited the alleged tendency of CARA to treat them differently when protesting an X rating on their films. When the independently produced horror film *Mother's Day* (1980) was initially rated X for such violent scenes as an on-screen beheading, the beating and strangling of a girl, and a character getting struck in the groin with an ax, Richard G. Hassanein, president of United Film Distribution Co., the film's distributor, wrote an angry letter to Heffner, accusing him of treating the film differently because of its pedigree: "It is quite apparent to us that the product of the major companies is rated differently than that of the independent distributor and that your decisions are discriminatory, capricious and aimed to the destruction of the independent distributor for the benefit of the majors who are the members of your Association" (Hassanein to Heffner, September 15, 1980, in Heffner, "Reminiscences," box 1, 2). Hassanein also compared his film to films with similar levels of violence that were released by major studios but were given an R rating, including *The Fury, Dressed to Kill,* and *Friday the 13th.*

Friday the 13th was frequently cited by angry horror filmmakers who felt that Sean S. Cunningham's film had gotten away with graphic levels of violence while theirs were being punished for similar representations, which was largely true. For Heffner, the fact that *Friday the 13th* had made it into the theatrical marketplace with an R rating was a genuine thorn in the side of CARA and the industry as a whole, and he took personal responsibility for what he viewed as a serious rating mistake. When Heffner first screened *Friday the 13th* in March 1980, he immediately felt that it should be rated X, as did the majority of the Rating Board. However, because the film was being distributed by Paramount, a major studio, it couldn't be released with an X rating or go unrated, so it went back into the editing room six or seven times before the Rating Board felt that it could be rated R. Heffner, however, believed that the violence that remained in the film, including a brief but graphic shot of an arrow being thrust through the neck of a character played by Kevin Bacon, still warranted an X rating, but he couldn't convince the majority of the board. The film was released in May 1980, and while it was financially successful, as we have seen it became a source of both controversy and criticism for Paramount. As for CARA, it became a source of complaint for other filmmakers who wanted to include the same levels of graphic gore in their films and still have a market-friendly R rating.

Heffner's regret over allowing *Friday the 13th* into the theatrical marketplace with an R rating was central to his renewed efforts to take a harder stand on screen violence, which Paramount felt the next year when it submitted *Friday the 13th Part 2* (1981) for a rating. When Heffner called Paul Hagger, who was CARA's contact at Paramount, he informed him that the first cut of *Friday the 13th Part 2* had been rated X and that "CARA was going to be increasingly tough on violence." He also warned Hagger that, even if each individual instance of graphic violence in *Friday the 13th Part 2* was trimmed, it might still be rated X due to the "accumulation" of violence throughout the film (Heffner, "RDH Pre–Oral History Memorandum 1981," box 1, 51). Frank Mancuso, president of Paramount at the time, then accused CARA of applying different standards to the film during the rating process, which would unfairly ensure a prohibitive X rating. Heffner responded with a letter in which he rebuked the accusations of treating the film differently but did admit that CARA was taking a harder line on violence: "The fact that the Rating Board's majority has now come to share my feelings of last year—that the first *Friday the 13th* should have been rated X, not R—does indeed mean that we are coming down much harder on explicit violence" (Heffner to Mancuso, February 13, 1981, in Heffner, "Reminiscences," box 1, 1).

However, despite Heffner's transparency in terms of CARA's approach to violence, the feeling still lingered that the major studios were given more preferential treatment when it came to the line between R and X. For example, when Wes Craven submitted *A Nightmare on Elm Street* (1984) to the rating administration, he was told to return to the editing room and remove some of the graphic gore before it could be rated R. One scene that was singled out involved a teen character played by Johnny Depp being pulled down into his bed by the hand of the villainous Freddy Krueger (Robert Englund), after which a torrent of blood explodes upward out of the bed and covers the ceiling. The scene is clearly over the top and in keeping with the film's surrealistic dreamscapes, particularly in the way the blood is clearly running against gravity as it pools on the ceiling. However, CARA believed that this much blood was simply excessive. Craven argued that the scene was "obviously symbolic," since we never see what happens to Depp's body. When that argument didn't work, he sent CARA a videotape of the famous dream image from Stanley Kubrick's *The Shining* in which a literal ocean of blood comes pouring out of an elevator, flooding a hotel hallway and eventually washing over the camera lens (this particular image is repeated at various points throughout the film). To Craven, these scenes were basically identical, as they both involved large amounts of blood fulfilling a symbolic purpose, which meant it made no sense that his use of such imagery was outside the bounds of an R-rated film whereas Kubrick's was not. Nevertheless, CARA "sent it back unwatched, saying it was apples and oranges and they don't compare one film with another" (Craven).

Craven eventually edited *A Nightmare on Elm Street* down to the point that it could receive an R rating and be commercially distributed, thus underscoring the necessity of the rating as a commodity that independent producers needed if they hoped to be viable in the marketplace. That is, not only is an MPAA-sanctioned rating required of its member studios and distributors like New Line Cinema, which distributed *A Nightmare on Elm Street*, but it also helps to mark a film as legitimate in the marketplace. Beyond the ratings' stated purpose of informing consumers about the age-appropriate content of a film (a somewhat dubious claim, as we will see in chapter 6), they also serve the practical purpose of branding a particular film as a product of the industry. Therefore, an independently produced film like *A Nightmare on Elm Street* can automatically be given a veneer of respectability via association with mainstream studio products simply by being branded with an MPAA rating. Kevin S. Sandler refers to this process as "the Incontestable R," which ensures a level of "respectable entertainment" for the public, therefore allowing the MPAA to appear without seeming contradiction as both moral watchdog and protector of free expression (205).

The importance of having the rating attached to one's film sometimes led producers to literally steal it. In 1972, when producer Sean S. Cunningham was preparing to distribute *The Last House on the Left,* also directed by Wes Craven, CARA repeatedly returned the film with an X rating. According to Craven:

> This process [of submitting the film to CARA] repeated itself for a week until the film was 75 minutes long and made absolutely no sense anymore. Finally Sean just swore under his breath, went down the hall to someone who'd made an "R" film and got their "This Film is Rated R" banner and spliced it onto the head of our totally restored, original cut, sent it across the street to the optical house for blow-up (we were in our 16mm days), and released it that way. (qtd. in Lewis, *Hollywood* 171)

A similar situation occurred in the early 1980s with Meir Zarchi's rape-revenge melodrama *I Spit on Your Grave* (1980), except this time within the new realm of home video distribution. CARA had rated *I Spit on Your Grave* X when it was originally submitted in 1978 under the title *Day of the Woman.* When it was re-released in 1980 under its new title by enterprising exploitation distributor Jerry Gross, seventeen minutes were cut out in order to secure a marketable R rating. Thus, the film was officially rated R and could carry the MPAA's trademarked R-rating label. However, when the film was distributed on video by Wizard Video, the deleted seventeen minutes were restored, but the R rating was not removed from the advertising. Thus, an X-rated film was marketed as an R-rated film, which led the MPAA to file a trademark infringement suit in the summer of 1984 that eventually resulted in all major video distributors agreeing to universal procedures for applying MPAA ratings (Prince, *New Pot of Gold* 366–67).

This situation again underscores how vitally important it was for distributors to get an R rating by any means, but also how equally important it was for the MPAA to protect the credibility of its rating system if it were to continue to be a viable means of controlling industry-sanctioned film content. This issue will be explored in more detail in chapter 6.

Horror Fandom in the 1980s

Despite mainstream Hollywood's attempts to curtail horror film production in the 1980s by not producing such films and by using CARA to put a brake on the extremity of the content in independently produced horror films, the genre flourished in the 1980s thanks in large part to a core of dedicated fans who not only enjoyed but demanded increasingly graphic and gory content. In terms of quantity, even with CARA's increasingly rigid restrictions, horror films of the 1980s upped the gore factor far beyond what had previously been seen, making horror and gore virtually synonymous.

Scholars have accounted for this shift in the genre with various explanations. Tony Williams argues that horror films became more grotesque during the Reagan years than in any previous era because "the greater the social repression, the more monstrous the repressed" (170). If the return of the repressed in 1970s horror was primarily ideological (R. Wood, "Introduction"), in the 1980s it became primarily visual. According to Walter Kendrick, the innovation of on-screen gore is not inherent to the horror genre but rather functioned as a way to refresh the genre when it was teetering into oblivion in the 1950s. Horror novelist Stephen King has suggested that there is something childish and primitive about the gore in horror films, what he calls the "'wanna-look-at-my-chewed-up-food?' level" of operation, although he also concedes that "the gross-out *is* art" and must be done well to be effective (189). John McCarty attributes the rise in splatter films to a combination of the crumbling of industry-enforced censorship and the development of more realistic special effects techniques.

However, the most useful explanation for the increase in gore in 1980s horror is that it was a product of the discursive interconnection between filmmakers and horror fans, the interplay described by Rick Altman in which genres come into existence only when there is a balance between what viewers want and what filmmakers produce. The pure action genre discussed in chapter 3 developed in the 1980s along the parameters established by Hollywood filmmakers catering to a mainstream audience who liked their blockbuster screen mayhem violent, but not too violent, and situated within a cartoonish context of winning at all costs that matched the ethos of the Reaganite economy. The horror film, on the other hand, having been relegated to the fringes of the industry and left largely in the hands of independent producers, developed according to the tastes of a different audience, one that was captivated, not repulsed, by "the sense of watching something that was forbidden, secretive, taboo" (Kermode, "Teenage Horror Fan" 56). This led to "a remarkable tightening of the bounds of the horror ghetto, along with the rise of a new kind of horror fan, one who makes a cult of the whole business and revels in arcane information that only fellow fans share" (Kendrick 255).

In this sense, horror fandom was crucial to sustaining the horror genre in the 1980s and not allowing it to devolve into self-parody as it did in the 1940s. Because the industry was pushing explicit horror films further and further to the fringes in an effort to protect its own sense of legitimacy in the public eye, the horror genre could survive only through the insistent devotion of its fan base, whose knowledge of and fascination with the genre and particularly the technologies used to create images of graphic violence and monstrosity fed the sensibilities of horror filmmakers.

Horror fans were deeply entrenched in their own form of cultural capital, which, in Pierre Bourdieu's terms, is knowledge or competence whose worth is directly related to the field in which an individual is functioning. Thus, arcane knowledge about horror films, the vast majority of which were deemed "low art" or "trash" by mainstream taste standards, had little worth outside the realm of the horror genre. However, within that field, the fans' cultural capital helped guide how they viewed horror films, setting them apart from average viewers who did not bring to the screen the same level of knowledge and appreciation. Similar to the paracinema fans discussed by Jeffrey Sconce who break down the boundaries between high and low divisions by appropriating the tactics of high-art aesthetes in their embrace of the lowest of low art, horror fans also self-consciously positioned themselves against the mainstream and defined themselves through the intricacies of their knowledge. Horror fans were able to see nuances, details, and levels of meaning in even the "cheapest" horror films that would be lost on a general audience not steeped in horror's cultural capital. As Joan Hawkins argues, the "'good tastes' of low culture are every bit as complex, nuanced, and acculturated as is the elite taste for classical music, European art movies, and modern art" (113).

Thus, more so than in any other genre in the 1980s, horror fans were closely tied to the films they watched and therefore influenced how they were made. Horror fans were self-aware, something the filmmakers understood and appreciated. Mark Kermode argues that the use of gore offers a way for horror filmmakers to self-consciously address their self-aware audience: "The truth is simply that the experienced horror fan understands the on-screen action in terms of a heritage of genre knowledge, which absolutely precludes the possibility of sadistic titillation" ("Teenage Horror Fan" 63). Because horror plays and feeds upon fans' knowledge, fans can view explicit gore symbolically, whereas mainstream audiences will take it literally. This is not to say that all horror gore is metaphorical, but horror fans are in a better position to appreciate the potential for it to have such dimensions. As an example, Kermode notes how horror fans will respond knowingly to the gory mayhem of Sam Raimi's *The Evil Dead* because they recognize Raimi's combination of well-worn horror film clichés with the slapstick style of the Three Stooges, whereas nonfans will just see gratuitous gore.

Similarly, horror fans can also appreciate gore technologically, in that they have accumulated knowledge about how the effects were created and how much effort and ingenuity went on behind the scenes to create the illusion. Thus, scenes of horrific screen violence become in fans' eyes moments of technological triumph, as they often find pleasure in looking beyond the torn flesh and splattering blood on-screen and imagining the invisible inner workings designed by a makeup effects artist. This, of course, leads to what Kermode calls "the absolute divide between horror fans and everyone else in the world" (59).

Because they are steeped in knowledge about the genre, horror fans are able to watch horror films differently than a mainstream audience would. Kermode describes the act of watching horror films with other fans as "something profoundly 'conversational' . . . something that joined us together as a group in our increasingly knowing reactions to what was happening on-screen" ("Teenage Horror Fan" 60). This is a particularly lucid example of what Altman terms a "constellated community," in which fans of a particular genre are drawn together in a symbolic group that is formed and maintained by shared knowledge. Unlike the filmmakers behind pure action films, horror filmmakers knew that they were addressing a specific, rather than broad, audience, and they catered to them accordingly, which resulted in a great deal of self-reflexivity in horror films that could be appreciated only by fans and went straight over the heads of nonfans. For example, the presence of makeup special effects artist Tom Savini in a cameo or bit role in the films for which he designed the effects was the filmmaker's way of "winking at fans in the audience" ("Teenage Horror Fan" 60).

Where critics derided many horror films for their formulaic nature, fans relished the ritualistic rehashing of familiar narrative and visual tropes, knowing it would lead to a gory payoff. "What horror films offer, after all, is the representation of violence—violence embedded in a generic, narrative, fictional, often highly stylized, and oddly playful context" (Waller 260).

Fangoria

In August 1979, O'Quinn Studios in New York City, publisher of the science fiction magazine *Starlog*, introduced *Fangoria*, a new bimonthly magazine with the subhead "Monsters • Aliens • Bizarre Creatures." As

Philip Brophy points out, the strange title of this new publication perfectly encapsulated the essence of modern horror films, breaking down and recombining semantic elements of the words "gore," "fantasy," "phantasmagoria," and, of course, "fan." "The title simultaneously expands a multiplicity of cross-references and contracts them into a single referential construct," one that would eventually become synonymous with horror fandom in the 1980s (277).

The timing of *Fangoria*'s debut was not in any way coincidental. Rather, it was introduced specifically in response to the desires of, and to give a voice to, fans who felt that there were no publications that spoke directly to their interests in contemporary horror films. *Fangoria* filled that need, "expand[ing] and contract[ing] a critical voice for a mutant market—that of the contemporary film: a genre about genre; a displaced audience; a short-circuiting entertainment" (Brophy 277). In the opening issue, publisher Kerry O'Quinn noted that the magazine was founded because readers of *Starlog*, a strictly science fiction magazine, kept asking for pictorial features on fantasy subjects. He described *Fangoria* as "a new publication whose *exclusive world* is the realm of monsters, aliens, and bizarre creatures." However, O'Quinn noted,

> FANGORIA is much more than just another cheap monster magazine; each issue will include full-color art, media news, techniques of special effects and makeup, important interviews—the same high quality you have come to expect from other STARLOG publications. Our intention is for FANGORIA to be the first classy, professional, pictorial news magazine covering the world of fantasy. (4)

It is ironic that O'Quinn felt the need to stress *Fangoria* as being "classy" and "professional," because the magazine has been thought of largely in terms of rebellion against mainstream tastes and acceptable content. Kermode describes the magazine's arrival in England and how it brought

> a garishly modern approach to horror which seemed oddly in tune with the post-punk nihilism blighting British youth culture. It wasn't for nothing that *Fango* earned the affectionate nickname "Exploding Heads Monthly." For all its up-market production values, *Fango* was the Sex Pistols of horror fanzines, loud, noisy, visually graphic and absolutely guaranteed to send your parents apoplectic with righteous indignation. ("Teenage Horror Fan" 59)

Fangoria, therefore, established itself in a strange space between the aesthetics of professional publications and the desires of "hard-core" horror fans who demanded imagery and content that was viewed as juvenile and gross at best and perverse and disturbing at worst. To complicate the bridging of this dichotomy even further, *Fangoria* utilized the glossiest element of each issue—a select number of full-color, slick-stock pages—to highlight the goriest of images, whereas the rest of each issue was printed on black-and-white rough paper stock.[8]

In this way, *Fangoria* is a perfect metonym for the horror genre in the 1980s: Trapped between the fan base's escalating desires for more and more socially unacceptable imagery in a culture that was policing such imagery with increasing fervor, it simultaneously celebrated gore through graphic color imagery and disavowed its impact and social significance by focusing on the techniques used to create the illusions rather than on their meaning. Because Hollywood had largely given itself over to such policing, *Fangoria* filled in the space left behind by packaging the most obscene elements of the horror genre in a way that spoke to fans but still maintained barely discernible connections to the mainstream industry in order to keep a sense of legitimacy, however tenuous.

Developing an Identity

Fangoria was not always single-minded of purpose in celebrating the grotesqueries of the contemporary horror film. In its first year of publication, the magazine struggled to find a coherent identity, varying wildly among interests in fantasy, science fiction, classical horror, and contemporary horror. While the first issue of *Fangoria* contained what would become its staple article, a detailed interview with a makeup effects designer—in this case, with Tom Savini about how he created the gory effects in *Dawn of the Dead*—most of the rest of the issue had little or nothing to do with the kinds of contemporary horror films that fans cherished. Rather, there was a lengthy article about Godzilla (who appeared on the cover and in a foldout poster in the middle of the issue), an article about unused alien designs in TV's *Battlestar Galactica*, and the first installment of a short-lived section titled "Fantasticart," which was to feature in each issue the fantasy artworks of an up-and-coming artist. In this issue, the artist was twenty-five-year-old Don Maitz of Connecticut, whose fantasy-inspired paintings included an image of an armored knight straddling a slain dragon and a wizard leafing through an enormous book of spells.

The second issue in October 1979 was not much more coherent in terms of content, although it featured two stories on contemporary horror films, one on John Frankenheimer's ill-fated ecological horror thriller *Prophecy* (1979), whose mutated grizzly bear appeared on the issue's front cover, and Don Coscarelli's cult favorite *Phantasm* (1979). The rest of the issue, however, was devoted mostly to classic horror and science fiction, including retrospective articles on Rouben Mamoulian's 1932 version of *Jekyll and Hyde* and George Pal's *War of the Worlds* (1953), as well as an article about the lost test footage of Bela Lugosi in the Frankenstein's monster makeup that would eventually be made famous by Boris Karloff.

The next few issues continued to struggle with this topical balancing act, and their covers highlight how contemporary horror was not only just one of many subjects included in the magazine but one that often took a backseat. On the cover of the December 1979 issue was a picture of horror icon Christopher Lee in the notoriously awful fantasy flop *Arabian Adventure* (1979); the February 1980 cover was of *Star Trek: The Motion Picture*'s (1979) Dr. Spock; and the April 1980 issue featured on the cover the marauding robot of the horror/science fiction thriller *Saturn 3* (1980). As final evidence of *Fangoria*'s struggling identity at this point, the cover of the June 1980 issue, which was the first anniversary issue and the first not to include "Starlog Presents" before the title, featured an image of C-3PO and R2-D2 from *The Empire Strikes Back* (1980), although the issue included articles on *Friday the 13th*, makeup special effects artists Tom Savini and Rob Bottin, and Vincent Price recalling his days starring in American International Pictures films. Perhaps the most bizarre inclusion in any of these early issues was the April 1980 issue's foldout insert poster of "The Legendary World of Faeries: An A to Z Encyclopedia."

It was with *Fangoria*'s seventh issue, the first of its second year of publication, that its identity as a pure horror magazine began to come together in a coherent shape. That issue, August 1980, featured on the cover the now iconic image of Jack Nicholson in Stanley Kubrick's *The Shining* as he trudges through the hedge maze at the end of the film, head lowered and eyes cast upward from beneath a demonically furrowed brow. It was the first issue in which every feature article focused on horror without a single nod to science fiction or fantasy. Chief among these was yet another article about Tom Savini (the third in seven issues), this one titled "These Guts for Hire or, Blood to Let—Behind the Scenes of 'Maniac' With FX Master Tom Savini," which included several pages of exceedingly gory photographs of Savini's gut-wrenching effects, including a girl in the process of being scalped, Savini himself being shot in the head by a shotgun through a car windshield, and star Joe Spinell's decapitated head lying next to his body.

From this point on, *Fangoria*'s identity began to cohere quickly around an intense fascination with the special effects that dominated the contemporary horror genre. Gore became *Fangoria*'s stock-in-trade, and the subsequent issues began to focus more and more on full-color images of the goriest moments of the films they covered.

14. The identity of *Fangoria* (August 1980) cohered in its seventh issue, which was the first in which every feature article focused on horror, without a single nod to science fiction or fantasy. "Fangoria" and articles and graphics copyright 2008 Starlog Group, Inc.

The Centrality of Gore

The tenth issue of *Fangoria*, January 1981, featured on its cover the kind of image that was to become synonymous with both the magazine and the horror genre in the 1980s: an exploding head, this particular one coming from David Cronenberg's *Scanners* (1981). It was the first time the editors of *Fangoria* had been bold enough to put such a graphic image of gory violence on the front cover, and it marked a significant turning point in the magazine's focus. Only three issues since the August 1980 issue that had set aside all pretenses toward fantasy and science fiction to focus primarily on horror, *Fangoria* had fully achieved the status worthy of the nickname "Exploding Heads Monthly."

Fangoria eagerly embraced the essence of horror defined by William Ian Miller as "fear-imbued disgust" (26). As Miller argues, horror is horrifying because it denies the fight-or-flight mechanism triggered by straight fear: "Because the threatening thing is disgusting, one does

15. It wasn't until the tenth issue (January 1981) that the editors of *Fangoria* made a graphic image of gory violence the central focus of the magazine's front cover, which helped it achieve the status worthy of the nickname "Exploding Heads Monthly." "Fangoria" and articles and graphics copyright 2008 Starlog Group, Inc.

not want to strike it, touch it, or grapple with it. Because it is frequently something that has already gotten inside of you or takes you over and possesses you, there is often no distinct other to fight anyway" (26). This is an adept literalization of the experience of watching a horror film, in which the viewer is essentially trapped in the theater as a parade of horrific imagery dances across the screen. There are always the options of closing one's eyes or simply leaving the theater, but that is to succumb to defeat. Most anyone who enters the theater for a gory horror film intends to bear through any imagery the film might offer; in a sense, it is a test of resilience in which the viewer is challenged to withstand the physical intensities generated by the visual excess of the genre (L. Williams). The horror genre is thus inseparable from *affect,* defined by Joan Hawkins as "the ability of a film to thrill, frighten, gross out, arouse, or otherwise directly engage the spectator's body" (4).

Not surprisingly, then, *Fangoria* focused much of its editorial attention on the horror subgenre that came to be known as the "splatter film," which "aim[s] not to scare their audiences, necessarily, nor drive them to the edges of their seats in suspense, but to *mortify* them with scenes of explicit gore" (McCarty 1). However, by isolating graphic moments of gory violence in its glossy color pages, *Fangoria* went beyond simply reproducing the affect of a splatter film's goriest moments. By pulling such moments out of the context of the film (even the minimalist plot context of a slasher film) and reproducing them in full color as still images, *Fangoria* heightened the visceral impact of the imagery. Turning these gory filmic moments into isolated still images extends their existence in time and space far beyond their presence in the films themselves because it allows the action to be held infinitely at the moment of maximum violence. While the exploding head in *Scanners* fills less than a second of screen time in the film itself, on the cover of *Fangoria* it becomes infinite, daring the spectator not just to see the image but to examine and absorb the details one could never see at twenty-four frames per second.

With CARA's increased policing of both the quantity and graphicness of screen violence in the 1980s, moments of shocking gore in horror films were becoming briefer and briefer, often reduced to a few seconds or less of screen time—just enough for the viewer to register the gist of what happened but not much else. *Fangoria* served as a corrective, then, allowing fans to see in detail for as long as they wanted what had been perhaps a flash of flesh and blood on the screen. This had the effect of making some horror films appear to be gorier than they actually were. It also allowed kids who were not able to get into R-rated horror films in the theater or were not allowed to watch them on cable at home to see what they were missing, thus subverting authorial attempts to keep young eyes from seeing such imagery. Not surprisingly, some bookstores and convenience stores began treating *Fangoria* like pornography by placing it behind the counter and selling copies only to customers of a certain age.

The still imagery of gore and descriptions of violence in the articles in *Fangoria* also served a watchdog purpose in that the magazine informed readers when they had seen censored versions of their favorite horror films. Because many of the articles were written during the films' production, oftentimes images and descriptions of events that appeared in the magazine never made it to the screen, having been cut out during the rating process, both in the United States and abroad. Thus, like Tim Lucas's *Video Watchdog*, although not with the single-minded focus of that publication, *Fangoria* could serve as a reference tool for horror fans for whom knowing the details was crucial. For example, in the third issue (December 1979), a reader wrote a letter to the editor in which he noted that an article about Tom Savini in the first issue had referenced in both text and still imagery several gory effects in *Dawn of the Dead* (including a zombie being stabbed in the ear by a screwdriver and another having the top of his head sliced off by whirling helicopter blades) that had been cut out of the prints distributed in Canada. There are also numerous articles that are specifically about how horror films were constantly being recut and shortened in order to achieve an R rating or to reach a wider audience. A good example of this is the article "Basket Case Update" in the February 1982 issue, which discusses how the low-budget, independently produced film *Basket Case* (1982), profiled in an earlier issue, had been significantly recut by its distributor, Analysis Film Releasing, in order to reach a wider audience.[9]

Although it became the magazine's defining characteristic, the emphasis on gore in *Fangoria* was not appreciated by all its readers, and part of the process of developing its identity involved some significant back-and-forth between various readers and the editors over just how much the magazine should focus on blood and guts. It started with a letter to the editor printed in "The Postal Zone" in the November 1980 issue. The letter was written by director John Landis, a longtime horror fan who was at the time in production on *An American Werewolf in London*. His letter generally praised the magazine for filling a niche for horror fans, but then he wrote: "I do have one small complaint, however: Gore, for its own sake, quickly grows tiresome. Please try to refrain from repeatedly printing the most gruesome stills you can get your hands on" (5). In that same issue, another reader wrote in complaining of the magazine's increased coverage of "all the cheap, sensational, blood-letting, gore-gushing, here-today-gone tomorrow, give us your money and puke, trash movies and make up techniques" (5). For the next two issues, "The Postal Zone" was filled with letters from readers debating the place of gore in the magazine, which was in essence a displaced debate about the role of gore in the horror genre itself. Some readers felt that explicit gore was exploitative, and they longed for an earlier era of horror films in which violence was suggested rather than shown, while other readers proclaimed their love of all things gory and noted that they weren't ashamed to say so.

In the April 1981 issue, *Fangoria* editor Bob Martin (who referred to himself as "Uncle Bob") noted in his editor's column that 50 percent of the letters to the editor in the previous two months had been about the magazine's focus on explicit gore and its support of films that were graphically violent. Martin defended *Fangoria*'s fascination with such disreputable imagery and, by proxy, the horror genre's. In a perfect summation of *Fangoria*'s disavowal of the realities of violence by fetishizing the technologies used to re-create it on-screen, Martin wrote: "Our pictures, however grisly, are accompanied by articles that stress the men *behind the scenes*—the screenwriters who conceive the horrors, the makeup men who produce the illusion, and the directors whose job is to convince us—just for a moment—that the illusion is real. Our message is that even the most terrifying film is only color, light and sound" ("Imagination").

It is easy to see such disavowal in Martin's defense of *Fangoria*'s emphasis on graphic gore, which stresses the momentary illusion of the imagery—it is not "real"; therefore, it's not truly threatening. At another point in the editor's note, he relates blood and guts in horror films to technological hardware in science fiction films: They are simply an iconographic element of the genre. Of course, in making this argument, Martin ignores the fact that explicit gore was not always part of the horror genre but rather a recent development that, at that time, was little more than a decade old. As Walter Kendrick argues, gore is not inherent to the horror genre but is rather a generic element that is used to varying degrees at different points in the genre's cycle, often as a way of refreshing it.

The appeal to the artificiality of gore was crucial to *Fangoria*'s strategy of packaging the most explicit of horrific screen violence in such a way that allowed the magazine to celebrate something socially subversive without being *too* subversive in the process. As Tony Williams notes, spectacular displays of gore are "remarkable for concealment as well as manifestation" (165). Citing Steve Neale, Williams argues that "contemporary special effects represent a concealing device veiling both the improbability of the representation and 'genuine trauma.' This genuine trauma may have social and historical links which cinematic spectacle attempts to conceal and disavow" (165).

Interestingly, this exact argument was also used by some producers and distributors of horror films to make their films seem more acceptable and less dangerous (and therefore more marketable). For example, after *When the Screaming Stops* was rated X by CARA for its graphic violence, Miles Nelson, the film's distributor, wrote a letter to MPAA president Jack Valenti protesting the rating by arguing that the film's violence is on a fantasy level, which negates any potential ideological or social impact:

> Our film does not deal in real life. It is simply a monster movie made to entertain by frightening and surprising the audience. It is obviously fantasy and the violence is not designed to be disturbing such as films like *Death Wish* or *Taxi Driver* which carry an "R" but have the potential of being psychologically damaging to children as well as adults. Those pictures attempt to deliver a message and manipulate the audience in a way that could possibly result in anti-social behavior. Our film, on the other hand, is just a good scare. (Nelson to Valenti, September 27, 1978, in Heffner, "Reminiscences," box 1, 1)

To reduce the impact of screen violence in horror movies—to further remove it from any association with "genuine trauma" or anything "disturbing"—*Fangoria* took a lighthearted tone toward its depiction of grisly mayhem, constantly prodding its readers to see the humor in all the excess. This often took the form of jokey captions that used knowingly bad puns and cheeky references to accompany gory photographs. For example, in the April 1981 issue, a picture of a victim in *Friday the 13th Part 2* with a machete buried in the middle of his face bears the caption: "Mark (Tom McBride) develops a 'split' personality during the counselors' night of terror" (13). Another photograph in that same issue, this one of a character having her head split in two while drinking a beer, carries the caption, "A nice cold beer—just the thing for those splitting headaches." Such silly captions have a subversive quality in that they make light of depictions of terrible events, but such subversion is undermined by the magazine's incessant focus on not just the artificiality of the imagery but on the fact that this is all supposed to be *fun.* In the third issue's editor's note, editor emeritus Joe Bonham cautioned that readers who took the horror genre too seriously should look someplace else: "If you're looking for transcendental criticism and long-winded analyss [*sic*] of the sociopolitical ramifications of *Mothra* in our pages, you might as well stop reading now." Instead, Bonham admonished readers, "Have fun. Enjoy the magic. It's all around you" (4).

Thus, *Fangoria* strove to disassociate the affect of horror film violence from the kind of psychological, mythical, or social work attributed to it by film scholars like Carol J. Clover and Robin Wood. Much as the Hollywood industry was working to separate screen violence from pressing and often controversial social issues by turning to pure action movies, the pages of *Fangoria*, garish and subversive as they appeared at first glance, were actually performing the conservative function of downplaying any social significance of horror violence by focusing on the "magic" of its production and insisting that it's all just "good fun."

The Makeup Special Effects Artist as Auteur

The disavowal of the social significance of horror violence in *Fangoria* was achieved primarily by the magazine's constant focus on the role of the makeup special effects artists, who were treated in its pages as auteurs who were often more important to the genre than writers, directors, and producers.

In the first few years of publication, *Fangoria* profiled literally dozens of special effects artists, in the process making household names of behind-the-scenes artisans who in previous generations were all but unknown. Names like Tom Savini, Rob Bottin, Dick Smith, Stan Winston, Craig Reardon, Chris Walas, and Tom Burman were repeated regularly in article after article and were often splashed across the front cover of the magazine, giving them the kind of luminous star power usually reserved only for recognized actors and actresses.[10] An excellent example of this is the cover of the August 1981 issue, in which four of the five headlines are about special effects artists: Rick Baker and *An American Werewolf in London*, Tom Savini and *The Prowler* (1981), Stan Winston and *Dead & Buried* (1981), and Chris Walas and *Caveman* (1981). Within the industry, *Fangoria*'s focus on special effects was clearly having an impact, as Bob Martin complained in his editor's note in the February 1982 issue that some producers were beginning to deny the magazine the right to publish effects photos "because they don't want the effects men to become well-known and raise their rates" (4).

Despite some producers' reluctance to work with the magazine, *Fangoria* was able to publish hundreds of effects photos, some still images from the films and many more behind-the-scenes shots of the artists at work on their craft, cutting foam latex, making molds, painting details on masks, and wiring blood squibs. The main goal behind this coverage was to show "how it's done," to profile the details of the artistry of makeup special effects—to reinforce the message that "even the most terrifying film is only color, light and sound" (Martin, "Imagination"). For example, Bob Martin's June 1980 article "Tom Savini: A Man of Many Parts" features a photograph of Savini working on a scene from George A. Romero's *Martin* (1976) to create the illusion of the titular character, a modern-day vampire, having a stake driven into his chest. The scene in the film is extraordinarily effective in the shock of seeing a stake pounded

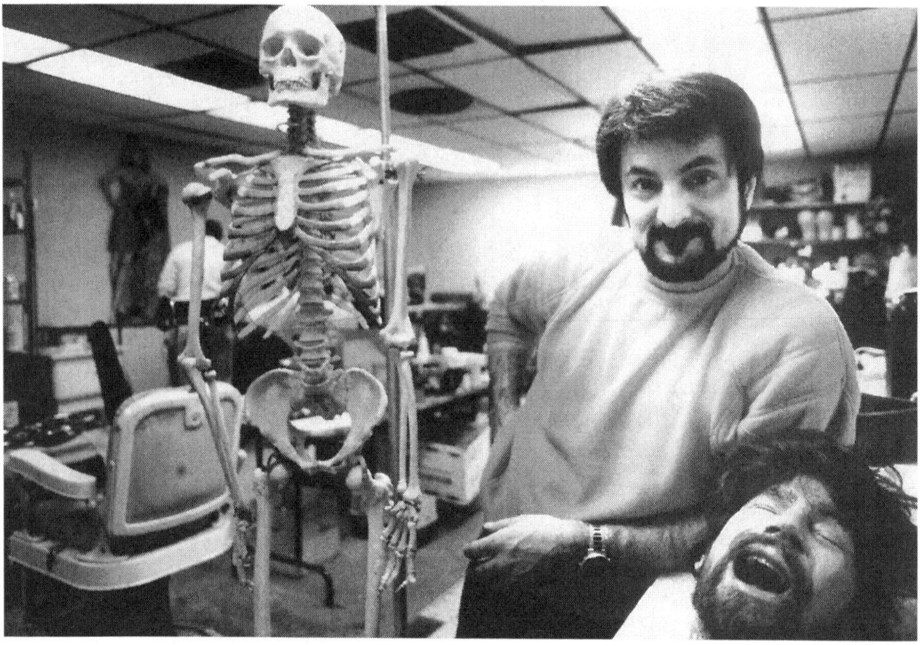

16. Photos like this one of special effects artist Tom Savini in his workshop on the set of *Day of the Dead* (1985) encouraged readers of *Fangoria* and other horror fanzines to treat effects artists like individual auteurs who had different visions, techniques, and specialties. Anchor Bay Entertainment/Photofest.

through the young man's heart, but the image of star John Amplas smiling as Savini douses him with fake blood is yet another reminder to the reader of the illusion. This article also includes a step-by-step eight-picture progression of how Savini turned actor Ari Lehman into the disfigured Jason Voorhees in *Friday the 13th*.

This coverage of makeup effects artists had two main results. The first is that it turned the artists themselves into auteurs. *Fangoria*'s focus on them and their work familiarized their names and faces to the magazine's readers, which gave fans one more means by which they could distinguish among horror films that nonfans saw as unoriginal and interchangeable. So, for example, to a nonfan, *Friday the 13th: The Final Chapter* (1984) was nothing more than the fourth reiteration of a hackneyed slasher formula, but to fans it was special because it marked the return to the series of Tom Savini, who had done the effects in the original *Friday the 13th*.

Fangoria encouraged fans to distinguish among the different effects artists by treating them like individual auteurs who had different visions, techniques, and specialties—artists who left their mark on the films on which they worked, regardless of how good the plot, director, or actors were. Articles in *Fangoria* discriminated among the different effects artists, giving them a sense of uniqueness and personality. For example, in an article about Tom Burman, the author states, "But, what makes Burman different from other notables such as Dick Smith or Rick Baker, is his ability to produce quality materials, sometimes in great quantity, in a minimum amount of time" (Carlomagno 20). Similarly, Savini was always discussed in terms of the realism of his effects, which was explained by his having served as a combat photographer in Vietnam. Thus, the quality and uniqueness of Savini's effects were understood as having been influenced by his past experiences; as an auteur, he brought himself to bear on his work, and this influenced how other scholars wrote about the horror genre. For example, in *The Zombies That Ate Pittsburgh: The Films of George A. Romero*, Paul R. Gagne devotes an entire chapter of the book to discussing Savini's makeup effects and their crucial role in Romero's films. Although the book clearly positions Romero as the auteur of his body of work, Gagne notes, "Tom Savini is considered by some to be the real 'star' of George Romero's films" (171).

Thus, makeup special effects artists were discussed in roughly the same terms that the French critics in *Cahiers du Cinéma* had used to discuss American directors via the "*politique des auteurs.*" As Andrew Sarris describes it, "The auteur theory is not so much a theory as an attitude, a table of values that converts film history into directorial autobiography" (30). In this case, then, horror films were converted into special effects artist autobiography, with films being defined primarily by the effects in them and the people who designed those effects. Virtually everything else in horror films was subverted to the effects, something that was understood by both fans and filmmakers, as evidenced in the following statement by William Lustig, director of *Maniac*: "[T]he *most* important element of a horror film is the special effects. They're your money stuff, so you can't scrimp on them; the audience has already seen the best and expects nothing less" (qtd. in Swires 45). It's not surprising, then, that a number of makeup effects artists who earned a reputation through *Fangoria* in the 1980s went on to become horror directors themselves, including Tom Savini, who directed several episodes of the TV series *Tales from the Darkside* and a 1990 remake of George A. Romero's *Night of the Living Dead*; Chris Walas, who directed *The Fly II* (1989) and an episode of HBO's *Tales from the Crypt*; Stan Winston, who directed *Pumpkinhead* (1989); and Tom Burman, who directed the comedic sci-fi fantasy *Meet the Hollowheads* (1989).

The second result of *Fangoria*'s coverage of makeup effects artists was that it made such work appear to be a viable means of entering into the world of Hollywood magic. The effects artists were often discussed in terms of their interconnections, and virtually all of them had begun as horror fans before becoming professional special effects artists. The articles that profiled these artists frequently included a paragraph about how they got involved in the business, and the recurring plotline begins with a childhood fascination with horror films, followed by voracious reading of monster magazines to find out who was responsible for the effects, and oftentimes a blind phone call to an effects artist asking for work. The role of the magazine itself was crucial in this respect, as it provided a means through which fans could learn about the process and develop a storehouse of knowledge before moving into the business. Savini admitted at one point that when he saw pictures of makeup pioneer Dick Smith in articles in *Starlog* or *Famous Monsters*, he'd "get a magnifying glass and study his shelves to see if there was some secret I could pick up from them" (qtd. in Martin, "Tom Savini" 52).

Thus, readers were further encouraged to distance themselves from the affect of horror film violence by seeing it as not just artistry and technique but artistry and technique that they could conceivably master themselves. This was also emphasized by the numerous advertisements in *Fangoria*'s pages for makeup effects kits that offered the tools of the trade to readers. The magazine even developed a subsidiary line of products called "The Blood Boutique," which offered derma wax, nose putty, spirit gum, liquid latex, and other tools of illusion-making that were foreign terms to nonfans who were put off by the extreme violence of horror films but signified to fans the magic of creating illusion, however gory that illusion may be.

Despite its seemingly central role in encouraging the subversive nature of horror described at the beginning of this chapter, *Fangoria* also played a barely disguised conservative role in the 1980s by disavowing the ideological in favor of the mechanical. That is, in celebrating the behind-the-scenes work that brought the gory images of the horror genre to life in the name of harmless "fun," *Fangoria* provided an alternate lens that stressed horror films' gory achievements as illusion. This is not to say that horror films in the 1980s were not at all subversive. Quite the contrary, in fact; were they not viewed as threatening to the social order, there would have been no need to disavow their affect in the first place. Particularly with their uninhibited display of spectacular moments of violence and gore that were often couched in a sexual context and designed to elicit a visceral, audible response from their audiences, horror films constantly threatened "good" taste and decorum. In a sense, horror films, with their increasingly realistic special effects, had become *too* effective, thus the need to police them even by those who would on the surface appear to be their strongest supporters.

Even though the major studios were generally unwilling to be involved in the production of horror films throughout most of the 1980s, it was still an incredibly popular and profitable genre. What is most interesting about it, though, is the way elements of the genre seeped into other films, fulfilling William Ian Miller's description of horror as "something that has already gotten inside of you or takes you over and possesses you" (26). While major studios shied away from producing horror films that could be easily labeled as such, many of their other films adopted some of the more spectacular elements of the genre, which resulted in a new round of controversies over film content in mid-decade. The next chapter will explore how the gross-out nature of horror violence worked its way into films conventionally understood as products for children and how Hollywood responded once again to protect itself from criticism.

6

CHILDREN IN DANGER

SCREEN VIOLENCE, STEVEN SPIELBERG, AND THE PG-13 RATING

THE THREAT THAT SCREEN violence posed to Hollywood's public image never seemed so dark as in the summer of the 1984, when two highly successful PG-rated films, *Gremlins* and *Indiana Jones and the Temple of Doom*, were at the eye of a storm of controversy over the role of violence in popular films. For the first time on a significant national scale, screen violence was at the heart of the debate between what constituted a PG-rated film and an R-rated film. The controversy was so intense that it threatened the public's perception of the Classification and Rating Administration's ability to label film content properly, and thus its stability as a protective institution was called into question, which in turn threatened the entire structure of the motion picture industry. Jack Valenti, president of the Motion Picture Association of America, eventually consented to do something he had vehemently resisted doing since the inception of the rating system sixteen years earlier: create a new rating category. The new rating, PG-13, would sit between the PG and R ratings. Like the PG rating, however, there was nothing restrictive about it; it was purely advisory in "strongly caution[ing]" parents that "some material may be inappropriate for children under 13."

The ratings controversy over *Gremlins* and *Indiana Jones and the Temple Doom* and the subsequent creation of the PG-13 rating was a crucial moment for Hollywood because it forced the industry to distinguish even more clearly between the films that were suitable for children and those suitable for adults by formally codifying the teenage audience into its rating system. More specifically, it forced the industry to deal formally and publicly with the centrality of screen violence to its most profitable films and reconcile the role of violence in "children's" entertainment. It is not surprising that this was accomplished with a change in the rating system because, from the outset, the rating system has always been about maximizing profits by standardizing and therefore legitimating Hollywood product through stable categorization (Lewis, "Those Who Disagree"; Sandler).

However, such an action was complicated by the fact that this controversy was taking place at a time when the American culture was, on the surface at least, in a mood of conservatism and a return to "values." Hollywood, in attempting to solidify its financial footing in the new blockbuster era, wanted simultaneously to cater to the culture's conservatism while also profiting from the audience's desire for escapist violent fare. The creation of the PG-13 rating, then, was the perfect solution because it was all surface; in establishing a new category, a new "genre" of film, it allowed the industry to "do something" about the problem of screen violence by more carefully labeling its age appropriateness without actually changing any of its practices. The industry could claim it was "warning" parents that a film might be unsuitable for children under thirteen, thus fulfilling its moral obligation, but those same children were in no way restricted during exhibition from seeing those films, which meant that the studios' profit potentials were not threatened. If anything, profits could be increased because the nonrestrictive PG-13 rating allowed for even more screen violence than a PG rating, thus making certain films more enticing to younger viewers.

This chapter will examine the controversies surrounding several films that eventually led to the creation of the PG-13 rating in the summer of 1984. Central to the debate is the figure of Steven Spielberg, who either produced or directed the three films—*Poltergeist, Indiana Jones and the Temple of Doom,* and *Gremlins*—that were most directly responsible for blurring the lines between what kinds of screen violence were acceptable in a PG-rated versus an R-rated film. The subsequent PG-13 rating was a perfect embodiment of the industrial mindset of Hollywood in the 1980s because it was yet another form of packaging—a brand that marked the violence of certain films as just illicit enough to entice curious viewers but not so illicit that some people (that is, children) had to be kept from viewing them outright, thus helping to bolster profits by having it both ways.

Rating Screen Violence

In "Movie Ratings as Genre," Kevin S. Sandler uses Rick Altman's semantic/syntactic/pragmatic approach to genre to argue that R-rated films constitute a film genre. As genres are defined by Altman not as deterministic textural structures but rather as sites of contest and struggle for meaning among filmmakers, studios, exhibitors, audiences, politicians, media watchdog groups, and others, the various rating categories are clearly generic in the way they "describe, label, and define films" (Sandler 203). Filmmakers and studios are well aware that it means something to consumers when they see a PG label at the bottom of a movie poster versus an R label; it establishes a set of generic expectations.

The key to the functionality of the rating system, Sandler argues, is its stability of meaning over time. Each rating category must be "historically stable, but always transitory" (209). That is, just as the specifics of what is deemed "obscene" or "tasteless" change over time while the general connotation of the words themselves remain stable, each rating category has to evolve to allow material that is deemed appropriate for that age level at that point in history without ever losing the fundamental essence of its meaning. Thus, even though different material has been allowed into the R or PG genres at different periods in history, the meaning of each rating remains relatively stable in the consumer's eyes. This is why, we will soon see, there was such controversy over *Gremlins* and *Indiana Jones and the Temple of Doom*: because they challenged consumers' understanding of what constituted the PG genre.

According to Sandler, there are six criteria the members of CARA use when rating a film: theme, language, violence, nudity, sex, and drug use. Sandler shows that, in terms of rating sexuality and nudity, there is "an overwhelmingly consistent formal structure" that results in an R rating. However, the manner in which CARA rates a film in relation to its depictions of violence involves more than just its formal characteristics. On the surface, it would seem that the graphicness of the violence, what Stephen Prince calls "stylistic amplitude," would be the key to distinguishing between PG-rated and R-rated violence (*Classical Film Violence* 35). For example, PG-rated films often include screen violence in the form of characters being shot, but in such films there are rarely overt displays of the bullet entering and/or exiting the body, whereas R-rated films involving the same kind of violence routinely use blood squibs to depict the bullet damaging the body.

In discussing the changing depictions of violence on-screen during the classical Hollywood era, Prince defines screen violence as "the stylistic encoding of a referential act" (*Classical Film Violence* 34). Thus, different forms of screen violence can be graphed in relation to their "referential component," that is, the actual behavior that is depicted (the x-axis), and the "stylistic design," or how that behavior is depicted (the y-axis). The stylistic design is composed of two elements—graphicness and duration—and the more intense the former and the longer the latter, the more likely it is that a film will cross rating boundaries from PG to R or R to

X. For example, for Sam Peckinpah's *The Wild Bunch* to earn an R rating instead of an X, editor Lou Lombardo had to reduce the violence of the scene in which General Mapache slits Angel's throat. He left in a quick, head-on shot of Mapache drawing the knife across Angel's neck and a brief spurt of blood, but by cutting out a side angle shot of the action that more graphically depicted the throat-slitting and the subsequent flow of blood, Lombardo reduced both the graphicness and the duration of the violence, thus making it acceptable for CARA to award the film an R rating (Prince, *Savage Cinema* 23–24).

However, beyond style and duration, the context in which the violence takes place is crucial to CARA when rating films. In fact, CARA has historically more often judged screen violence according to its context than it has judged depictions of sexual activity or use of vulgar language according to their contexts. For example, there is no quantitative body count limit that determines whether a film is rated PG or R. However, in terms of language, there have historically been finite, quantitative limits to the usage of certain words. One of the few steadfast rules CARA has admitted to using when rating films is the so-called one-use rule involving the word "fuck" (Greydanus). According to the rule, "fuck" can be used once in its nonsexual sense in a PG-rated film (as in, for example, *Sixteen Candles* [1984], *Nothing in Common* [1986], and *Big* [1988]), although there have been a few instances in which a PG-rated film has used it more than once (as in, for example, *Reds* [1981] and *Racing with the Moon* [1984]). In general, a third usage of the word would absolutely merit an R rating, as would any use of the word in its sexual meaning. Similarly, with nudity, a certain amount is deemed acceptable (although that amount has fluctuated over time), usually involving above-the-waist nudity on women or rear nudity on men. But, if a shot were held too long or if the nudity were full-frontal, an R rating would be automatic.

The depiction of violence, however, is frequently considered in relation to its context when assigning ratings. This is perhaps one of the reasons why CARA has been historically more lenient in its approach to rating screen violence than sexuality (Sandler). In discussing his six-month tenure with CARA in the early 1970s, Stephen Farber notes that the context in which violence took place was routinely taken into account when rating films. In one instance, Farber wanted to rate an Italian western titled *Kill Them All and Come Back Alone* (*Ammazzali tutti e torna solo*, 1968) X, but "the other board members felt it was too exaggerated to warrant such a strong reaction" (*Ratings Game* 29).

Even graphically explicit violence can be deemed acceptable for unrestricted audiences by CARA if it is done within a comic framework. The Black Knight sequence in the medieval comedy *Monty Python and the*

Holy Grail (1974) is a good example. In this sequence, King Arthur (Graham Chapman) battles a mysterious Black Knight (John Cleese) for the right to pass over a bridge. During the fight, Arthur manages to chop off both of the knight's arms and both of his legs as well, and the sequence's comedy emerges from the knight's refusal not only to back down after such serious wounds but to even acknowledge their severity. The depiction of the knight's maiming is certainly graphic: All four appendages are cut off in full view of the camera, and there is the requisite spurting of large amounts of blood. But, because it is done within a comical context in which the audience is asked not to take the violence seriously, the graphic nature of its depiction is ameliorated through laughs. The power of humor to overcome the graphic effects of screen violence is also illustrated in television networks' Standards and Practices Departments allowing similar sequences to play on broadcast television, such as the spurting blood when Dan Aykroyd accidentally cuts off his own finger in the *Saturday Night Live* spoof of Julia Child's cooking show or Monty Python's over-the-top parody of bloody Sam Peckinpah–style violence at a refined racquet club on *Monty Python's Flying Circus*.

Of course, there is a balance to be had, and comedy does not automatically mitigate all forms of screen violence, rendering them acceptable. Even though Sam Raimi's *The Evil Dead* and *Evil Dead II* were essentially slapsticky homages to Three Stooges–style comedy, their gore factor was both so graphic and so unrelenting that CARA slapped both films with X ratings, causing their distributors to release them unrated in the theatrical market.

Context can also work *against* a film, making the screen violence seem more extreme than it is, as we have seen in the cases of both *Cruising* and *Dressed to Kill*. The former's setting in the gay S&M underworld and the latter's fascination with gender-bending sexual psychosis surely affected how the CARA board members viewed the depictions of violence in each film, and it is not surprising that each had to be trimmed significantly before it was given an R rating. As the decade of the 1980s wore on, CARA became more and more stringent in demanding cuts to the graphic screen violence in slasher films, which was certainly a result of the ongoing public debate about how such films were seen as dehumanizing their teenage audience. Similarly, Farber points out that, in his experience with CARA, the board frequently noted whether or not the violence depicted in a film was "imitable," which is why CARA was harder on rating motorcycle films, which were particularly popular with the youth audience in the late 1960s and early 1970s, than most other violent genres. "These films were usually rated R, because the idea of presenting realistic *antisocial* behavior that might be imitated by young people obviously upset the board members, whereas they were more tolerant of violence that had a social sanction—the violence of soldiers, for example" (*Ratings Game* 29).

As we will see, the context of *Poltergeist, Gremlins,* and *Indiana Jones and the Temple of Doom* as films associated with Steven Spielberg had a significant impact on how they were rated. At the time those films were rated, Spielberg was so heavily associated with family-friendly blockbuster entertainment—he was, in Robert Kolker's words, "the ultimate, arbitrating patriarch" (212)—that the Rating Board was unable (or unwilling) to recognize the complexities of the screen violence in those films. In effect, they were unable to reconcile the two sides of Steven Spielberg.

The Two Sides of Steven Spielberg: *Poltergeist* and *E.T.*

Because of his virtually unrivaled popularity at the box office and consistent acclaim with mainstream film critics, Steven Spielberg has been frequently dismissed as a simplistic filmmaker whose works are popular and therefore profitable because they comfort the audience with glib reassurances about redemption and patriarchal family values. Kolker has summarized this viewpoint best in his critique of Spielberg's ideological tendencies:

> [Spielberg] is the grand modern narrator of simple desires fulfilled, of reality diverted into the imaginary spaces of aspirations realized, where fears of abandonment and impotence are turned into fantasy spectacles of security and joyful action, where even the ultimate threat of annihilation is diverted by a saving male figure. The problem with Spielberg is that the security and joy offered by his films are rarely earned but rather forced on the viewer, willing or not, by structures that demand complete assent and emotional compliance in order to survive. (285)

Robin Wood notes a similar tendency in what he labeled "The Lucas-Spielberg Syndrome," the keynote of which is "reassurance" (*Hollywood* 162).

Kolker is not off base to say that Spielberg's films "transcend the function of responding or giving shape to ideology and instead become the ideology, the very shape and form of the relationships we desire for our world" (257). However, while the foundation of so many of Spielberg's films reinforce simple patriarchal notions of comfort and safety, notions that are all the more powerful and appealing to the audience because, as Kolker argues, they are *available,* there is also a tension in many of them that is not so easily recuperated by the "fantasy spectacles of security and joyful action" (285).

While most of Spielberg's films rely on the all-embracing "happy ending" in which the wrongs are put right, sometimes the trauma of enacting those wrongs is so severe that the happy ending cannot fully contain them. For their arguments to work, Spielberg's critics tend to assume that the reassurance of neoconservative values in his films overwhelm and therefore mitigate the violence in them, when in fact that violence is often so severe that the happy ending is hollow. In this sense, many of his films are similar to modern horror films, which also tend to feature beginnings and endings that seem conservative on the surface narrative level but are undermined by the transgressive ideological subtext (Clover). This is not necessarily intentional on Spielberg's part; rather, it is the best evidence of the tension between his two sides, one of which desires to reassure conventional, middle-class patriarchal structures of power and the other of which desires to tear them down and expose their weaknesses and fragility.

These two sides of Spielberg were on display in the summer of 1982, when two films were released that bore his immediately recognizable thumbprint: *E.T.: The Extra-Terrestrial* and *Poltergeist.* Both films were blockbusters in their own right, although *E.T.* was clearly the more successful of the two.[1] In a sense, the films were extremely similar, as they both dealt with the intrusion of the fantastical into a modern, middle-class California neighborhood. In fact, the neighborhoods depicted in the two films were so similar that one might imagine the stories were taking place in the same location at the same time, perhaps just on different streets.

However, where *E.T.* is a science fiction fantasy about a benevolent three-foot-tall alien who is accidentally left behind on Earth and befriends a small boy, *Poltergeist* is an unrelieved horror film about the violent intrusion of a ghostly presence that doesn't merely haunt but actively attacks the family. In essence, both films are children's narratives, as they deal with emotions on a level with which children most readily identify. But, while *E.T.* is a child fantasy that reassures by offering redemption and wholeness at the end, *Poltergeist* is its nightmare inverse that ends in defeat.

E.T. is Spielberg's ultimate children's film, not just because it features a ten-year-old child as a protagonist but because it was conceived of and shot entirely from the child's point of view. The emotions in *E.T.* are woven out of fears of abandonment and loneliness and are redeemed through kindness, friendship, and dedication.

E.T. is found by Elliott (Henry Thomas), a young boy who is dealing with his own feelings of abandonment and loneliness since his father left, leaving a gaping, still raw wound in the family structure. E.T. fills that void for Elliott just as surely as Elliott fills the void for E.T., thus creating a closed circuit of intimacy and redemption between the two of them that is threatened only by outside forces in the adult world. Those forces are represented from a child's (or E.T.'s) point of view—low shots that capture the men only from the waist down as they track the deserted alien and eventually locate him in Elliott's house. The men are large and menacing, sometimes represented only by their shadows, as monsters often are in the early stages of a horror film.[2]

The alignment of E.T.—wondrous, fantastical, both ancient-wise and childlike but always gentle—with children is emphasized when Elliott tells his little sister Gertie (Drew Barrymore) that only children can see him. This is, of course, a fabrication, something Gertie knows because the sinister men eventually find E.T., and it is up to Elliott, his older brother Michael (Robert MacNaughton), and other kids from the neighborhood to outsmart the government operatives and help E.T. rendezvous with his spaceship, thus completing the fantasy of children trumping adults. In *E.T.*, childhood is the essence of life, a time of purity, energy, and innocence in which the world can be made right. It is important that the one adult character aside from Elliott's mother (Dee Wallace) who is depicted with any sympathy is the lead government agent (Peter Coyote), who is at first portrayed menacingly via low shots that are connected by the jingling of the keys he keeps on his belt. Once he is given a face, though, we learn that he is still a child at heart when he tells Elliott that E.T.'s arrival on Earth is "a miracle," something he's been waiting for since he was a "ten-year-old boy." Thus, he is, in a sense, Elliott as an adult, which is why it is so natural that he would take his place alongside Elliott's mother at the climactic moment of E.T.'s return to his spaceship, standing in for Elliott's lost father.

If *E.T.* represented Spielberg's "optimism," as he put it, then *Poltergeist* represented the darker side of his nature, something he readily admitted (Kakutani). Although Spielberg did not direct *Poltergeist*, he had a significant hand in its creation as producer and co-writer of the script from a story he had originally concocted. In fact, there were rumors that he had, in fact, directed much of the film, with the film's credited director, Tobe Hooper, functioning in little more than a technical capacity. According to an article in the *New York Times*:

> Although "Poltergeist" was directed by Tobe Hooper, the movie is widely considered to be the work of Steven Spielberg, its co-writer and executive producer. Mr. Spielberg chose the cast and locations and did the storyboarding—the setting up of the way scenes should be shot. Mr. Spielberg has said he was the creative force behind the movie and that it came out of his typewriter and his imagination. He was also on the set almost every day and supervised the editing. (Harmetz, "Film Rating System")

More important, though, Spielberg was understood by both audiences and critics as the film's true author, something the distributor, MGM, attempted to emphasize in its advertising. In fact, MGM was so eager to market the film via Spielberg that it was ordered to pay $15,000 for violating a section of the 1981 Directors Guild of America Basic Agreement involving the size of a director's credit in a trailer. The trailer for *Poltergeist* opens with a title card noting in large type that the film is "A Steven Spielberg Production," and at the end of the trailer the "A Steven Spielberg Production" credit is twice as large as all the other credits, including director Tobe Hooper's ("MGM Is Ordered to Pay").

In writing about the film, critics tended to couch it in terms of a Spielberg film rather than a Hooper film, and many went out of their way to defend that position. For example, in the *Washington Post,* Gary Arnold wrote, "The premise and the technique of systematically juxtaposing comic and scary touches may be easily recognized as Spielberg trademarks. The suburban setting in 'Poltergeist' and the upcoming 'E.T.,' an acknowledged Spielberg credit, are obviously similar and identifiable as his characteristic social terrain."

Poltergeist tells the story of the Freelings, a typical middle-class family whose lives are disrupted by an invasion of angry poltergeists that take over their suburban home. While the traumatizing violence inflicted by the poltergeists is aimed at the family in general, the majority of it is relentlessly and systematically directed at the two youngest children, eight-year-old Robbie (Oliver Robbins) and five-year-old Carol Anne (Heather O'Rourke). The older daughter, a teenager (Dominique Dunne), is largely absent from the narrative after the first poltergeist attack, and no violence is ever directed specifically at her at any point, leaving the two youngest children to be the primary victims. Additionally, the only time any violence is directed specifically at the parents (JoBeth Williams and Craig T. Nelson) is when they are trying to protect Robbie and Carol Anne.

Thus, if *E.T.* is a fantasy about childhood empowerment, *Poltergeist* is its inverse nightmare about childhood victimization, which is brought to a climax when the house literally takes Carol Anne prisoner, reducing her to a terrified, disembodied voice. Carol Anne is presented as a victim of her own innocence, as she is the only family member who doesn't seem concerned at first about the presence of the "TV People." This metaphysical abduction resonates traumatically with real child abductions, which were a significant concern in the early 1980s ("Child Abductions"), particularly with the media coverage of the kidnapping and murder of six-year-old Adam Walsh in 1981 and his parents' subsequent campaign that led to the passage of the Federal Missing Child Act.[3] This also accounts for the film's true source of horror, which is the random nature of violence and the inability of the American family to do anything about it. Robin Wood downplays the horror in *Poltergeist* on the grounds that the family is absolved of any responsibility for the horror because they were unaware that their house was built on top of a cemetery (*Hollywood* 182). The idea of the neighborhood being constructed on top of the bones of others suggests how modern middle-class comfort has been built at the expense of other, non-European cultures. However, what Wood doesn't see is that the horror in *Poltergeist* isn't radical because of its source (that is, something external rather than within the family itself, as in much 1970s horror) but rather because it can't be defeated.

Poltergeist is scary because it invites the audience to identify with the victims in the film—both children and parents. For both, much of the film's horror emerges from the parents' inability to do anything about the violence being inflicted on the children; for parents, it is frightening because it reminds them that they can't do everything to protect their children in a scary world, and for children it is scary because they are reminded that they will not always be protected. The Freeling parents are constantly depicted in a state of panic as they race about the house, trying to save their children from the clutches of the poltergeists, which possess physical objects in order to inflict bodily harm on the house's residents. At one point, Robbie is attacked by a possessed clown doll that tries to strangle him, and he has to save himself because the poltergeists are so successful in keeping his mother out of the room. Thus, as much as it is a children's nightmare, *Poltergeist* is also a parental nightmare.

17. A beastly poltergeist blocks Diane Freeling's (JoBeth Williams) attempt to save her children, Robbie and Carol Anne, from the possessed house in *Poltergeist* (1982). Such scenes underscore how much of the film's horror emerges from the parents' inability to do anything about the violence being inflicted on their children. DVD still.

It is not surprising that *Poltergeist* is often given only cursory treatment or left out entirely of critical accounts of Spielberg's work that take him to task for his conservative idealism and overtly stated moral certainty (for example, Kolker), because it doesn't fit neatly into the Spielbergian paradigm. One could make the argument that it adheres to Spielberg's worldview because the family survives in the end and remains intact. However, the family's survival is only in the most basic physical meaning of the word: they are still alive. The poltergeists have clearly won in the sense that they successfully drove the family out of the house and, their work done, folded the house in on itself, leaving only a gaping scar in the suburban neighborhood that was once a source of comfort and ease. The final shot of the film shows us the Freeling family, haggard, battered, and looking completely defeated, shuffling wordlessly into the Holiday Inn motel room where they will spend the night. It is a dreary final shot punctuated by the visual joke of the father rolling the TV—the source of the poltergeists in their house—out the door. It is a closing moment that is hardly typical of Spielberg's desire to comfort his audience with easy answers.

Not surprisingly, when it was initially submitted to CARA, *Poltergeist* was rated R. The intensity of the scares, the gore of a nightmare-fantasy in which a paranormal investigator hallucinates that he's ripping his own face off, the hordes of rotting corpses, and the consistent direction of violence against children was enough to warrant the restrictive rating. Interestingly, though, CARA chairman Richard Heffner insisted that the film should be rated R, not for "violence," but for "terror," which he felt was increased dramatically by the film's impressive use of Dolby surround sound to envelop the viewer. However, because MGM/UA, the film's financier and distributor, saw teenagers as the film's target audience, it appealed the decision with the Appeals Board, which is comprised of representative members of the major studios, distributors, and exhibitors. The Appeals Board voted overwhelmingly to rate *Poltergeist* PG, and just like that, an R-rated film became a PG-rated film without having to remove a single frame.

The appeals process itself was fraught with internal conflict and was seen as an example of how the studios could manipulate the system to their own advantage in a way that independent producers and distributors could not. Immediately after the appeals hearing for *Poltergeist*, William Nix, counsel for CARA, wrote a memo to Jack Valenti outlining his concerns about what had happened (in Heffner, "Reminiscences," May 6, 1982, box 1). Chief among these was the fact that United Artists (UA) had insisted that it be allowed to vote on the appeal. This was the first appeal for an MGM film since MGM and UA had merged in 1981; however, despite the merger, UA was still a legally separate member of the MPAA. Thus, even though UA had a financial stake in the film, which was normally considered a conflict of interest and reason for the studio to abstain from voting in the appeal,[4] it voted anyway. UA was so determined to cast its vote that the company sent Alan Benjamin, a senior member of the studio's legal staff, to vote on UA's behalf, even though he was not the studio's designated Appeals Board member and had never appeared before the board. UA's insistence in being included in the vote and the overwhelming support of the other members of the Appeals Board to rate *Poltergeist* PG were rooted almost entirely in economics. MGM/UA was in financial trouble at the time and was in need of a significant hit. If the studio did end up going under, the other studios would be affected because they would have to fill in MGM/UA's financial responsibilities to the MPAA.

Thus, the Appeals Board overturned CARA's R rating of *Poltergeist* for short-term economic reasons without paying much heed to the long-term social and political consequences that were involved in allowed such a terrifying film into the theatrical marketplace with what many perceived to be a misleading rating. Not surprisingly, *Poltergeist* led to some controversy because what most viewers understood the PG rating to mean was challenged by the film's frightening and violent content. Internally, Jack Valenti received a letter from Reverend James M. Wall, editor of the *Christian Century* and chairman of the National Council of Churches' Government and Industry Committee. In his letter, which also included a review of *Poltergeist* that he intended to publish, he told Valenti that the film, with its PG rating, "reflects negatively on the industry and suggests that we have reached one of those developmental moments in the life of the ratings system when a major change is in order." Far more disturbing for Hollywood, Wall suggested that such films make "it very difficult for those of us in the Protestant church who want to ward off censorship and block the irresponsible behavior of the New Right" (Wall to Valenti, June 14, 1982, in Heffner, "Reminiscences," box 1, 1). In the public sphere, many critics made special note in their reviews, as they believed that the PG label did not fully inform viewers of what the film contained. In his review, Gary Arnold noted, "Parents should probably be alerted to the fact that the PG rating is a borderline call. . . . Although I've certainly seen more ghoulish and terrifying spectacles erupt from the screen, 'Poltergeist' seems grisly enough to be approached with caution and kept offbounds for younger children."

The fact that *Poltergeist* was labeled as a horror film from the outset may have mitigated potential controversy because that generic label alone was enough to keep many parents from taking their small children, despite Spielberg's association with the film and its PG rating. Although there was some rumbling from viewers who thought the film was too intense for its PG label, it was not enough to warrant the MPAA making any changes to the rating system. Two summers later, however, the story was much different.

The Summer of Kiddie Violence: *Indiana Jones and the Temple of Doom* and *Gremlins*

On June 18, 1984, *U.S. News and World Report* published an article with the headline asking "Movie Violence Getting Out of Hand?" (Bronson and Hawkins). Although this headline would seem to suggest that the article was concerned with screen violence in general, it was really concerned about a specific kind: the violence in films aimed at children. This article, and many others like it, were written in response to the uproar surrounding the release of two films in the summer of 1984, *Indiana Jones and the Temple of Doom* and *Gremlins*, both of which were positioned by the industry in terms of both marketing and their PG ratings as children's entertainment.

The 1980s marked a significant rise in both the levels and explicitness of violence and frightening imagery in films that were marketed to children and young adolescents. Although *Gremlins* and *Indiana Jones and the Temple of Doom* were singled out for their dark content and often gruesome violence, there had been a number of films in the early 1980s that paved the way, many of which were produced and distributed by the Walt Disney Corporation, which had been known and revered for decades as a haven of safe family entertainment. For example, in the early 1980s, Disney partnered with Paramount Pictures on a pair of expensive coproductions, the second of which was the medieval fantasy film *Dragonslayer* (1981).[5] It tells the story of Galen (Peter MacNicol), a young and ambitious sorcerer's apprentice who is tasked with ridding a medieval kingdom of a fearsome dragon after his mentor, the aging and cantankerous sorcerer Ulrich (Ralph Richardson), is killed. With its youthful hero and groundbreaking special effects,[6] *Dragonslayer* was clearly intended to be a youth-centric blockbuster in the mold of *Star Wars*, yet it includes several scenes of gruesomely bloody violence. Particularly notable is Galen's descent into the dragon's lair, which includes the horrific imagery of the dragon's progeny feasting on the bloody remains of the king's daughter, who had earlier been sacrificed to appease the dragon. There are several shots of a young dragon gnawing the flesh from the dead girl's leg down to the bone, and when Galen lops its head off, it has the girl's severed foot in its mouth. Part of the disturbing effectiveness of this scene is how it runs so directly counter to expected conventions:

Usually when a beautiful princess is threatened by a monster, the hero saves her in the nick of time rather than finds her corpse being chewed on by the monster's babies.

Several years later, Disney produced *Return to Oz* (1985), a dark, in-name-only sequel to *The Wizard of Oz* (1939), whose horror movie overtones include early scenes of Dorothy being confined to a mental institution and an evil sorceress who maintains a roomful of disembodied heads. The same year also marked the release of Disney's *The Black Cauldron*, an animated sword-and-sorcery movie based on Lloyd Alexander's popular *The Chronicles of Prydain* series. *The Black Cauldron* was intended to raise Disney's animation department out of the doldrums into which it had sunk over the previous decade by jettisoning the company's increasingly stale musical formula and emphasizing action and spectacle, the hallmarks of 1980s blockbuster filmmaking. The most expensive animated film produced by Disney since *Pinocchio* (1940), it was shot in 70mm and was one of the first films to utilize Dolby's six-channel surround sound process. And, because of its frightening imagery and violent content, which some critics connected to the darker aspects of early Disney films like *Snow White and the Seven Dwarfs* (1937) and *Pinocchio*, it was also the first animated Disney film to be rated PG.

The use of violence in children's entertainment has a long and storied history, and it has been seen at different times, in different cultures, and by different scholars as either productive or dangerous. In his classic study of fairy tales, Bruno Bettleheim argues that the often gruesome stories serve a crucial social function in helping children cope with and manage their own violent tendencies. Reading fairy tales helps children deal with issues of chaos, powerlessness, and social integration, an argument that Gerard Jones updated by replacing fairy tales with movies, TV shows, and video games (*Killing Monsters*). Similar to Bettleheim, Jones argues that "exploring, in a safe and controlled context, what is impossible or too dangerous or forbidden for [children] is a crucial tool in accepting the limits of reality" (11). Jones also points out that children and adults tend to respond to mediated violence differently, and "in the gap between juvenile and adult reactions, some of our greatest misunderstandings and most damaging disputes are born" (11).

Maria Tatar, however, has taken a contrary view to Bettleheim's thesis, namely because Bettleheim (and, by extension, Jones) assumes an inherent human violence and concomitant need to use violent entertainment to deal with it. Tatar argues that, because fairy tales are the products of adults, they better reflect adult sensibilities: "Fairy tales may now belong to the culture of childhood, but they have always been of adult making. The violence in the tales is driven by the psychological needs of the adult or by the narrative exigencies of the plot, not by the supposedly anarchic, innately aggressive nature of the child" (71).

Similarly, *Gremlins* and *Indiana Jones and the Temple of Doom*, as they were initially understood during their theatrical release, were meant to "belong to the culture of childhood," particularly because, as we have seen, Spielberg was so closely associated with children and the childlike. Thus, they shocked many viewers because they so clearly reflected an adult sensibility that was perceived to be damaging to preadolescents. Robin Wood argues that one of the chief characteristics of filmmaking in the 1980s was "the curious and disturbing phenomenon of children's films conceived and marketed largely for adults" (*Hollywood* 163). In the case of *Temple of Doom* and *Gremlins*, they were children's films conceived for adults but then marketed to children—thus, interstitial, neither kids' films nor adult films—which was the source of their controversy.

Indiana Jones and the Temple of Doom

Indiana Jones and the Temple of Doom was the highly anticipated sequel to *Raiders of the Lost Ark*, which had earned $250 million at the theatrical box office and had been the top-grossing film of 1981. *Temple of Doom* was released on May 23, 1984, the Wednesday before Memorial Day weekend, which meant that it kicked off the summer movie season, a time that, since the massive success of *Jaws* in the summer of 1975, has been associated with blockbuster movies aimed primarily at preadolescents and adolescents.

Inspired by the cliffhanging Republic serials of the 1930s in both form and style, *Raiders of the Lost Ark* had been the brainchild of George Lucas and Spielberg. Set in the mid-1930s and following the adventures of a rough-and-tumble archaeologist named Indiana Jones (Harrison Ford), *Raiders* was the antithesis of the serious-minded irony and despair that had characterized so much American filmmaking in the 1970s. It was a loud, fast, unrepentant throwback to an earlier cinematic era, and it evoked fantasy and nostalgia with a larger-than-life hero who could get in the most calamitous circumstances but never lose his hat.

A globe-trotting fantasy character brought down to earth in a rumpled leather jacket, beaten fedora, and five-day beard, Indiana is part Humphrey Bogart and part Superman. He evokes Bogart in his coolness under pressure and absolute self-assuredness, even as he tweaks the icon with his comic tendency to get in way over his head. Simultaneously, he evokes the idea of the superhero, complete with an alter ego as a mild-mannered, bespectacled, tweed-suit-wearing professor of archaeology who stumbles for words when one of his female students writes "Love You" on her eyelids and bats them flirtatiously. As a character, Indiana

Jones is a nostalgic recreation of a bygone era of über-masculine heroes with the modern twist of sly self-awareness. He is a perfect embodiment of the "ideal male" Robin Wood notes is so central to American genre filmmaking: "the virile adventurer, the potent, untrammeled man of action" ("Ideology" 61).

In *Raiders of the Lost Ark,* Indiana is pitted against nothing less than the Nazis in a race to discover the biblical ark of the covenant. The screenplay, penned by Lawrence Kasdan (*Body Heat,* 1981) from a story by George Lucas and Philip Kaufman (*The Unbearable Lightness of the Being,* 1988), is a model of streamlined efficiency, as is Spielberg's direction. Coming off the elegant and moody sci-fi hit *Close Encounters of the Third Kind* (1977) and the ambitious comic dud *1941* (1979), Spielberg was getting back to his roots as an action director, and it paid off with a massive hit. Naturally, the pressure to make a sequel was intense.

Both Lucas and Spielberg wanted the sequel to be different, although they differed in terms of what they thought the tone should be. Following the phenomenal success of *Raiders of the Lost Ark, Temple of Doom* had a heavy weight of expectations riding on it, and Lucas dealt with those expectations by going directly against them, similar to what he had done with *The Empire Strikes Back,* the much darker sequel to *Star Wars.* In many ways, *Temple of Doom* is only tangentially related to its predecessor, with the only real link being the character of Indiana Jones. The arc of the story and the mood and tone of its telling are completely different; *Temple of Doom* is more comedic horror movie than action-adventure yarn, and some amusingly dubbed it "Indiana Jones Goes to Hell." According to Lucas, "It was meant to be a little darker, then we sort of got carried away. I was going through a divorce and was not in a very good mood, so it turned out a lot darker than probably it should have" (qtd. in Matloff 76). Spielberg did not agree with the film's dark tone: "I wasn't inspired by the story. It was really dark and scary. In those days that kind of stuff wasn't on my diet, and it didn't interest me" (76). Yet, Lucas was intent on his vision of what *Temple of Doom* should be, so Spielberg relented and agreed to direct it.

In *Temple of Doom,* Indiana Jones, a spoiled American singer named Willie (Kate Capshaw), whom he picks up in Beijing, and Indy's sidekick, a precocious twelve-year-old Chinese orphan named Short Round (Ke Huy Quan), wind up on the northern edge of India, where they are taken into a dusty, destitute village of starving men and women and no children. Indy is informed that evil members of the Thugee cult have stolen the village's sacred stone that protects them and also abducted all of their children, which links the film's underlying uneasiness to the child abduction narrative in *Poltergeist.* Thus, rather than chasing after an artifact, *Temple of*

Doom positions Indiana Jones as an unlikely rescuer, sent on a mission by the starving village elders to Pankot Palace, which he discovers is just a facade for the eponymous Temple of Doom, where the Thugees worship the evil god Kali with human sacrifice and use enslaved children to dig in the mines for another missing sacred stone. It is here that the story's inherent darkness truly envelops the film, casting it in dark shadows and blood-red light that underscore its horror connotations. A good half of the film takes place in the Dante's inferno–like Temple of Doom, and when Indy, Willie, and Short Round finally escape into the daylight for the big climax (as opposed to all the smaller climaxes scattered throughout the film), it's like waking up from a claustrophobic nightmare.

Like *Raiders, Temple of Doom* was rated PG, which meant that anyone could see it without a parent, although the vote from the Rating Board was not unanimous. Of the six members of the board, four thought it should be rated PG and two thought it should be rated R. Richard Heffner felt that it was neither a PG nor an R, but without a middle rating, he ultimately believed that it should be rated PG if only because, had the Rating Board given it an R, it would have resulted in an appeal that, given Spielberg's stature, the box-office expectations riding on the film, and Heffner's previous experiences in the appeals process, the Rating Board would have lost. Heffner was personally troubled by the film's dark violence, and he wrote in his notes after the screening, "I see the film at Paramount and am terribly upset by it. As I tell Frank Mancuso, the innocence and fun of *Raiders* [*of the Lost Ark*] is gone, and what is left is the manipulative meanness of spirit, violence that runs through the film (particularly the heart on-fire scene in reel four). No matter the happy ending; this I note is a perfect R-13" (Heffner, "RDH Pre–Oral History Memo 1984," box 2, 53).

Of course, *Raiders of the Lost Ark* had not been an easy PG either. When the Rating Board first screened that film in May 1981, two voted for R and three voted for PG, citing the film's "considerable violence," which includes a frightening climax in which the ark of the covenant is opened, releasing spirits that cause two villains' faces to melt on-screen and one villain's head to explode. There are also a number of shoot-outs featuring bloody squibs and some indirect gore when a Nazi villain finds himself in the way of a spinning plane propeller, which results in a copious splattering of blood across the plane in two different shots. However, Heffner voted PG with the others because he felt that the majority of the violence had a "James Bond quality," which suggests that, even when bloody, as long as screen violence had a slightly unrealistic quality and was apolitical, it had more leeway. Still, when Heffner reported the Rating Board's PG decision to Paramount, he noted, "But the fact remains, we are still very disturbed

18. Members of the Classification and Rating Administration were split when they first screened *Raiders of the Lost Ark* (1981), with two members voting for R and three voting for PG. The board cited the film's "considerable violence," which includes a frightening climax in which two villains' faces melt on-screen and one villain's head explodes. DVD still.

that the classification system will be damaged by the violence" (Heffner, "Reminiscences," vol. 5, box 5, 833). Although there were some complaints, there was little to suggest that most parents felt the violence in *Raiders* was too much. The same could not be said for *Temple of Doom.*

Because of *Temple of Doom*'s PG rating and the fond memories of *Raiders*, many of the parents who took their children to see *Temple of Doom* were expecting a lighthearted, swashbuckling adventure. Instead, they were faced with an almost schizophrenic film, one that married adventurism with unnerving horror and slapstick comedy. The scene that was singled out above all others for crossing a line between acceptable fantasy and unrelieved horror is the one where Indiana and the others witness a Thugee ceremony in which the high priest, Mola Ram (Amrish Puri), reaches into a living man's chest and tears out his still-beating heart. Although the heart-ripping is shown in full view of the camera and leaves nothing to the imagination, it is not particularly well done from a special effects standpoint, as it is obvious that an actor is tearing into a hollow rubber chest cavity. However, such details did not placate the parents who were incensed that they had taken their children to a PG-rated film that included a scene of such graphic violence, one that they felt clearly deserved an R rating.

The critics who reviewed the film generally praised the action and Spielberg's direction, but they were all cautionary about the effect the film might have on children. Associated Press critic Bob Thomas noted that the film demonstrated some of Spielberg's more "excessive" tendencies, particularly in a comically gross-out banquet sequence in which characters dine on live eels, oversized roaches, eyeball soup, and chilled monkey brains eaten directly out of the skull. He also noted that the film had "less humor and character involvement" than *Raiders of the Lost Ark,* which is crucial when one considers the importance of context in determining how screen violence plays. This is probably why Thomas ended his review by proclaiming that "the movie is almost guaranteed to give [children] any number of nightmares" ("*Indiana Jones*").

Writing in the *New York Times,* Vincent Canby seemed torn regarding how he thought children would react to the film. On the one hand, he felt that some of the film's grosser aspects, particularly the banquet sequence, would be better received by children than by adults because kids have an affinity for the gross that is not encumbered by such adult concepts as taste and maturity. Interestingly enough, Canby also felt that the heart-ripping scene would play better with older kids than adults. As he wrote, the scene "is not only a film-making trick but a trick within the film itself, something that older children may understand more readily than their adult guardians" ("'Indiana Jones'"). On the other hand, like Bob Thomas, Canby noted that the film, "in addition to being endearingly disgusting, is violent in ways that may scare the wits out of some small patrons." However, Canby pointed specifically to the context of the violence as being the source of scaring children, particularly the fact that the film hinges on the kidnapping of hundreds of Indian children and their being forced into slave labor in the mines. Even though Canby thought the violent scenes of children being beaten and whipped were "so exaggerated that it seems less real than cartoon-like," the exaggeration was clearly not enough to ameliorate the shock some viewers felt at seeing small children as the targets of direct violence in a film supposedly intended for preadolescents.

Jack Kroll of *Newsweek* also noted the exaggeration of the violence in *Temple of Doom,* but rather than functioning to take the edge off the violence, he cited it as the main problem. Starting with the heart-ripping scene, Kroll complained that "at this point the movie loses its stylish integration of violence and humor and becomes a careening juggernaut of beatings, gougings, and crunchings." Although he described the violence as "comic-book carnage," he criticized it for not being "imaginative or witty." Ultimately, Kroll felt the film was little more than "kinetic pornography—quantity annihilating quality."

Indiana Jones and the Temple of Doom was intended to be a blockbuster from the start, and it required a PG rating to reach its intended audience. Yet, the PG rating, which was a net cast so wide by the mid-1980s that it was beginning to lose its stability of meaning, was interpreted by parents as meaning that the film was safe for their children. After all, if

19. Many parents were incensed after they took their children to the PG-rated *Indiana Jones and the Temple of Doom* (1984) only to discover that it included scenes of arguably R-rated graphic violence, such as the one in which the high priest Mola Ram (Amrish Puri) tears a man's heart from his chest during a nightmarish ritual. DVD still.

the film had contained anything that might be disturbing to children, surely CARA would have given the film a restrictive R rating. Unfortunately, *Temple of Doom* was a film whose contents, in Jack Valenti's words, placed it "awkwardly beyond PG but not clearly within the R" (qtd. in Sanello, "New PG-13 Film Rating Hits Theaters"). Although critics of the film pointed to specific, isolated moments, particularly the heart-ripping scene, it was the film as a whole that was truly unsettling to some audience members. The juxtaposition of a beloved big-screen hero and a disturbing scenario involving child slave labor, human sacrifices, and black magic was ultimately at the heart of the controversy, especially when one considers the film in light of the twin social panics of child abduction and Satanism that were crystallizing in the early 1980s. Specifics such as eyeball soup and a heart being torn from a man's chest were easy, graspable signifiers of the film's less tangible context of pervasive horror.

In a sense, *Temple of Doom* represented the convergence of the two most popular genres of the 1980s: the pure action film, which was viewed at the time as simple, unproblematic escapism, and the horror film, which was disreputable. The influx of horror into *Temple of Doom* disrupted audience expectations that had been created through fond memories of the swashbuckling adventurism of *Raiders of the Lost Ark*, the view of George Lucas and Steven Spielberg as cherished cinematic icons who had created some of the most memorable "family-friendly" entertainment of the past decade, and the security of a PG rating. This created a tension between what audiences expected and what was ultimately delivered, which was even more severe in the case of *Gremlins*, released a few weeks later.

Gremlins

Gremlins was released on June 8, 1984, just two and a half weeks after the release of *Indiana Jones and the Temple of Doom* and thus still in the heat of that film's controversy. There had been a significant amount of pre-release hype around the film, mainly because Steven Spielberg's name was prominently associated with it (even though he was one of three executive producers, the advertising billed the film as "Steven Spielberg presents *Gremlins*") and because there was a great deal of secrecy involving the film's actual contents.

The advertising campaign for *Gremlins* was structured around secrecy, with hints and suggestions about what might be in it but nothing absolute. "From an advertising point of view, we're going to tease them," said Joel Wayne, vice president of creative advertising for Warner Bros., the studio that produced and distributed the film in association with Spielberg's recently formed Amblin Entertainment (qtd. in Maslin, "At the Movies"). The film's advertising one-sheet is a perfect example of this approach. It shows a medium close-up of a young man from the chest down. He is holding a box, the lid of which is slightly ajar, revealing the two furry paws of a small creature, one of which is delicately touching the young man's hand. Above the box is a list of words—"Cute. Clever. Mischievous. Intelligent. Dangerous"—that hint at the nature of the film's gremlins without being overtly specific. The film's trailer informed audiences of the three rules that must be followed with the film's creatures: (1) Don't expose them to direct light; (2) don't get them wet; and (3) don't feed them after midnight. It was suggested that bad things would happen if these rules weren't followed, but exactly what was left tantalizingly unclear.

The furry paws on the one-sheet belong to Gizmo, the pet Mogwai who is the inadvertent source of the film's mayhem. Gizmo was immediately likened to E.T. by critics and audiences, as he was an irresistible mixture of child and wise old man, adorable in a so-ugly-he's-cute sort of way but heightened because he was furry. Vincent Canby described him as "something like a cuddly teddy bear with the ears of a rabbit, a Bambilike nose, eyes as round and deep and dark as glass buttons, a sweet disposition, and a physical nature more unstable than hydrogen gas" ("'Gremlins'"). David Ansen described him as "E.T. and Yoda rolled into a koala bear . . . heart-meltingly huggable in the best Spielbergian manner" ("Little Toyshop"). Many audience members, including parents with small children, entered the theater thinking that the adorable Gizmo was one of the gremlins of the title, unaware that his offspring would actually morph into scaly green creatures with enormous teeth and vicious cat eyes. This misunderstanding extended to press coverage of the film prior to its release; for example, *New York Times* critic Janet Maslin, in an article about the film's advertising campaign, mistakenly referred to Gizmo as "a leading gremlin," apparently unaware that the film was to feature an entirely different set of creatures that were significantly more menacing ("At the Movies").

This secrecy surrounding *Gremlins* turned out to be its major problem because, similar to the situation with *Indiana Jones and the Temple of Doom,* many viewers went into the theater expecting one thing and ended up seeing something entirely different. And when those viewers were parents with small children who had expected another version of *E.T.* but saw a subversive horror-comedy hybrid about green creatures run amok in an idyllic small town, they weren't happy.

The story in *Gremlins* involves a well-meaning father named Randall Peltzer (Hoyt Axton), a comically inept inventor who brings Gizmo home from a curio shop in Chinatown to give to his teenage son, Billy (Zach Galligan), as a Christmas present. The first rule is broken when water is spilled on Gizmo, causing him to multiply spontaneously. His five offspring, who are clearly sneaky and malicious in a way that Gizmo is not, trick Billy into feeding them after midnight, after which they metamorphose into the demonic green gremlins of the title. The gremlins then go on a rampage in Billy's small hometown, creating chaos and disaster.

As with *Indiana Jones and the Temple of Doom,* viewers tended to point to specific moments of gore as the reason for their being upset with *Gremlins.* The most talked-about sequence involved Billy's mother (Frances Lee McCain) first discovering the gremlins in her house. In a scene of violent maternal protectiveness, she fends off the monsters and dispatches them in ways that are outlandishly gory. In one instance, a gremlin is curiously sticking its head into a blender, and the mother quickly switches it on, resulting in the top half of the gremlin being shredded inside the blender and splattered all over the kitchen cabinets. The other most talked-about moment in this sequence is when the mother forces one of the gremlins into a microwave and then turns it on, resulting in the gremlin exploding in a mass of green goo inside the appliance. Interestingly, less mentioned was the sequence's most overtly violent moment, when the mother stabs one of the gremlins to death with a large kitchen knife while screaming hysterically, "Get out of my kitchen!"

However, it is entirely conceivable that it was less the violence of the actions than the context in which they took place that really upset viewers, even if that was not what they articulated. First, *Gremlins* is a profoundly anti-nostalgic film in that it derives most of its satire from subverting cherished American values surrounding idyllic small towns, close-knit nuclear families, and, most of all, the Christmas season. This made *Gremlins* an anomaly, particularly for a mainstream studio film, as nostalgia "was pecu-

20. While a gremlin being shredded in a blender and another exploding in a microwave were frequently cited as over-the-top gory moments in *Gremlins* (1984), the scene's most overtly violent moment is rarely mentioned: Billy's mother (Frances Lee McCain) stabbing one of the gremlins to death with a large kitchen knife while screaming hysterically, "Get out of my kitchen!" DVD still.

liarly strong [in the 1980s] because of the uncertainties and fragmentation that had typified preceding decades" (Slocum, "Screening Violence" 256).

By situating the gremlin-created mayhem in a small town during the Christmas season, the film went out of its way to undermine all of the traditional and familiar warmth associated with that time of year. Director Joe Dante, who was hired by Spielberg on the strength of his werewolf film *The Howling* (1981), first establishes the film's familiar mise-en-scène via snow-covered streets, Christmas lights, gingerbread cookies, and, most important, *It's a Wonderful Life* (1946) playing on TV, and then dismantles it through violence and pandemonium.

Familiar Christmas decorations become deadly, as the gremlins use Christmas lights to string up Billy's dog and another attacks Billy's mother from inside the family Christmas tree, making it appear as though the tree itself is trying to devour her. The subversion of Christmas extends to the soundtrack, as well, as composer Jerry Goldsmith utilizes familiar Christmas music in ominous ways, notably by playing "Away in a Manager" as Billy surveys the seemingly apocalyptic damage done to the town. However, Christmas takes its hardest hit from the film's heroine, Kate (Phoebe Cates), who doesn't celebrate Christmas because, when she was nine years old, her father attempted to climb down the chimney dressed as Santa Claus and died of a broken neck. This is arguably the film's most disturbing scene, as Kate relates the grotesque story during a lull in the gremlin mayhem, suggesting that it is not just fantastical green creatures that can bring terror into the holidays. Kate telling of how she smelled her father's rotting corpse when she opened the chimney flu and how his dead body was the evidence that shattered her belief in Santa Claus brings a level of chilling everyday horror to the film, particularly since it is told from a child's point of view.

Another aspect of the film that disturbed audiences was its freewheeling shifts between comedy and horror. For the most part, the comedy in *Gremlins* is invariably connected to its moments of horror, resulting in a slippage between the two, something William Paul points out as being central to both modern Hollywood "animal comedy" and horror films. Such films are like roller coasters in that they "make us both laugh and scream" and "present a constant shifting back and forth between extreme states" (423). For example, much of the humor in *Gremlins* derives from moments of "gross out," such as the aforementioned gooey killing of the gremlins in the kitchen. There is also the clearly comical sequence in which the gremlins take over the local tavern, which is really just a cartoonish montage of silly images of gremlins filling their bellies with beer to the point of being grossly bloated, a gremlin pulling a long string of snot from its nose, and so forth. At the same time, though, the film's shifts between obvious comedy and something more disturbing is palpable, as this raucous tavern scene is followed directly by the scene in which Kate tells of her father's death, resulting in a strange disconnect that some audiences members didn't know what to make of.

Although it was originally written as a straight horror movie by Chris Columbus when he was a screenwriting student at New York University, the combined influence of Spielberg, who wanted to make it more accessible to a larger audience, and Dante, who wanted to add levels of social satire and parody, changed it into something that couldn't be easily categorized. According to Dante, the original screenplay was much more gruesome than what ended up on-screen:

> [The gremlins] cut [the] mom's head off and bounce it down the stairs, they eat the dog, it was pretty gruesome. And when we were making the movie, it just seemed that they were actually so funny—the puppets were so funny when they were doing human things, putting on clothes—that it took a whole different direction. It became much more of a horror-comedy than it was a straight horror picture. (qtd. in Klein)

Had the film remained "a straight horror picture," it is entirely conceivable that it would have met no controversy because it would have been rated R and marketed to the horror audience. That is, it would have been easily categorized, which is how the industry protects itself. Instead, it became a hybrid film, one that was designed to appeal to children even though it contained material that many parents felt was inappropriate for them. The gremlins themselves are good metonyms for the film as a whole, as they are alternately scary and funny, threatening and ridiculous. They kill people, but often in silly ways (for example, when one gremlin dispatches the high school science teacher, he sticks a hypodermic needle in the corpse's rear end as payback for the teacher having drawn blood from him earlier). Further confounding this balancing act was the fact that all the gremlins were spawns of Gizmo, the innocuously cute and furry hero. Thus, the violence inflicted by the gremlins could not be completely separated from Gizmo, who most people thought of as a huggable plush toy (of which thousands were sold in the film's subsequent blitz of marketing tie-in products, making the film all the more attractive to children).

However, Dante, as well as some critics,[7] believed that, because much of the violence was done in an over-the-top cartoonish manner, it would be understood better by children than by adults:

> It's more Road Runner-y than anything. But the great thing with that picture was that it was so apparent to me that kids understood the level of fantasy involved. And parents often didn't. There was actually an incident at the screening of the picture at the studio where, after the microwave scene, some woman stormed out with her child. She just came running right past me. The kid didn't want to go, and a couple of minutes went by, and the kid runs back in the theater having apparently escaped her mother, and goes and hides somewhere in the theater. And the mother comes and stands next to me fuming by the door, because there's no way she's going to be able to find her kid. She's going to have to stick around and finish the picture. (qtd. in Klein)

Of course, that was ultimately a moot point because, as far as the film industry was concerned, it was parents' opinions, not children's, that mattered, and many of them were vocally upset that the rating system was not doing its job.

A New Genre: The Creation of the PG-13 Rating

The controversies around *Indiana Jones and the Temple of Doom* and *Gremlins,* as well as the lingering sentiments about *Raiders of the Lost Ark* and *Poltergeist,* were directly related to viewers believing that the films' PG ratings were misleading in terms of the extent and graphicness of their violent content. The fact that people were openly questioning whether CARA was capable of making proper distinctions in terms of rating movies was threatening to the stability of the industry's system of guidance-based self-regulation, the core of its interface with the public. Thus, the MPAA knew that something finally had to be done.

At least in concept, the idea of a rating in between PG and R to distinguish between content that was potentially not appropriate for children but that most parents would be comfortable with young adolescents being exposed to was not a specific product of the 1980s. In fact, it has been one of Richard Heffner's most passionate arguments since he became chairman of CARA in 1974. In a series of letters and memos to Jack Valenti as well as in conversations with him over the ensuing decade, Heffner took various approaches to arguing for the necessity of a rating between PG and R. He claimed that it was necessary to maintain goodwill with the public, that it would keep more films out of the restrictive rating and thus increase their box-office potential, and that it would better reflect the changing mores and values of America's parents. Over the years, Valenti wavered back and forth on the issue, at times expressing his support of a change to the rating system, only to retreat with counterarguments of why it might not work.

In a 1977 letter soliciting responses from key industry figures about the idea of a rating between PG and R, Valenti noted a number of benefits, including "More accurate pinpointing of advice to parents," "It would solve this vexing problem of [the automatic language rule]," "It would allow the system to be a little more flexible" by creating a space for films that legitimately fall in a "no man's land" between PG and R, and "It doesn't require further restrictive categories, which might prove inefficient and unworkable at the [movie theater] since it is another age group to monitor." On the other hand, Valenti listed a number of liabilities to the proposed rating: "Some groups, the religious ones come to mind, would count this revision as an 'escape from the R' category," "Some would argue with us that this new category ought to be restricted in some fashion for younger children," and "There would be criticism that we are going 'liberal' in the [movie ratings]" (Valenti to G. Johnson, B. Scott, S. Schreiber, R. Heffner, K. Clark, S. Schartz, February 18, 1977, in Heffner, "Reminiscences," box 2, 2–3). Thus, according to Valenti, the benefits of the middle rating would help alleviate some of the decision-making burden on the Rating Board and also allow more films to fall into an unrestricted category, which could conceivably increase their box-office potential. The liabilities, however, are almost entirely couched in terms of controversy and criticism of the industry, and the fact that the MPAA did not adopt the middle rating for another seven years is indicative of just how leery the studios were of opening themselves to public criticism and outcry.

Nevertheless, Heffner worked relentlessly to convince his boss that a middle rating was needed, and his primary argument was that it would help smooth over criticism of the rating system and, by proxy, the industry itself. For example, in a memo from February 1982, Heffner responded to Valenti's claim that a new rating would not eliminate criticism of the film industry by noting that that was not the primary concern; criticism could never be completely eliminated. Instead, he wrote, "The question at hand is whether such changes will improve the industry's lot. And to that question, my dear friend, I have no doubt that the answer is YES" (Heffner to Valenti, February 12, 1982, in Heffner, "Reminiscences," box 1, 1). Heffner then went on to argue that the new rating was necessary to maintain goodwill with the public:

> [If the rating system] were more accurate the industry would suffer less! Again, no one is looking for perfection or for a refuge from criticism. But why should an industry that ultimately depends upon the good will of the American public . . . fail to take those simple steps that will work to improve rather than diminish the industry's public reputation? . . . [These are] changes that will never in a million years eliminate criticism of the industry in our pluralistic society, but will more adequately and accurately reflect what has happened to our society over these extraordinarily volatile years since you created CARA and thus mute criticism. (2)

Over the years, a number of alphabetical possibilities were floated for an intermediary rating, some of which were age restrictive and some of which were merely cautionary: RR, R-13, PG/13, PG-M, PG-Mature, and Mature-M, to name a few. Valenti at one point suggested that the PG and R ratings be stratified with three gradations—Soft, Medium, and Hard—which would effectively create six ratings where there had been two. Heffner rejected this as too rhetorically complicated in terms of practical application by the Rating Board and instead suggested a system in which PG and R movies could also be given an "intensity signal" in the form of an asterisk, thus creating two new ratings. He also suggested two-tiered PG and R ratings that would differentiate between PG1 and PG2 and R1 and R2 (Heffner to Valenti, May 5, 1980, in Heffner, "Reminiscences," box 1).[8] At the same time, many of the discussions regarding a rating between PG and R were also conflated with other suggested changes to the system, including a rating between R and X and the inclusion of brief, one-word descriptions explaining to parents why a movie had received a certain rating. However, Heffner's chief concern was the "no man's land" between PG and R, which by the 1980s were virtually the only two ratings used since fewer and fewer G-rated films were being made and no Hollywood producer would release an X-rated film.

In May 1981, Jack Valenti circulated a draft of a proposed press release that would change the rating system by adding a PG/13 rating between PG and R that would restrict children under thirteen from attending without a parent or guardian and an NC rating between R and X that would serve essentially the same function as the X (no children under seventeen would be admitted) but without that rating's stigma of pornography. Earlier that month, the National Association of Theater Owners, the MPAA, and Independent Film Distributors had circulated a draft of a statement calling for a new M rating between PG and R, the lowering of the restrictive age limit for R from seventeen to sixteen, and the replacement of the X rating with a less-stigmatizing Adult-A rating (Draft Statement by the National Association of Theater Owners, the Motion Picture Association of America, and Independent Film Distributors, May 8, 1981, in Heffner, "Reminiscences," box 1). By November 1981, the M rating between PG and R had been dropped and was instead being used between R and X to rate "those films whose depictions of violence, sensuality, language or combination of these elements, go beyond the range of the 'R' but do not in the judgment of the Rating Board invade the 'X' category" (Heffner to Valenti, December 11, 1981, in Heffner, "Reminiscences," box 1, 1). However, these changes were never made; according to a letter from Frank E. Rosenfelt, chief executive officer of MGM, the idea of an M rating had been suggested and rejected by the MPAA board of directors (Rosenfelt to Heffner, December 31, 1981, in Heffner, "Reminiscences," box 1).

Thus, the idea of an interstitial teenage rating had been kicking around the industry for a decade, with at least a few moments in which it had been seriously considered. However, its ultimate implementation in the summer of 1984—the first addition to the MPAA rating system since its inception in 1968—was the result of specific industrial and cultural circumstances in the mid-1980s. While some people had thought that, if there were to ever be any changes to the rating system, they would "come slowly and softly, creeping in the back door" (Harmetz, "Movie Ratings"), the implementation of the PG-13 rating was almost dizzying in its suddenness, especially after so many years of Jack Valenti and the MPAA board of directors refusing to yield on the issue.[9]

According to Steven Spielberg, he was the instigator of the rating's creation. In one interview, he even said, "I created the problem and I also supplied the solution. . . . I invented the rating" (qtd. in Breznican). This is, of course, an exaggeration, since the idea of the PG-13 rating or something similar had been discussed among industry insiders for a decade. However, it is not far-fetched to believe that a filmmaker of Spielberg's power and influence could have been instrumental in getting the gears moving to make practice out of theory. Spielberg agreed with the criticisms that were being leveled at the violence in *Temple of Doom* and *Gremlins*—not so much that the violence didn't belong or that it was too extreme for the subject matter but that the films should have been labeled in such a way that parents had a better understanding of what they contained. He was also concerned about the PG rating that had been given to *Poltergeist,* even though he had been involved in ensuring that it received that rating. Spielberg had personally driven Heffner to the airport after the *Poltergeist* appeal and told Heffner that he felt there should be some kind of rating between PG and R (Heffner to Spielberg, July 23, 1982, in Heffner, "Reminiscences," box 1). In early 1984, Spielberg and Heffner exchanged a series of letters and met for lunch to discuss the need for a rating between PG and R (Heffner, "RDH Pre–Oral History Memo 1984," box 2, 23). After the intensely negative reactions to the PG-rated *Temple of Doom* and *Gremlins,* Spielberg personally called Valenti and suggested that the PG-13 rating be created (Breznican; Matloff 80).

Serious discussion within the MPAA about the creation of a new rating began less than a month after the release of *Indiana Jones and the Temple of Doom* and only a few weeks after the release of *Gremlins.* By early June, the decision had already been made to create the PG-13 rating, although Jack Valenti formally announced on June 25 that he planned to hold a meeting with studios, distributors, and exhibitors for the sole purpose of discussing the creation of the new rating (Sanello, "New PG-13 Movie Rating Likely"). According to Valenti at the time, the new rating would "contain more information and a strong admonitory caution so parents will know if the movie is something more than PG and less than R" (qtd. in Sanello, "New PG-13 Movie Rating Likely"). Earlier in the month, news had leaked that the MPAA was planning on a new rating, but at that time it was understood that the rating would be restrictive (meaning that no one under thirteen could attend the film without a parent or adult guardian) rather than simply advisory, which ultimately caused some confusion with viewers as to what the PG-13 rating meant. On June 27, Valenti and Joel Resnick, president of the National Association of Theater Owners, made a joint announcement that any films submitted to CARA after July 1 would be eligible for the new PG-13 rating (Sanello, "New PG-13 Film Rating Hits Theaters"). Just over a month later, on August 10, the hyperviolent, hyperpatriotic *Red Dawn,* whose extensive and bloody violence would have warranted an R rating a month earlier, became the first film to be released theatrically with a PG-13.[10]

The Meaning of PG-13

In "Movie Ratings as Genre," Kevin S. Sandler argues that the controversy over the R rating given to *Cruising* in 1980 was "an isolated case" and that "no other MPAA-distributed or NATO-exhibited film since, not even *Natural Born Killers* (1994), has dramatically undermined the industry's system of self-regulation and commitment to respectable entertainment" (210). While this is generally true in the sense of R-rated versus NC-17-rated films, the controversy over the PG ratings awarded to *Indiana Jones and the Temple of Doom* and *Gremlins* called into serious question the industry's system of self-regulation because it revealed a division between what kinds of screen violence parents and the members of CARA felt were appropriate in a PG-rated film. Thus, the creation of the PG-13 rating was really about three things: (1) attempting to resolve the complexities of screen violence, (2) fully embracing the teenage marketplace by creating another brand name that marked the product, and, most important, (3) avoiding conflict while still protecting the industry's profit potential.

The creation of the PG-13 rating was largely about resolving the disparity between the simultaneous popularity of screen violence and reservations about its supposed nefarious effects on small children. CARA seemed to have successfully resolved the boundaries between what constituted R-rated sexuality and PG-rated sexuality, but that line had not been clearly demarcated in regard to screen violence. For example, Reverend Wall, editor of the *Christian Century*, complained, "PG means there are bad words in it. It doesn't cover nonstop violence. It's reprehensible" (qtd. in Bronson and Hawkins).

In the case of *Indiana Jones and the Temple of Doom* and *Gremlins*, the all-important context of the films' violence came into play, although that was rarely mentioned in the press. It is arguable that the controversy around those films and their inappropriateness within the strictures of a PG rating had less to do with the isolated moments of graphic violence (the heart being ripped out, the gremlin being diced in the blender) than with the general tone of both films. *Temple of Doom* is a dark, foreboding film, especially compared to *Raiders of the Lost Ark*, and *Gremlins* is essentially a black comedy that mercilessly lampoons traditional American values and Christmas spirit à la *It's a Wonderful Life*. This is something that both George Lucas and Steven Spielberg recognized, and in response to the outcry over *Temple of Doom*, they issued a joint statement that read in part, "'Indy' is less violent than 'Raiders,' but it's more intense. A story with children in jeopardy is going to get a more emotional reaction than a story with Indiana Jones battling Nazis" (qtd. in Canby, "PG Says Less").

Both *Temple of Doom* and *Gremlins* also defied the boundaries of what parents thought they could expect in terms of violent content from a film associated with Steven Spielberg, whose name brought its own set of connotations and expectations. Of course, Spielberg, like the other wunderkinds of the New Hollywood, has a notable history of working with screen violence, particularly in his breakthrough film *Jaws*.[11]

However, despite the gore in *Jaws*, Spielberg's association with his then most recent film, the blockbuster *E.T.*, seemed to have wiped the audience's memory and situated Spielberg within the collective cultural mindset as a single-minded purveyor of safe, hopeful family entertainment. Therefore, *Temple of Doom* and *Gremlins* were seen as rebellious shockers from Hollywood's perennial favorite man-child genius, which is what made them so disconcerting to those both inside and outside the industry. They were uncanny in that they didn't fit into any categories. They broke boundaries in a way that other blockbusters hadn't; it was as if the goose that laid the golden egg was suddenly biting at its master's hand. Despite Jack Valenti's claims that CARA doesn't give preference to particular filmmakers or films, it's hard not to imagine that the board members were more lenient on rating Spielberg's films and that, had *Gremlins* been directed by David Cronenberg or Wes Craven, it would have been rated R.[12]

Thus, it was screen violence that was at the forefront of everyone's mind in the summer of 1984 when the PG-13 rating was created. This was widely acknowledged in both press reports and in the rhetoric used by Valenti and other film industry officials. When United Press International entertainment reporter Frank Sanello wrote about the introduction of the PG-13 rating, he described it as being intended, according to movie officials, "to warn parents that a film may be too violent for children under 13" ("New PG-13 Film Rating Hits Theaters").

Professed intentions about warning parents aside, the PG-13 rating turned out to be a brilliant marketing device for the film industry because it allowed filmmakers and studios to fully embrace the profitable teenage marketplace by creating another brand name with which they could package their products. Particularly to older children and adolescents, a film's rating is a crucial label that marks a film as being desirable or not. G-rated movies are not desirable to teenagers because they carry with them the connotation of being a "kid's movie." Part of growing up and shedding childhood is taking part in activities marked as "adult," and one of the easiest and most obvious activities is watching "adult" films. Thus, a PG- or PG-13-rated movie will immediately seem more desirable to adolescents than one that bears a G rating.

Once the rating system became part of the collective cultural mindset, the industry began to realize that the G rating, while fine for films aimed at very small children, was an obstacle to marketing films to older children and adolescents. To some extent, this flew in the face of the reality of the movie marketplace. During the first decade of the rating system, from 1969 to 1979, PG-rated films had the highest success ratio at the box office (26.7 percent), followed not by R-rated films, as producers seem to think, but rather by G-rated films (24.2 percent success ratio). During this time period, R-rated films had a success ratio of only 13.7 percent, almost half that of PG-rated films (Austin, Nicolich, and Simonet 28). Nevertheless, the production of G-rated films in the United States dropped off sharply throughout the decade, from eighty-one in 1969 to twenty-two in 1979. The resistance to the G rating on anything other than clearly defined "children's films" was so strong by the early 1980s that filmmakers often went out of their way to include just enough "adult" material to garner a PG rating in a film that would otherwise be G-rated. For example, in both *Annie* (1982) and *E.T.*, a few select obscenities were added in order to get a more market-friendly PG-rating (Sanello, "New PG-13 Movie Rating Likely"). When CARA rated the Oscar-winning British film *Chariots of Fire* (1981) G, the film's producer, David Puttnam, wrote a letter to Richard Heffner complaining about the rating and the fact that he now felt the need to add additional language, which would "compromise the quality of a film that has been three years in the making" in order to get a more marketable PG rating. In his letter, Puttnam wrote, "You will be better versed than I in the rationale as how a G rating can adversely affect an adult picture, and, irritating though it must be to you, I would have hoped that as members of the same industry, you would have accepted an obligation to help those films of merit which fall into this problem area" (Puttnam to Heffner, June 15, 1981, in Heffner, "Reminiscences," box 1).

Because the G rating had come to automatically signal a "children's film" and X-rated films were simply not financially feasible after the early 1970s, there were essentially two ratings for the vast majority of mainstream feature films until 1984: PG and R. Of the 342 films rated by CARA in 1983, the year before the controversy that led to the creation of the PG-13 rating, 11 films were rated G, 123 rated PG, 207 rated R, and 1 rated X (Bronson and Hawkins). Thus, 96 percent of all studio films released theatrically were rated either PG or R, and the variety of content in those 330 films was enormous. For example, in 1983 alone, the PG rating was able to contain a family-oriented film such as *A Christmas Story*, whose only "adult content" was the mostly suggested use of curse words that were cleverly replaced with stand-in nonsensical words (or, in the case of the dreaded "f-word," the word "fudge"), and *Jaws 3-D*, which featured such gory images as a severed arm floating underwater (in 3-D, no less, so that the severed stump was literally right in the audience's face), a decomposing, half-eaten corpse, and several scenes of characters being eaten whole by the titular shark. On the far end of the R-rated spectrum in 1983, there were films such as *Scarface*, which featured a record number of uses of the word "fuck" in addition to extreme levels of violence, including a character being dismembered by a chainsaw (mostly offscreen), and *Videodrome*, which featured a litany of David Cronenberg's trademark disturbing imagery, including a shot of James Woods reaching his hand into a gaping, vagina-like wound in his stomach.

By creating the PG-13 rating, then, the MPAA not only developed another marker of film content, which allowed it to maintain the veneer of moral responsibility in an increasingly conservative culture, but in the process created a specific teenage niche for the film industry. On the surface, the MPAA created a label that was meant to "warn parents," thus fulfilling the industry's public obligations to protect children, but actually it functioned to attract adolescents with the siren call of illicit content. "In effect, if not intent, PG-13 exacerbates generational tensions, warning the parent while seducing the child" (Mundy).

Just as it had when it raised the age limit of the R rating from sixteen to seventeen in 1970 in order to allow the R rating to absorb content that would have previously been rated X (Sandler), the MPAA allowed the PG-13 rating to absorb content that, prior to 1984, would have resulted in an R rating. In reality, then, the PG-13 rating actually made *more* illicit content available to younger viewers. Of course, Valenti and other officials explicitly denied this, as it would negate the public perception of why the PG-13 rating was created in the first place. But, the fact that there were concerns about the levels of screen violence allowed in *Red Dawn*, the very first film released with a PG-13 rating, suggests otherwise.

As mentioned earlier, the PG-13 rating did not restrict anyone from entering the theater; thus, the MPAA could avoid conflict and protect the industry's profit potential at the same time. There is no reason why the rating couldn't have been restrictive as it was originally intended, thus barring anyone under the age of thirteen from attending a PG-13-rated film without an accompanying adult, but the choice was clearly made to make the rating advisory rather than restrictive, thereby ensuring that anyone could still attend. In fact, Valenti wanted such films to be perceived as having a restricted rating, even though it was not. At one point, he told Heffner, "Talk about it as a restricted rating, because then the public will feel that we didn't do them in," and when Heffner refused, Valenti threatened to "get another Rating Board" (in Heffner, "RDH Pre–Oral History Memo 1984," box 2, 36, 45).

As applied, there was no downside to a film being rated PG-13; it was the best of both worlds. Parents were given the perception of protection by the industry, while adolescents were given the opportunity to indulge in material that they would have been barred from seeing the year before. There is an old B-movie saying: "An older child will *not* watch anything a younger child will watch, but a younger child will watch *anything* an older child will watch" (Breznican). In this sense, PG-13 was the perfect brand to suggest a film that has edge but is still attainable by any child. Profit potential is thus protected, and if a child is in any way traumatized by material in a PG-13-rated film, the industry's moral obligation is covered because it has dutifully warned parents to be cautioned.

It is not surprising that PG-13 is now the rating that every blockbuster movie aims for. The PG rating has become the new G rating in that it doesn't suggest any edge. According to Steven Spielberg, "In a way it's better to get a PG-13 than a PG for certain movies. Sometimes PG, unless it's for an animated movie, it turns a lot of younger people off. They think it's going to be too below their radar and they tend to want to say, 'Well, PG-13 might have a little bit of hot sauce on it'" (qtd. in Breznican). And Spielberg would know: Of the seventeen movies he's directed since the creation of the PG-13 rating, more than half of them (ten) have been rated PG-13. And, if one doesn't consider his four R-rated adult films (*Schindler's List*, 1993; *Amistad*, 1997; *Saving Private Ryan*, 1998; *Munich*, 2005), then more than three-quarters of his post-1984 films have achieved the desired PG-13 rating, and he hasn't directed a PG-rated film since 1991. It is probably also worth noting that his three PG-rated films of that era—*Empire of the Sun* (1987), *Always* (1989), and *Hook* (1991)—were the least successful at the box office.

In the end, the creation of the PG-13 rating is just one more instance in the long history of Hollywood's tug-of-war between the desire to include illicit content and the need to avoid controversy, a struggle that dates back to the very beginnings of the cinema. This particular episode highlighted the inherent problem of the MPAA rating system, which relies on the ability to quantify particular kinds of content as a means of categorizing films in terms of age appropriateness, and the complexities of screen violence, which resist simple quantification and description. Such complexity includes not only the myriad forms in which screen violence can be presented visually and aurally but also the narrative and thematic context in which it is embedded and external factors associated with it, such as the reputation of the filmmaker and the film's genre.

The primary lesson Hollywood learned during the creation of the PG-13 rating and throughout the decade of the 1980s was that violence sells, just not too much of it. With the right context, the right filmmaker, and the appropriate rating, screen violence could be immensely profitable. The trick was finding just the right amount of hot sauce.

CONCLUSION

FASHIONING A NEW SCREEN VIOLENCE FROM THE OLD IN THE 1990S

IN THE INTRODUCTION, I noted that the 1980s closed with a series of blockbuster action movies—*Batman, Indiana Jones and the Last Crusade,* and *Lethal Weapon 2*—that topped the box-office charts in the summer of 1989 and epitomized how the major Hollywood studios tended to treat screen violence throughout the 1980s: as one of many components in a high-concept package explicitly designed to attract as many of the most sought-after demographic as possible while simultaneously avoiding controversy and public outcry. Each of these three films is a slick, polished, well-crafted action vehicle with big stars, big budgets, and at best minimal attention paid to the real-life consequences of their many violent actions. *Batman*'s hyperbolic, film-noir-on-steroids vision of a world infested with crime is not terribly far removed from *Indiana Jones*'s cartoonish Nazi villains and *Lethal Weapon 2*'s nefarious South African diplomat-criminals. Each film is bulging with violent action and death, yet by 1989 such content was expected, if not routine, in Hollywood productions.

Yet, 1989, the same year that gave us the largely trouble-free, audience-pleasing violence of *Batman, Indiana Jones,* and *Lethal Weapon,* also produced a handful of studio-produced films that suggested a return to a more troubling and thought-provoking use of violence on the big screen. If one had to mark a specific moment when it seemed that the tide might turn, it would have to be the premiere of Spike Lee's incendiary *Do the Right Thing* at the Cannes Film Festival. Lee had made one independently financed film (1986's *She's Gotta Have It*) and one studio film for Columbia that was unceremoniously dumped in theaters (1988's *School Daze*), so it was something of a gamble that Universal Studios, which had a pair of top 10 box-office hits in 1989 with *Back to the Future Part II* and *Parenthood*, was willing to finance and distribute *Do the Right Thing*, even on its modest budget. It was a film that had great potential for generating the kind of controversy the studios had mostly avoided since the first few years of the 1980s;[1] in fact, one could argue that Lee designed the film specifically to evoke controversy, which is exactly what it did.

The divisiveness the film created among viewers is neatly encapsulated in the opening paragraph of the liner notes Roger Ebert wrote for the film's release on laser disc by the Criterion Collection:

> Leaving the theater after the tumultuous world premiere of *Do the Right Thing* at Cannes in May of 1989, I found myself too shaken to speak, and I avoided the clusters of people where arguments were already heating up. One American critic was so angry she chased me to the exit to inform me, "This film is a call to racial violence!" I thought not. I thought it was a call to empathy, which of all human qualities is the one this past century seemed most to need.

That *Do the Right Thing* could be understood by one viewer as a "call to racial violence" and another as "a call to empathy" is evidence of its profoundly complex nature, which finds its fullest realization in the violent climax in which the death of an African American youth at the hands of white police officers tips the film's boiling racial tensions into a full-scale riot. When answering questions from the press following the film's screening at Cannes, Lee summarized his approach to cinema in a way that both immediately reverberates with the troubling 1970s-era cinema of Scorsese, Coppola, Altman, and others and also rejects the primary thrust of the majority of mainstream Hollywood cinema: "It isn't the job of movie makers to offer solutions. All we can do is to present the problems" (qtd. in Canby, "Spike Lee"). Thus, while Bruce Wayne, Indiana Jones, and Martin Riggs were solving the country's problems with violence, Lee was presenting it as a question to be pondered.

In *Do the Right Thing*, which takes place over a single blistering hot summer day in a small area of the Bedford-Stuyvesant section of Brooklyn, Lee uses violence—physical, verbal, and emotional—to examine the boiling-point nature of race relations. Throughout the film, Lee plays with the film's tone by shifting between elements of comedy and drama, even as he constantly raises the tension among the primary characters. It all explodes at the end when a race riot arguably instigated by Mookie (played by Lee himself), the film's most roundly sympathetic and likable character, results in the complete destruction of a popular and long-standing pizzeria owned by an Italian American family in the predominantly African American neighborhood. Like everything in the film, the precise meaning of these violent actions is left vague and open-ended. In other words, Lee used violence to provoke discussion in his viewers, to drive at controversial issues that don't have simple, neat, or clean answers. As he put it, "I don't make the kind of movie that is going to be a Walt Disney–Steven Spielberg view of life. We don't have everybody joining hands and singing, 'We're all God's children.' Color always has and will play a part. It shouldn't, but in the real world it does make a difference, no matter what people say" (qtd. in Van Gelder).

However, *Do the Right Thing* was not the only film released in 1989 that suggested that the door was creaking open and allowing a wider expanse of possibilities for screen violence in mainstream Hollywood films. Oliver Stone directed *Born on the Fourth of July*, which did literal violence to romanticized notions of the American spirit in telling the true-life story of Ron Kovic, whose experiences fighting in Vietnam and his subsequent treatment by both the government and his family and friends when he returned home paralyzed changed him from an all-American idealist to one of the most notable antiwar activists. *The War of the Roses*, Danny DeVito's unexpectedly dark and financially successful black comedy about a marriage gone terribly sour, uses violence not only to satirize the cherished institution of marriage (made all the more striking by DeVito's subversive casting of stars Michael Douglas and Kathleen Turner, who had played the romantic leads in 1984's *Romancing the Stone* and its 1985 sequel, *The Jewel of the Nile*) but also to make a strong statement about the nature of materialism. While the film shows how far people who have pledged their lives together will sink when they grow to hate each other, the core of the conflict is the fact that their happiness together hinges on the material life they have built rather than on a genuine emotional connection. Thus, filmmakers like Lee, Stone, DeVito, and David Lynch—who shocked audiences a year later with his graphically violent crime-romance *Wild at Heart* (1990), the same year that Martin Scorsese returned to full form with his stylishly brutal mafia saga *GoodFellas* (1990) after making mostly nonviolent films throughout the 1980s—slowly but surely worked their way into the cracks of the dominant Hollywood ideology and used various forms of screen violence to challenge audience expectations and responses.

Even though the majority of films released by the Hollywood studios during the 1980s suggest that the industry was trying to contain screen violence in order to avoid controversy and protect the studios' profit potential, whether it was through the win-at-all-costs conservative ideological framework of the pure action film, the marginalization of the subversive horror genre, or the creation of the PG-13 rating to help push the responsibility of protecting children away from the industry and onto parents, such efforts were ultimately doomed to failure because screen violence in all its various manifestations is, by its very nature, uncontainable. In fact, by trying so hard to restrict screen violence—to control its excesses, limit its subversive potential, and otherwise keep it contained within a set of parameters defined by the worldview of a conservative cultural mindset—the Hollywood studios unwittingly opened the door for an even more violent and ideologically unruly cinema, one fueled by fiery independent filmmakers working on the edges of the industry. As Judy Stone, film critic from the *San Francisco Chronicle*, noted in her yearly roundup at the end of 1989, "Independent spirits made their mark everywhere this year—from those tearing down the Berlin Wall to the inventive film makers breaking down big-budget barriers. Although not all of the imaginative, low-budget films appear on the Top 10 lists, it's remarkable how many movies made with sheer determination, comparatively few bucks and lots of true grit have caused critics and audiences to take notice in 1989."

Independent filmmakers and distributors have forever been the bane of those in control of the U.S. film industry because they show how the mechanics of control can be, if not truly subverted, at least bypassed under the right conditions. Independence from the Hollywood studio system is a strange tie that binds, bringing together serious-minded artists and exploitative opportunists into a single category defined simply by their outsider status. In the big picture, there is little difference among the pioneering studio-era exploitation filmmakers who, unencumbered by the need to abide by the strictures of the Production Code, dealt with "taboo" or "forbidden" subject matter (Schaefer); trash auteurs like John Waters who didn't care about having their films rated by the MPAA and mined the fringes of popular culture in the 1960s and 1970s to feed midnight audiences with explicit sex, violence, and humor; and provocative contemporary filmmakers like Abel Ferrara whose independently produced films are constantly pushing the boundaries of otherwise conventional genres. All of these filmmakers have in common the simple fact that they supply what Hollywood doesn't, and since the consolidation of U.S. filmmaking into an industry in the 1920s, there has always been a demand for something different. Thus, the attempts by the major studios to maintain control over representations of violence throughout the 1980s eventually had the opposite effect by propelling more extreme depictions of screen violence into the arena of "art cinema," which then influenced the depictions of screen violence in studio films.

In the late 1980s and early 1990s, independent studios reemerged as a viable market force to contend with the hegemony of the major Hollywood studios, arguably for the first time since the "instant majors" in the late 1960s. As Thomas Schatz has argued, this has created a governing paradox of the New Hollywood of the 1990s: "the consolidation of power by a cartel of global media conglomerates geared to franchise-scale blockbusters on the one hand, and the steadily increasing diversification, fragmentation and localization of both media products and media audiences on the other" ("Introduction" 8). While the 1980s is often thought of as an era of complete corporate dominance, independent production of films that played in the mainstream movie marketplace saw a significant increase during the later years of the Reagan era. For example, the number of independently produced films submitted to the MPAA for a rating rose from 193 in 1986, to 277 in 1987, to 393 in 1988 (Wyatt, "Formation" 74), and "independent majors" such as Miramax and New Line became viable market forces, partially because they embraced the kinds of controversy from which the major studios had been running and found a way to market it.

Miramax, in particular, made its name in the late 1980s and early 1990s by "selling a product which lends itself to media-induced controversy" (Wyatt, "Formation" 80). Several foreign films distributed in the United States by Miramax, including *Scandal* (1989), *The Cook, the Thief, His Wife, and Her Lover* (1989), and *Tie Me Up! Tie Me Down!* (*¡Átame!*, 1990), ran into problems securing an R rating from the MPAA due to their explicit sexual content, which would have been seen as a significant problem by a major studio. Miramax, however, used the conflict to its advantage to raise awareness of these films, which might have otherwise been mired on the margins of art cinema, available only to those cineastes with the wherewithal to seek them out. Each of these films was the subject of a certain amount of controversy, with many conservative pundits using them as examples of how morally subversive content can masquerade as "art." Justin Wyatt suggests that Miramax "has thrived due to its marketing savvy, particularly the ability to apply 'exploitation' techniques to art house product" (83). Such techniques were perfectly timed to offer something different and unique in response to the control of content exercised by the conservative commercial dictates of the studios throughout the 1980s.

Not surprisingly, the studios couldn't sit back and allow independent filmmakers and distributors to define American cinema throughout the 1990s, so they flexed their muscle by buying the most successful independents. Independent cinema became "a victim of its own success" (Schamus 103) as the major studios slowly but surely brought the independents into the fold throughout the 1990s, allowing them to maintain an outward aura of autonomy but keeping them firmly within the control of Hollywood's collective worldview (see Wyatt, "Formation" 84–87). In a span of four years in the mid-1990s, all the significant independent distributors had been bought by major studios, beginning in 1993 with Disney's purchase of Miramax and Turner Broadcasting's purchase of New Line and ending in 1997 with Universal's purchase of October Films. Major studios that weren't able to buy up one of those distributors were not to be left out, as they created their own "independent" divisions, such as Paramount Classics and Sony Pictures Classics, to produce and distribute smaller films that are routinely described as "independent." While the studios claimed in press releases that the purchasing of these independent distributors was their way of broadening their product line to reach more audiences, it was also a way of reasserting control over the marketplace, thus illustrating the tenuous nature of the long-standing balancing act the major studios have played in trying to cash in on audience desire for edgier films while also restricting the indulgence of such desires lest it lead to too much controversy.

Many of the most notable and economically successful independent films of the early 1990s engaged screen violence in a way that most films had not for the past decade. These independently produced films featured what B. Ruby Rich termed "neo-violence" that was often ideologically complicated and always aesthetically brutal. In many ways, they were reminiscent of the hard-edged films of the 1970s, but amplified. In the United States, Abel Ferrara's *Bad Lieutenant* (1992) and Quentin Tarantino's *Reservoir Dogs* (1992) arguably led the way, and these were soon joined by increasingly violent and disturbing studio-produced films, including Joel Schumacher's *Falling Down* (1993), Tony Scott's *True Romance* (1993), Allen and Albert Hughes's *Menace II Society* (1993), Oliver Stone's *Natural Born Killers*, Kathryn Bigelow's *Strange Days* (1995), and David Fincher's *Seven* (1995). Steven Spielberg also gravitated toward increasingly graphic and troubling forms of historical realist screen violence in *Schindler's List*, a rare mainstream studio film to tackle the Holocaust; *Amistad*, which deals with the brutal realities of the American slave trade; and *Saving Private Ryan*, which helped reignite interest in World War II. All of these films feature levels of disturbing graphic violence that led many industry insiders to question whether their R ratings were a direct result of Spielberg's power and influence in the industry. Yet, all three films were also made in close proximity to the audience-pleasing, blockbuster-style screen violence of Spielberg's *Jurassic Park* movies (one in 1993 and one in 1997). This suggests that Spielberg was self-consciously straddling a divide, continuing to produce enjoyable blockbuster-style screen mayhem while also experimenting with the limits of violent representation as a way of bringing some of recent history's darkest days to the big screen. Even though critics took Spielberg's historical films to task on many levels, they nonetheless represent a crucial willingness on the part of major studios to fund such troubling films. As Ed Guerrero writes, the force of both *Schindler's List* and *Amistad* "resides in [their] visual shock value, and in those resistant images, currents, and arguments that escape the policing of Hollywood's liberal, paternalist discourse" (224).

In a sense, the 1990s was like a return to the 1970s in which brash young filmmakers fought to make a name for themselves by "reinventing" American cinema, often by reworking traditional representations of violence while mainstream filmmakers turned out audience-pleasing disaster epics and action movies. And, like in the 1970s, the innovative American filmmakers were often inspired by foreign films, which, in turn, had been inspired by classical American films. These violent films challenged audiences' expectations and caused a great deal of ink to be spilled on editorial and op-ed pages in newspapers and magazines either praising or decrying their deployment of screen violence. Returning to the point at which this book began, the April 1, 1991, issue of *Newsweek* summed it up well with its eye-grabbing cover that stated "Violence Goes Mainstream: Movies, Music, Books—Are There Any Limits Left?"

Chief among the new American purveyors of screen violence was Quentin Tarantino, whose *Reservoir Dogs* and *Pulp Fiction* (1994) were heralded as new masterpieces of a gritty, ironic, and extremely violent crime genre. Tarantino, a former video store clerk with an encyclopedic knowledge of cinematic ephemera ranging from obscure film noir, to Hong Kong martial arts films, to exploitation classics, became the poster boy for the new violence of the American art cinema, which was a self-conscious reworking of the screen violence that had revolutionized American filmmaking in the late 1960s and early 1970s. In writing about *Reservoir Dogs*, for example, critics repeatedly compared it to films of that era. Todd McCarthy, writing for *Variety*, noted influences coming from Martin Scorsese's *Mean Streets* and specifically pointed out the similarities of the criminals in *Reservoir Dogs* emerging from the restaurant during the credit sequence to the titular group in Sam Peckinpah's *The Wild Bunch*. He also compared Tarantino's bloody and ironic ending to Sergio Leone's spaghetti westerns *For a Few Dollars More* and, especially, *The Good, the Bad, and the Ugly*.

Other films of this period also consciously evoked the violent films of the 1970s. Director Tamra Davis explained her 1992 film *Guncrazy* as having less to do with its namesake, Joseph H. Lewis's 1949 noir classic, than with Arthur Penn's *Bonnie and Clyde* and Terrence Malick's *Badlands* (1973), the latter of which was already a self-conscious reworking of the criminal-couple-on-the-run myth (Rich). These comparisons extended to foreign films, as well, particularly John Woo's *The Killer* (*Dip huet seung hung*, 1989) and *Hard Boiled* (*Lat sau san taam*, 1992), which were seen as hyperkinetic extensions of Sam Peckinpah's violent stylistics. Woo then imported his style of violent aesthetics to the United States in films such as *Hard Target* (1993), which ran into trouble with the Rating Board due to its graphic violence, *Broken Arrow* (1996), and *Face/Off* (1997). On another front, a wave of young African American filmmakers such as John Singleton (*Boyz N the Hood*, 1991), Allen and Albert Hughes (*Menace II Society*), and Mario Van Peebles (*New Jack City*, 1991) began translating the violence of the ghetto into its own genre (Guerrero). These ghettocentric films were very much like the violent films of the 1970s in that, for the most part, their filmmakers were genuinely interested in using the cinema to explore the complex webs of social violence that informed their subjects, but their films could just as easily be seen as thrilling and escapist.

The violence in the films by Tarantino and many others of the early 1990s has been referred to as "new violence" or "neo-violence," and it has been seen as particularly characteristic of a postmodern age in which style is elevated over narrative and thematic coherence, morality, and even meaning. The new violence of the 1990s has been defined primarily by its technical and stylistic sophistication and its self-consciousness. And, while many scholars (for example, Giroux; Prince, *Savage Cinema*; and Sobchack) have largely decried this "new violence," placing it in opposition to the "socially meaningful screen violence" of the late 1960s, it was not really "new" at all. Rather, it was a logical reformulation of trends in screen violence that have been with the cinema since its origins.

Hollywood's attempts to package screen violence in order to avoid controversy throughout the 1980s constituted a form of repression that was bound to erupt at some point, which it did in the early 1990s with a rash of independently produced "art house" movies that effectively replaced sex with graphic violence as their source of appeal (Rich). The primary distinction here, and the moment at which the screen violence of the 1980s morphed into the screen violence of the 1990s, has less to do with direct representation—that is, the style of the violence, which is what most critics have focused on—and more to do with the openness of the content. Rather than trying to downplay these films' violence, filmmakers and producers made it the central selling point, which kicked off a fresh round of debate and controversies—exactly what the studios had largely avoided during the previous decade.

So, as the 1980s began in controversy regarding screen violence, so did the 1990s, and the cycle continues.

Notes
Works Cited
Index

Notes

Introduction: The Mainstreaming of Hollywood Screen Violence

1. The eight major studios during the 1980s were Columbia, Disney, MGM/UA, Orion, Paramount, 20th Century-Fox, Universal, and Warner Bros.

2. For example, following the success of *Beverly Hills Cop* (1984), Don Simpson and Jerry Bruckheimer were signed to a long-term deal with Paramount Pictures. Brian Grazer signed a deal with Tri-Star Pictures following the success of *Splash* (1984), and Aaron Russo, who produced *Trading Places* (1983), made a $72 million multifilm deal with Producers Sales Organization, an independent production/distribution company that was vying for mainstream success (Ansen, "Producer").

3. *An American Werewolf in London* earned just over $30 million at the domestic box office and became the twenty-third highest grossing film of 1981. It was the only horror movie to place in the top 25 box-office earners that year, likely due to Landis's previous success with the youth-oriented comedies *National Lampoon's Animal House* (1978) and *The Blues Brothers* (1980).

1. A Bloody Renaissance: Screen Violence and the Rise of the New Hollywood Auteurs

1. Most other notable examples of graphic violence in silent-era films come from other countries, such as Danish director Benjamin Christensen's *Häxan* (*The Witch*, 1922), which includes memorably gruesome reenactments of witch-scare stories. One of the scenes shows a witch pulling a rotting, dismembered hand from a bundle of sticks and snapping off a finger to make a potion, while another scene shows a demon holding aloft a dead baby that he then proceeds to bleed into a cauldron (the impact of which is somewhat diminished by the patent fakery of a doll substituting for the baby). Another example is Sergei Eisenstein's *Potemkin* (1926), whose famous Odessa Steps sequence features a brief but graphic image of a woman who has been shot in the eye.

2. The original 1968 set of classifications—G for general audiences, M for mature audiences, R for restricted to those under sixteen without an accompanying adult, and X restricted to anyone under sixteen—was revised several times. In 1970, the M rating was changed to GP, then changed again in 1972 to PG (parental guidance suggested). Around the same time, the R

and X ratings had their age limits raised to seventeen. In 1984, the PG-13 rating (may by unsuitable for children under thirteen) was added as an in-between rating for those movies that were beyond PG material but not quite R (for a more in-depth discussion of this rating, see chapter 6). Finally, in 1990, the un-copyrighted X rating, which had become synonymous with pornography and was therefore deemed no longer commercially viable for Hollywood productions, was replaced with the copyrighted NC-17 rating, although this move was strictly symbolic and ultimately had little effect on the industry's output.

3. To put this astoundingly low number in better perspective, Hollywood's all-time high weekly attendance was 78.2 million in 1946.

4. This is the primary reason why Stanley Kubrick's proposed biopic of Napoleon, which was supposed to follow his critical and commercial hit *2001: A Space Odyssey* (1968), fizzled at several studios and never saw the light of day. Instead, he went on to make *A Clockwork Orange* (1971), one of the seminal violent films of the early 1970s.

5. While there was no nudity in the early Hammer films, Boot describes the sexual suggestiveness of the films in terms of "milky white bosoms and throats exposed for biting, and lots of orgasmic gasping at the moment of penetration" (89–90).

6. *The Curse of Frankenstein*, which was distributed worldwide by Warner Bros., made $5 million. The film's budget was a mere $160,000 (McCarty 22).

7. When the reviews first came out, they were almost uniformly negative, and even those critics who wrote positively about the movie as a whole still had negative things to say about Marion's murder. Philip T. Hartung of *Commonweal* called the shower scene "one of the bloodiest scenes ever shown in a movie" (469); Moira Walsh of *America* said it was "the bloodiest bathtub murder in screen history," suggesting that Hitchcock's "chief sources" of subject matter were "Krafft-Ebing and the Marquis de Sade"; an unnamed critic at *Time* described it as "one of the messiest, most nauseating murders ever filmed" ("Cinema"); and Stanley Kauffman, writing for the *New Republic*, called the two murders in *Psycho* "among the most vicious I have ever seen in films, with Hitchcock employing his considerable skill . . . to shock us past horror-entertainment into resentment " (22). Writing in the *Nation*, Robert Hatch did little to conceal his feelings about the film: "I am shocked, in the sense that I am offended and disgusted." Bosley Crowther of the *New York Times* warned, "You had better have a pretty strong stomach and be prepared for a couple of grisly shocks when you go see Alfred Hitchcock's 'Psycho.'" Despite these negative reviews, the film was a box-office hit, earning $15 million in domestic rentals alone and breaking opening day attendance records in Boston, Philadelphia, and Chicago (Rebello 161).

8. This was the first (but hardly the last) time one of Steven Spielberg's films was given a lesser rating than many thought it deserved. In 1984, the PG rating given to *Indiana Jones and the Temple of Doom*, ostensibly an ac-

tion movie aimed at kids, helped spur the MPAA to create the PG-13 rating (which will be discussed in depth in chapter 6), and many complained that, had a less powerful director made *Saving Private Ryan* (1998), its graphically violent war sequences would have earned an NC-17 rating.

2. Retreating from the World of Revolution: Controversies over Screen Violence at the Dawn of the Reagan Era

1. *Sorcerer* had the misfortunate of opening one week after *Star Wars,* just as the Lucas juggernaut was taking off. The trailer for Friedkin's film played in front of *Star Wars,* and according to editor Bud Smith, "When our trailer faded to black, the curtains closed and opened again, and they kept opening and opening, and you started feeling this huge thing coming over your shoulder overwhelming you, and heard this noise, and you went right off into space. It made our film look like this little, amateurish piece of shit. I told Billy [Friedkin], 'We're fucking being blown off the screen. You gotta go see this" (qtd. in Biskind 337). *Sorcerer,* which cost $22.5 million to make, ultimately grossed only $9 million worldwide.

2. According to Friedkin, the quasi-subliminal frames of anal penetration "were inserted . . . mainly as a snub to the censors who kept telling us we had to cut down the number of stab wounds" (Kermode, "Cruise Control" 24).

3. Blind bidding was a process that dates back many decades and functioned as a way for studios to maintain control over exhibitors and ensure that their product had an outlet, no matter how shoddy it was. Under this system, exhibitors had to bid for films before they saw them. This practice is now outlawed in twenty-three states, and the flap General Cinema made over *Cruising* is largely responsible for the change in policy.

4. United Artists Theaters was not related to the film's distributor, despite having the same name.

5. De Palma already had a relationship with Arkoff, as AIP had distributed his film *Sisters* in 1973.

6. The distributor, Sigma III, eventually withdrew its appeal and distributed the film with the X rating ("First Appeal").

7. For a more in-depth detailing of all the changes made to *Dressed to Kill,* see Bouzereau, *Cutting Room Floor* 137–50.

8. The rhetoric of the feminist protesting of *Dressed to Kill* was reminiscent of the protests that attended the 1976 release of *Snuff,* a low-budget exploitation film that earned worldwide notoriety for claiming to include footage of an actual murder that was clearly a staged hoax. According to Beverly LaBelle, *Snuff* can be credited with making "the misogyny of pornography a major feminist concern" (qtd. in Hawkins 137). For more on feminist concerns with fictional depictions of violence against women, see Clover, *Men, Women, and Chainsaws*; L. Williams, "Film Bodies"; and Vance, *Pleasure and Danger.*

9. On the August 17, 1980, broadcast of WBCN's *Boston Sunday Review* program, Ellen Herman of Women Against Violence Against Women summed

up her view of just how dangerous *Dressed to Kill* was: "*Dressed to Kill . . .* is killing us on the streets, in our homes, and at our workplaces" (qtd. in Schiff 46).

10. Not long after the *White Dog* debacle, Fuller moved to Europe where he lived and worked until his death in 1997.

3. Pure Action, Packaged Violence: The Role of the Action Film in 1980s Hollywood

1. Particularly by the mid-1980s, the list of the top 10 highest grossing films of each year was frequently dominated by action films or films from other genres with significant amounts of action. In the years 1980, 1981, 1983, 1984, 1986, and 1989, an action-oriented film was the top grossing film of the year: *The Empire Strikes Back, Raiders of the Lost Ark, Return of the Jedi, Beverly Hills Cop, Top Gun,* and *Batman,* respectively. Of the top 100 highest grossing films of the 1980s, thirty-three were action films (and this does not count science fiction films like *The Empire Strikes Back*). The only genre with more box-office hits was comedy, which accounted for thirty-five of the hundred highest grossing films of the decade.

2. Almost the exact reverse had happened with John Milius's involvement in Francis Ford Coppola's *Apocalypse Now* (1979). Milius had written the script in 1968 for George Lucas and Coppola's newly established production company, American Zoetrope. When United Artists green-lighted the film for production in 1976, the script had to be significantly reworked without Milius's involvement. According to Jon Lewis, Milius's "right-wing script for a $1.5 million, 16-mm Vietnam movie" had to be rewritten by Coppola "to make it a big studio feature" and "to make it more politically correct for 1976" (*Whom God Wishes* 41).

3. His contracts stipulated that part of Milius's payment for directing a film was that the studio had to buy him an exotic gun.

4. For example, in *Rambo: First Blood Part II* (1985), the enemies are Soviet officers working with the Communist Vietnamese army; in *Rambo III* (1988), the enemies are again the Soviets, except this time in Afghanistan; in *Die Hard,* Bruce Willis's John McClane fights against European thieves posing as terrorists, mostly from Germany; and in *Lethal Weapon 2,* the villains are South African, a mild sop to director Richard Donner's political causes, much like his inclusion of animal rights messages. Even when the villains were businessmen, as in *Beverly Hills Cop* and *Beverly Hills Cop II,* they had accents marking them as somehow foreign.

5. It is significant that in the United States, the early 1980s was a period of tension and fear about potential war. On the Left, there was a significant anti-nuclear movement and constant concern that Reagan intended to invade South American countries like Nicaragua and El Salvador, which could potentially lead to another Vietnam (of course, the United States *did* invade

Grenada in 1983). From that perspective, *Red Dawn* works like a Red menace film, showing what will happen if we don't take a proactive, militaristic approach to wiping out Communism.

6. *Red Dawn* placed number 20 on the box-office chart for 1984, making it the second most successful of MGM/UA's films that year, the other being *2010*, which placed number 17 with a $40 million gross. Otherwise, MGM/UA didn't have a single film in the top 30, which lends some credence to Milius's assertion that *Red Dawn* "saved" the company that year.

7. Only two James Bond feature films, 1967's *Casino Royale* and 1983's *Never Say Never Again*, were not produced by Broccoli, due to his not having the rights to the original Ian Fleming novels.

8. One can see that, on a narrative and thematic level, action movies of the 1980s were becoming much like video games, and it would be only a few more years before the visual correspondence between the two media through the increasing reliance on digital effects in the 1990s took hold.

9. The western had seen something of a resurgence in the 1970s, but most westerns made at that time were deconstructive in nature, questioning the themes of regenerative violence and moral standing that had defined the genre for so long. As audiences in the 1980s were no longer interested in either classical western stories or postmodern critiques of them, the western wound up "the most miserably performing genre of the decade" (Prince, *New Pot of Gold* 309).

10. In her qualitative study of viewer responses to screen violence, Annette Hill notes how the scene in *Pulp Fiction* (1994) in which a character is shot in the head split the audience down the middle. One person she interviewed said, "When Marvin gets his head blown all across the back of the car, I thought that was really funny, but it seemed the audience were divided. Half burst into laughter and another half thought it was absolutely shocking" (29).

11. Elizabeth Cowie's basic argument is that the tenets of classical Hollywood narrative have been overstated and that numerous films made during Hollywood's classic era did not conform to its dictates. Thus, the kind of narrative rupture typical of the pure action film is not a particularly new development, which would explain why audiences had little trouble accepting it and weren't jarred out of the cinematic experience à la Brecht.

4. Fighting Outward, Looking Inward: Violence in the 1980s Vietnam Film

1. The U.S. military clearly understood *M*A*S*H* as a film about Vietnam, as well; the film was banned from army and Air Force theaters because the brass was afraid it "might lower the confidence of soldiers in military medicine" (Wetta and Curley 190).

2. The Cannon Group was formed in 1979 when Israeli producer Menahem Golan and his cousin Yoram Globus bought a controlling interest in Cannon Films. They had a successful run throughout the 1980s making

relatively low-budget, no-frills action and adventure movies that petered out in the early 1990s when such films became the virtually exclusive province of the straight-to-video realm. Cannon was known for working with second-tier action stars like Chuck Norris, Michael Dudikoff, Dolph Lundgren, Jean-Claude Van Damme, and Charles Bronson, although the company also produced two films with Sylvester Stallone (1986's *Cobra* and 1987's *Over the Top*) when he was at the height of his popularity. Films produced by the Cannon Group during the 1980s included two *Missing in Action* sequels (1985's *Missing in Action 2: The Beginning* and 1988's *Braddock: Missing in Action III*), *American Ninja* (1985) and its four sequels (released in 1987, 1989, 1990, and 1993), and three sequels to the prototypical vigilante film *Death Wish* (1982's *Death Wish II*, 1985's *Death Wish 3*, and 1987's *Death Wish IV: The Crackdown*).

3. The word "Rambo," as well as the related terms "Ramboesque," "Ramboism," and "Rambo-like," were officially added to the *Oxford English Dictionary* in 1989. The entry for "Rambo" reads: "Characteristic of Rambo; aggressive, violent. . . . A person resembling or displaying characteristics of Rambo; an exceptionally tough, strong, and uncompromising man (esp. in militaristic contexts); one who is characteristically aggressive and violent."

4. The bill included legislation that would provide aid to anti-Communist insurgents in Cambodia, Afghanistan, and Angola.

5. When he first arrives in Vietnam, Rambo is confronted by a huge snake that sneaks up behind him on a tree limb. Quickly and without comment, Rambo spins around, grabs the snake by the neck, and stares it down. Vincent Canby noted this scene in the first paragraph of his review in the *New York Times* but did not comment on any potential significance beyond demonstrating Rambo's physical prowess. However, in broadly symbolic terms, one can see the snake as a commentary on Murdock and Rambo's strong response as a foreshadowing of things to come.

6. The ironic use of the name "Hope" for a town unwelcoming to Vietnam veterans was also used in *Welcome Home, Soldier Boys*, a film that prefigures much of *First Blood*. In that film, a group of recently discharged Vietnam veterans embark on a cross-country road trip full of dreams but eventually wind up broke and disillusioned in the small town of Hope, New Mexico, which they completely destroy after being shot at by a gas station owner for stealing gasoline.

5. Disavowing Horror: Independent Production, Fandom, and the Fetishizing of Makeup Special Effects

1. A few examples included the scene of a witch pulling a dismembered hand out of a bundle of sticks and snapping off a finger in *Häxan* and the detailed, gory depiction of a scientist cutting a woman's face off with a scalpel in Georges Fanju's *Eyes without a Face* (*Les yeux sans visage*, 1959).

2. This sentiment was not lost on Roger Ebert, one of the slasher genre's most vocal critics. He quoted McDowell's line in the opening paragraph of his three-star review of *Fright Night.*

3. The heavy use of this song in advertising *Cat People,* as well as in the film itself, is evidence that the Jerry Bruckheimer/Don Simpson ancillary market approach to connecting high-concept movies with pop songs was bleeding outside the boundaries of the pure action genre. It is particularly telling that the film's director, Paul Schrader, had previously worked with Bruckheimer and Simpson on *American Gigolo,* which prominently featured the hit Blondie song "Call Me."

4. As Carol Clover and others have shown, the slasher genre is much more ideologically complex in terms of violence and gender than it is traditionally given credit for.

5. *Friday the 13th* was among the twenty highest grossing films of 1980, earning $39 million at the theatrical box office. The year 1982 saw several slasher films in the top 50, including *Halloween II* ($25 million; number 30) and *Friday the 13th Part* 2 ($22 million; number 35) (*Box Office Mojo*).

6. An editorial in the *Chicago Tribune,* the home of Gene Siskel, proudly trumpeted that neither that newspaper nor the *Chicago Sun-Times* "publish[es] movie advertising that uses sadistic illustrations or suggests sexually-explicit violence" ("Sick Films for Sick People").

7. Ironically, when *The Wild Bunch* was re-released in a restored director's cut to theaters in 1994, CARA re-rated it NC-17, even though it was the same version of the film that had been rated R in 1969, albeit not the same one that played in theaters. Virtually all of the restored footage, however, had no violent content. Once the film's distributor, Warner Bros., was able to provide proof to CARA that the most graphic violence in the restored director's cut was exactly the same as it had been in the version that had been rated R in 1969, CARA let the rating stand.

8. *Fangoria* eventually became a full-color magazine printed entirely on slick stock.

9. Analysis Releasing had also distributed *Caligula* in its uncut form, as well as *Maniac,* in 1980. It is tempting to note the irony, then, that a distributor who would take on such visceral films in their unrated, uncut state would then re-edit *Basket Case* to make it more appealing to a wide audience. But, it is more accurate to note that this is just another example of how producers were responding to the increased pressure by both society at large and the film industry itself to reduce controversial screen violence.

10. Interestingly, images of actors and actresses, the bread and butter of most film-related publications, almost never appeared on the cover of *Fangoria* after the first year of publication. The only time an actor would appear on the cover was if he or she were in some form of makeup, such as Robert Englund made up as Freddy Krueger.

6. Children in Danger: Screen Violence, Steven Spielberg, and the PG-13 Rating

1. *E.T.* was the biggest draw of the 1980s, with an astounding box-office take of $359 million. For a while, it was the biggest box-office earner in the history of cinema, a crown it held until it was dethroned fifteen years later by the re-release of George Lucas's *Star Wars: Special Edition* in 1997. *Poltergeist* ranked eighth at the box office in 1982, earning $76.7 million, an impressive sum for a horror movie.

2. Beyond this obvious horror imagery, *E.T.*, despite being a childhood fantasy on the surface, often operates like a horror film, which again suggests that Spielberg's films are not as one-dimensional and conservative as many think. Particularly notable is the absence of the father, which results in a fractured family structure that is more susceptible to invasion, a frequent trope in horror films, particularly in the 1970s. Although the arrival of E.T. could hardly be an invasion, the surreal and frightening imagery of the government agents invading the home near the end has strongly horrific overtones.

3. JoBeth Williams also starred as the mother of the abducted boy in the based-on-a-true story TV movie *Adam* (1983).

4. In his memo, Nix cites Article III, Section II-E of the CARA Rules: "(1) No member of the Appeals Board shall participate in an appeal involving a motion picture in which the member or any company with which he or she is associated has a financial interest" (Nix to Valenti, May 6, 1982, in Heffner, "Reminiscences," box 1, 2).

5. The other Disney/Paramount co-production was a live-action musical version of the cartoon *Popeye* (1980) starring Robin Williams and Shelley Duvall and directed by Robert Altman. An expensive flop at the box office, it surely ranks as one of the strangest hybrids of high-concept Hollywood mentality and the subversive artistry of one of New Hollywood's most revered and difficult auteurs.

6. The major innovation was a process developed by Industrial Light & Magic known as Go-Motion, a variation on stop-motion animation that uses computer-timed movements to smooth out the motion, effectively eliminating the jerkiness inherent to the process. Comparing the Go-Motion in *Dragonslayer* with Ray Harryhausen's stop-motion work on *Clash of the Titans*, another fantasy movie released that same year, is a testament to the former's superiority.

7. For example, *Newsweek* critic David Ansen wrote, "'Gremlins' is sure to arouse outrage in some circles over its gleeful carnage. But 'Gremlins's' violence, always spiked with wit, will probably be better understood by kids than by their parents" ("Little Toyshop").

8. A few examples of films that Heffner thought would warrant the "intensity signal" were *Airplane!* (1980) and *The Big Red One* (1980), which would be rated PG*, and *Cruising* and *Friday the 13th*, which would both be rated

R*. Heffner had received some letters complaining about the PG rating for *Airplane*, which featured brief nudity and crude humor about drugs and sex. *The Big Red One*, which was directed by the legendary Sam Fuller and based on his own experiences in World War II, featured significant amounts of war-related violence that made it a good candidate for the "no-man's land" between PG and R (Heffner to Valenti, May 5, 1980, in Heffner, "Reminiscences," box 1). The controversies around the copious amounts of violence and their frequent association with sexuality in *Cruising* and *Friday the 13th* have already been well documented in chapters 2 and 5, respectively.

9. According to Heffner, "Valenti's singular unwillingness to tolerate any changes whatsoever in his system" was related to the fact that "a change in the rating system in 1984 would mean that Jack Valenti, creator of the rating system in 1968, had been fallible, hadn't seen something that needed to be done or that would ever need to be done. Anything less than absolute omniscience in 1968 was very tough for him to take" (Heffner, "RDH Pre–Oral History Memo 1984," box 2, 23–24).

10. According to Heffner, *Red Dawn* and *The Lady in Red*, two of the first films to be rated PG-13, would have been rated R and were promised the PG-13 rating during June before the new rating was officially announced. However, when Heffner promised the rating, he was under the assumption that PG-13 would be a "restricted" rating (Heffner, "RDH Pre–Oral History Memo 1984," box 2, 33).

11. The addendum to the PG rating of *Jaws*—that it may be "too intense" for younger children—had also been added to the G rating of *The Andromeda Strain* (1970). However, the advertising one-sheet for *The Andromeda Strain* featured this warning across the top of the poster in significantly large font, whereas the one-sheet for *Jaws* placed the text in the bottom right-hand corner of the design in small font beneath the credits.

12. There were similar accusations leveled at Spielberg with the release of *Saving Private Ryan*, a World War II film whose graphic depiction of warfare set a new standard for gory verisimilitude in a mainstream film. It was suggested by many that the film was rated R, rather than NC-17, only because Spielberg had directed it, something Spielberg adamantly denied (see Ebert, "Movie Answer Man"; Persall).

Conclusion: Fashioning a New Screen Violence from the Old in the 1990s

1. The one major exception is Martin Scorsese's *The Last Temptation of Christ* (1988), which was also, not incidentally, produced and distributed by Universal Pictures after Paramount backed out of making it earlier in the decade.

Works Cited

Adair, Gilbert. *Vietnam on Film: From The Green Berets to Apocalypse Now.* New York: Proteus, 1981.

Alloway, Lawrence. *Violent America: The Movies 1946–1964.* New York: Museum of Modern Art, 1971.

Altman, Rick. *Film/Genre.* London: BFI, 1999.

Anderson, Christopher. *Hollywood TV: The Studio System in the Fifties.* Austin: U of Texas P, 1994.

Ansen, David. Rev. of *Cruising. Newsweek* 18 Feb. 1980.

———. "Little Toyshop of Horrors." Rev. of *Gremlins. Newsweek* 18 June 1984: 90.

———. "The Producer Is King Again." *Newsweek* 20 May 1985: 84.

Armstrong, Nancy, and Leonard Tennenhouse, eds. *The Violence of Representation: Literature and the History of Violence.* London: Routledge, 1989.

Arnold, Gary. "Horror with the Spielberg Touch." Rev. of *Poltergeist. Washington Post* 4 June 1982: D1.

Atkins, Thomas R. *Graphic Violence on the Screen.* New York: Monarch, 1976.

Attanasio, Paul. "'Rambo': New Blood, Old Moves Stallone's Righteous Rabble-Rouser." *Washington Post* 22 May 1985: F1.

Austin, Bruce A., Mark J. Nicolich, and Thomas Simonet. "M.P.A.A. Ratings and the Box Office: Some Tantalizing Statistics." *Film Quarterly* 35.2 (Winter 1981–82): 28–30.

Bach, Steven. *Final Cut: Art, Money, and Ego in the Making of* Heaven's Gate, *the Film That Sank United Artists.* Updated ed. New York: Newmarket, 1999.

Barker, Martin. "Violence Redux." Schneider 57–79.

Bart, Peter. *Fade Out: The Calamitous Final Days of MGM.* New York: Morrow, 1990.

———. "'Red Dawn': Shooting the McVeigh Way." *Daily Variety* 16 June 1997: 34.

Bart, Peter, and Peter Guber. *Shoot Out: Surviving Fame and (Mis)Fortune in Hollywood.* New York: Putnam's, 2002.

Base, Ron. "*Platoon*'s Director Tastes Victory." *Toronto Star* 18 Dec. 1986: C1.

Beale, Lewis. "Troubled Times: How Producers Pander to the Public's Paranoia." *San Francisco Chronicle* 8 Dec. 1985: 32.

Bell, Arthur. "Bell Tells." *Village Voice* 16 July 1979.

Belton, John. *Widescreen Cinema.* Cambridge: Harvard UP, 1992.

Bettleheim, Bruno. *The Uses of Enchantment: The Meaning and Importance of Fairy Tales.* New York: Random, 1975.

Birkland, Thomas A. *After Disaster: Agenda Setting, Public Policy, and Focusing Events.* Washington, DC: Georgetown UP, 1997.

Biskind, Peter. *Easy Riders, Raging Bulls: How the Sex-Drugs-and-Rock-'n'-Roll Generation Saved Hollywood.* New York: Simon, 1998.

Bok, Sissela. *Mayhem: Violence as Public Spectacle.* New York: Addison-Wesley, 1998.

Boot, Andy. *Fragments of Fear: An Illustrated History of British Horror Films.* London: Creation, 1996.

Bordwell, David, Janet Staiger, and Kristin Thompson. *The Classical Hollywood Cinema: Film Style and Mode of Production to 1960.* New York: Columbia UP, 1985.

Bourdieu, Pierre. *Distinction: A Social Critique of the Judgement of Taste.* Trans. Richard Nice. Cambridge: Harvard UP, 1984.

Bouzereau, Laurent. *The Cutting Room Floor: Movie Scenes Which Never Made It to the Movies.* New York: Citadel, 1994.

———. *The De Palma Cut: The Films of America's Most Controversial Director.* New York: Dembner, 1988.

———. *Ultraviolent Movies: From Sam Peckinpah to Quentin Tarantino.* Secaucus, NJ: Citadel, 1996.

Box Office Mojo. <http://www.boxofficemojo.com>.

Breznican, Anthony. "How 'Gremlins' and 'Indiana Jones' Remade Hollywood." *Associated Press State and Local Wire* 24 Aug. 2004.

Britton, Andrew. "Blissing Out: The Politics of Reaganite Entertainment." *Movie* (Winter 1986): 1–42.

Bronson, Gail, and Steve Hawkins. "Movie Violence Getting Out of Hand?" *U.S. News and World Report* 18 June 1984: 70.

Brophy, Philip. "Horrality—The Textuality of Contemporary Horror Films." Gelder 276–84.

Callahan, Jean. "Hot *Dog.*" *American Film* May 1983: 10.

Canby, Vincent. "Are Video Games About to Zap the Action Movie?" Rev. of *Blue Thunder. New York Times* 15 May 1983, sec. 2: 13.

———. "As a Rating, PG Says Less Than Meets the Eye." *New York Times* 10 June 1984, sec. 2: 1.

———. "Cockeyed at *Red Dawn.*" *New York Times* 16 Sept. 1984, sec. 2: 19.

———. "Film View: How Should We React to Violence?" *New York Times* 11 Dec. 1983, sec. 2: 23.

———. Rev. of *The Godfather. New York Times* 16 Mar. 1972: 56.

———. "Screen: 'Gremlins,' Kiddie Gore." *New York Times* 8 June 1984: C10.

———. "Screen: 'Indiana Jones,' Directed by Spielberg." *New York Times* 23 May 1984: C21.

———. Rev of *Sisters. New York Times* 27 Sept. 1973: 44.

———. "Spike Lee Stirs Things Up at Cannes." *New York Times* 20 May 1989, sec. 1: 11.

———. "Sylvester Stallone Returns as Rambo." *New York Times* 22 May 1985: C23.

Carlomagno, Ellen. "The Burman Studio." *Fangoria* Aug. 1981: 20–24.

Cawelti, John G. *The Six-Gun Mystique.* 2nd ed. Bowling Green, OH: Bowling Green State U Popular P, 1984.

Charney, Leo. "The Violence of a Perfect Moment." Slocum, *Violence and American Cinema* 47–62.

"Child Abductions a Rising Concern: With 150,000 Incidents Each Year, Units Are Forming to Aid Victims' Families." *New York Times* 5 Dec. 1982: 77.

Childs, Mike, and Alan Jones. "De Palma Has the Power!" *Brian De Palma Interviews.* Ed. Laurence F. Knapp. Jackson: UP of Mississippi, 2003. 37–45.

"Cinema: The New Pictures." Rev. of *Psycho. Time* 27 June 1960: 51.

Clagett, Thomas D. *William Friedkin: Films of Aberration, Obsession, and Reality.* Jefferson, NC: McFarland, 1990.

Clover, Carol J. *Men, Women, and Chainsaws: Gender in the Modern Horror Film.* Princeton, NJ: Princeton UP, 1992.

Collins, Glenn. "Is the Violence in 'Blade Runner' a Socially Destructive Element?" *New York Times* 30 June 1982: C19.

Cook, David A. "Ballistic Balletics: Styles of Violent Representations in *The Wild Bunch* and After." *Sam Peckinpah's* The Wild Bunch. Ed. Stephen Prince. Cambridge: Cambridge UP, 1999. 130–54.

———. *Lost Illusions: American Cinema in the Shadow of Watergate and Vietnam, 1970–1979.* Vol. 9 of *History of the American Cinema.* New York: Scribner, 2000.

———. "*The Wild Bunch,* Fifteen Years After." *North Dakota Quarterly* 51 (Summer 1983): 123–30.

Corrigan, Timothy. "Auteurs and the New Hollywood." Lewis, *New American Cinema* 38–63.

———. *A Cinema without Walls: Movies and Culture after Vietnam.* New Brunswick, NJ: Rutgers UP, 1991.

Cowie, Elizabeth. "Storytelling: Classical Hollywood Cinema and Classical Narrative." Neale and Smith 178–90.

Craven, Wes. "MPAA: The Horror in My Life." *Films in Review* 47.9–10 (Sept.–Oct. 1996): 34–39.

Crowdus, Gary, and Richard Porton. "The Importance of a Singular, Guiding Vision: An Interview with Arthur Penn." *Cineaste* 20.2 (Jan. 1994): 4–16.

Crowther, Bosley. "Psycho." Rev. of *Psycho. New York Times* 17 June 1960: 37.

———. "A Smash at Violence." *New York Times* 30 July 1968: 10.

"'Cruising' Gets Sole Screening for Press Feb. 4." *Daily Variety* 11 Jan. 1980: 3.

Darnton, Nina. "At the Movies: A New Hit Has the Industry Asking Why." *New York Times* 3 Apr. 1987: C8.

Davenport, Robert. *The Encyclopedia of War Movies: Wars 1900 to the Present.* New York: Facts on File, 2004.

Dittmar, Linda, and Gene Michaud, eds. *From Hanoi to Hollywood: The Vietnam War in American Films.* New Brunswick, NJ: Rutgers UP, 1990.

Doherty, Thomas. *Teenagers and Teenpics: The Juvenilization of American Movies in the 1950s.* Boston: Unwin Hyman, 1988.

Dominick, Joseph R. "Film Economics and Film Content: 1964–1983." *Current Research in Film: Audience, Economics, and Law.* Vol. 3. Ed. Bruce A. Austin. Norwood, NJ: Ablex, 1987. 136–53.

Do the Right Thing. Dir. Spike Lee. Universal, 1989. Laser disc. New York: Criterion Collection, 1995.

Dyer, Richard. "Action!" *Action/Spectacle Cinema: A Sight and Sound Reader.* Ed. José Arroyo. London: BFI, 2000. 17–20.

Ebert, Roger. Rev. of *Fright Night. Chicago Sun-Times* 2 Aug. 1985. <http://rogerebert.suntimes.com/apps/pbcs.dll/article?AID=/19850802/REVIEWS/508020301/1023>.

———. "The Movie Answer Man." *Chicago Sun-Times* 26 July 1998, Show sec.: 5.

———. Rev. of *Open Range. Chicago Sun-Times* 30 Aug. 2003. 10 May 2007 <http://rogerebert.suntimes.com/apps/pbcs.dll/article?AID=/20030815/REVIEWS/308150304/1023>.

———. Rev. of *Platoon. Chicago Sun-Times* 30 Dec. 1986. 10 May 2007 <http://rogerebert.suntimes.com/apps/pbcs.dll/article?AID=/19861230/REVIEWS/612300301/1023>.

———. "Russ Meyer: Ten Years after the 'Beyond.'" *Film Comment* 16.4 (July–Aug. 1980): 43–44.

Farber, Stephen. *The Movie Ratings Game.* Washington, DC: Public Affairs, 1972.

———. "Peckinpah's Return." *Film Quarterly* 23 (1969): 2–11.

———. "Shelf Life: The Hard Part, II: Getting It Shown." *Film Comment* 19.3 (June 1983): 39–43.

"First Appeal on 'X' Rating." *Variety* 27 Nov. 1968: 7.

Fleming, Charles. *High Concept: Don Simpson and the Hollywood Culture of Excess.* New York: Doubleday, 1998.

Fraser, John. *Violence in the Arts.* Cambridge: Cambridge UP, 1974.

French, Philip. "Violence in the Cinema." *Violence and the Mass Media.* Ed. O. N. Larsen. New York: Harper, 1968. 59–70.

Gagne, Paul R. *The Zombies That Ate Pittsburgh: The Films of George A. Romero.* New York: Dodd, 1987.

Gates, David. "Comic Books Go Hollywood." *Newsweek* 5 Jan. 1987: 3.

"GCC Stands on View 'Cruising' Needs X Rating; Won't Show It." *Daily Variety* 12 Feb. 1980: 2.

Gelder, Ken, ed. *The Horror Reader.* London: Routledge, 2000.

Ginsberg, Steven. "Demonstrations in Major Cities Seen as 'Cruising' Opens Wide." *Daily Variety* 15 Feb. 1980: 3.

———. "General Cinema Screens Won't Be 'Cruising.'" *Daily Variety* 1 Feb. 1980: 1+.

Giroux, Henry A. "Racism and the Aesthetic of Hyper-Real Violence: *Pulp Fiction* and Other Visual Tragedies." *Social Identities* 1.2 (Aug. 1995): 333–55.

Gitlin, Todd. *The Sixties: Years of Hope, Days of Rage.* New York: Bantam, 1987.

Goodman, W. "Is There a Moral Limit to the Violence in Films?" *New York Times* 18 Dec. 1983, sec. 2: 133.

Graham, Jefferson. "NBC Collars 'White Dog': Fuller Film Pulled from Cable in 1st-Ever Sweeps Maneuver." *Hollywood Reporter* 16 Jan. 1984: 1+.

———. "NBC Pulls 180 on 'White Dog'; Deems Feature as 'Inappropriate.'" *Hollywood Reporter* 19 Jan. 1984: 1+.

Grant, Barry Keith, ed. *Film Genre Reader II.* Austin: U of Texas P, 1995.

Grenier, Richard. "Stallone on Patriotism and 'Rambo.'" *New York Times* 6 June 1985: C21.

Greydanus, Steven D. "Ratings Creep? What Ratings Creep?" *Decent Films Guide* 7 Dec. 2004 <http://www.decentfilms.com/commentary/ratingscreep.html>.

Grover, Ronald. "You Don't Know Them—But They Know Moviegoers." *Business Week* 25 May 1987: 166.

Grover, Stephen. "Blood Flows Freely as Hollywood Goes Horrific." *Wall Street Journal* 11 Feb. 1981: 29.

Guerrero, Ed. "Black Violence as Cinema: From Cheap Thrills to Historical Agonies." Slocum, *Violence and American Cinema* 211–25.

Harmetz, Aljean. "The Figures Don't Lie: Hollywood's Audience Is Older and Pickier." *New York Times* 7 Mar. 1988: C13.

———. "Film Rating System under New Fire." *New York Times* 2 June 1982: C21.

———. "Movie Ratings—Too Much of a Mystery?" *New York Times* 3 May 1978: C17.

Hartung, Philip T. "The Screen: All That a Mother Can Mean." *Commonweal* 72 (Sept. 1960): 469–70.

Hatch, Robert. "Films." Rev. of *Psycho. Nation* 2 July 1960: 18–19.

Hawkins, Joan. *Cutting Edge: Art Horror and the Horrific Avant-Garde.* Minneapolis: U of Minnesota P, 2000.

Hayward, Susan. *Cinema Studies: The Key Concepts.* 2nd ed. London: Routledge, 2000.

Heffner, Richard D. "RDH Pre–Oral History Memorandum to Charles Champlin for 1981." In "Reminiscences of Richard D. Heffner," box 1. Columbia University Oral History Research Office Collection, Butler Library, Columbia University, New York.

———. "RDH Pre–Oral History Memo to Chuck Champlin for the Year 1984." In "Reminiscences of Richard D. Heffner," box 2. Columbia University Oral History Research Office Collection, Butler Library, Columbia University, New York.

———. "Reminiscences of Richard D. Heffner" (oral history and associated papers). 20 vols. Columbia University Oral History Research Office Collection, Butler Library, Columbia University, New York.

Hill, Annette. *Shocking Entertainment: Viewer Response to Violent Movies.* Luton, England: U of Luton P, 1997.

Hoberman, J. "The Fascist Guns in the West: Hollywood's 'Rambo' Coalition." *Radical America* 19.6 (1985): 52–62.

Hoberman, J., and Jonathan Rosenbaum. *Midnight Movies.* New York: Harper, 1983.

Hobsbawm, Eric J. *The Age of Extremes: A History of the World, 1914–1991.* New York: Pantheon, 1994.

Horsley, Jake. *American Chaos: From* Touch of Evil *to* The Terminator. Vol. 1 of *The Blood Poets: A Cinema of Savagery 1958–1999.* Lanham, MD: Scarecrow, 1999.

Hunter, Stephen. *Violent Screen.* New York: Delta, 1995.

IGN FilmForce. "An Interview with John Milius." *IGN.com FilmForce* 7 May 2003. 24 Aug. 2004 <http://filmforce.ign.com/articles/401/401150p1.html >.

Jacobs, Lea, and Richard Maltby. "Rethinking the Production Code." *Quarterly Review of Film and Video* 15.4 (1995): 1–3.

Jeffords, Susan. *Hard Bodies: Hollywood Masculinity in the Reagan Era.* New Brunswick, NJ: Rutgers UP, 1994.

Jenkins, Henry. *Textual Poachers: Television Fans and Participatory Culture.* New York: Routledge, 1992.

Jones, Gerard. *Killing Monsters: Why Children Need Fantasy, Super Heroes, and Make-Believe Violence.* New York: Basic, 2002.

———. "The Man Who Gave an 'X' Rating to Violence." *New York Times* 11 May 1975: D1.

Jowett, Garth S. "Books." *Film Comment* 7.1 (1971): 70–72.

Kael, Pauline. "The Current Cinema: Fear of Movies." *New Yorker* 25 Sept. 1978: 137–57.

———. *Kiss Kiss Bang Bang.* Boston: Little, 1968.

———. *Taking It All In.* New York: Holt, 1984.

———. *When the Lights Go Down.* New York: Holt, 1980.

Kakutani, Michiko. "The Two Faces of Steven Spielberg—Horror vs. Hope." *New York Times* 30 May 1982: D1+.
Kapsis, Robert E. *Hitchcock: The Making of a Reputation.* Chicago: U of Chicago P, 1992.
Karlen, Neal, with Lee Goldberg. "The Sons of Rambo." *Newsweek* 14 Oct. 1985: 50.
Kauffman, Stanley. "Several Sons, Several Lovers." Rev. of *Psycho. New Republic* 29 Aug. 1960: 21–22.
Kendrick, Walter. *The Thrill of Fear: 250 Years of Scary Entertainment.* New York: Grove, 1991.
Kent, Nicholas. *Naked Hollywood: Money and Power in the Movies Today.* New York: St. Martin's, 1991.
Kermode, Mark. "Cruise Control." *Sight and Sound* 8.11 (Nov. 1998): 22–24.
———. "Horror: On the Edge of Taste." *Film and Censorship: The Index Reader.* Ed. Ruth Petrie. London: Cassell, 1997. 155–60.
———. "I Was a Teenage Horror Fan: or, How I Learned to Stop Worrying and Love Linda Blair." *Ill Effects: The Media/Violence Debate.* Ed. Martin Barker and Julian Petley. London: Routledge, 1997. 57–66.
King, Geoff. "'Killingly Funny': Mixing Modalities in New Hollywood's Comedy-with-Violence." Schneider 126–43.
King, Stephen. *Danse Macabre.* New York: Berkley, 1982.
Klain, Stephen. "Weintraub 'Cruising' His Way, Bars *Variety* from Screening." *Daily Variety* 6 Feb. 1980: 1+.
Klein, Joshua. "Joe Dante." *The Onion A.V. Club* 29 Nov. 2000. 1 June 2006 <http://www.theavclub.com/feature/index.php?issue=3643&f=1>.
Knight, Arthur. *The Liveliest Art: A Panoramic History of the Movies.* Rev. ed. New York: Mentor, 1979.
Kolker, Robert. *A Cinema of Loneliness: Penn, Stone, Kubrick, Scorsese, Spielberg, Altman.* 3rd ed. New York: Oxford UP, 2000.
Kramer, Peter. "'Clean, Dependable Slapstick': Comic Violence and the Emergence of Classical Hollywood Cinema." Slocum, *Violence and American Cinema* 103–16.
Krämer, Peter. "Would You Take Your Child to See This Film? The Cultural and Social Work of the Family-Adventure Movie." Neale and Smith 294–311.
Kroll, Jack. "Indy Strikes Again." *Newsweek* 4 June 1984: 78.
Leff, Leonard J., and Jerold L. Simmons. *The Dame in the Kimono: Hollywood, Censorship, and the Production Code from the 1920s to the 1960s.* New York: Anchor, 1990.
Lev, Peter. *American Films of the 1970s: Conflicting Visions.* Austin: U of Texas P, 2000.
Lewis, Jon. *Hollywood v. Hard Core: How the Struggle over Censorship Saved the Modern Film Industry.* New York: New York UP, 2000.

———, ed. *New America Cinema.* Durham, NC: Duke UP, 1998.

———. "Those Who Disagree Can Kiss Jack Valenti's Ass." *The End of Cinema as We Know It.* Ed. Jon Lewis. New York: New York UP, 2001. 23–32.

———. *Whom God Wishes to Destroy: Francis Coppola and the New Hollywood.* Durham, NC: Duke UP, 1995.

Litwak, Mark. *Reel Power: The Struggle for Influence and Success in the New Hollywood.* Los Angeles: Silman-James, 1986.

Lyons, Charles. "The Paradox of Protest: American Film, 1980–1992." *Movie Censorship and American Culture.* Ed. Francis C. Couvares. Washington, DC: Smithsonian Institute, 1996. 277–318.

MacKinnon, Kenneth. *Misogyny in the Movies: The De Palma Question.* Newark: U of Delaware P, 1990.

Maltby, Richard. "'Nobody Knows Everything': Post-classical Historiographies and Consolidated Entertainment." Neale and Smith 21–44.

Martin, Bob. "Imagination, Inc." *Fangoria* Apr. 1981: 4.

———. "Tom Savini: A Man of Many Parts." *Fangoria* June 1980: 11+.

Maslin, Janet. "At the Movies." *New York Times* 13 Apr. 1984: C8.

———. "Film View: Bloodbaths Debase Movies and Audiences." *New York Times* 21 Nov. 1982: H1+.

———. "*Red Dawn,* on World War III." *New York Times* 10 Aug. 1984: C11.

———. "Screen: Norris in 'Missing in Action.'" *New York Times* 17 Nov. 1984: 11.

———. "Short on Talk, Big at the Box Office." *New York Times* 2 Dec. 1984, sec. 2: 17.

———. "Tired Blood Claims the Horror Film as a Fresh Victim." *New York Times* 1 Nov. 1981, sec. 2: 15.

Matloff, Jason. "Serial Thrillers." *Premiere* Oct. 2003: 72–80.

McCarthy, Todd. Rev. of *Reservoir Dogs. Variety's Film Reviews 1991–1992.* New Providence: Bowker, 1993.

McCarty, John. *Splatter Movies: Breaking the Last Taboo of the Screen.* New York: St. Martin's, 1984.

Merritt, Greg. *Celluloid Mavericks: A History of American Independent Film.* New York: Thunder's Mouth, 2000.

"MGM Is Ordered to Pay $15,000 to the Directors Guild of America and to Director Tobe Hooper for Violating Guild Credit Size Requirements in Trailer Advertising for 'Poltergeist.'" *Entertainment Law Reporter* 1 Aug. 1982.

Michelson, Herbert. "New Movie about Vietnam War 'Honors Soldiers, Not Conflict.'" *Oregonian* 31 Aug. 1987: C06.

Miller, Frank. *Censored Hollywood: Sex, Sin, and Violence On Screen.* Atlanta, GA: Turner, 1994.

Miller, William Ian. *The Anatomy of Disgust.* Cambridge: Harvard UP, 1997.

Morgenstern, Joseph. "The Thin Red Line." *Newsweek* 28 Aug. 1967: 82–83.

Mundy, Liz. "Do You Know Where Your Children Are? Most Likely, They're Watching PG-13 Movies." *Washington Post* 16 Nov. 2003.

Murphy, A. D. "Week-by-Week Cumulative Tix Sales Parallel Over 20 Years." *Variety* 2 Dec. 1981: 5+.

Musser, Charles. *The Emergence of Cinema: The American Screen to 1907.* Vol. 1 of *History of the American Cinema.* New York: Scribner, 1990.

Nadel, Alan. *Flatlining on the Field of Dreams: Cultural Narratives in the Films of President Reagan's America.* New Brunswick, NJ: Rutgers UP, 1997.

Naremore, James. *More Than Night: Film Noir in Its Contexts.* Berkeley: U of California P, 1998.

National Commission on the Causes and Prevention of Violence. *Mass Media Hearings: A Report to the National Commission on the Causes and Prevention of Violence.* Washington, DC: GPO, 1969.

Neale, Steve. *Genre and Hollywood.* London: Routledge, 2000.

———. "'You've Got to Be Fucking Kidding!' Knowledge, Belief, and Judgment in Science Fiction." *Alien Zone: Cultural Theory and Contemporary Science Fiction.* Ed. Annette Kuhn. London: Verso, 1990. 160–68.

Neale, Steve, and Murray Smith, eds. *Contemporary Hollywood Cinema.* London: Routledge, 1998.

Newman, David, and Robert Benton. "Now Let the Festivities Begin." *Esquire* July 1967: 55–57.

Norris, Chuck (with Ken Abraham). *Against All Odds: My Story.* Nashville, TN: Broadman, 2004.

O'Quinn, Kerry. "Welcome to the World of *Fangoria*." *Fangoria* Aug. 1979: 4.

Osborne, Robert. "Rambling Reporter." *Hollywood Reporter* 23 Nov. 1983: 2.

———. "Rambling Reporter." *Hollywood Reporter* 9 Dec. 1983: 2.

Pampel, Fred, and Dan Fost. "Marketing the Movies." *American Demographics* 16.3 (Mar. 1994): 48–53.

Paul, William. *Laughing Screaming: Modern Hollywood Horror and Comedy.* New York: Columbia UP, 1994.

Persall, Steve. "2 High-Profile Films Dodge NC-17 Rating; Raise Threshold on Raunch and Gore." *Record* 18 July 1998: Y07.

Plagens, Peter, Mark Miller, Donna Foote, and Emily Yoffe. "Violence in Our Culture." *Newsweek* 1 Apr. 1991: 46–52.

Plantinga, Carl. "American Documentary in the 1980s." Prince, *New Pot of Gold* 370–89.

Pollock, Dale. "*Cruising:* Protests on the Picket Lines." *Los Angeles Times* 18 Feb. 1980: 1.

"Poll Supports Changes in Film Ratings." *San Francisco Chronicle* 23 Dec. 1987: E1.

Prince, Stephen. *Classical Film Violence: Designing and Regulating Brutality in Hollywood Cinema, 1930–1968.* New Brunswick, NJ: Rutgers UP, 2003.

———. "Graphic Violence in the Cinema: Origins, Aesthetic Design, and Social Effects." Prince, *Screening Violence* 1–46.

———, ed. *A New Pot of Gold: Hollywood under the Electronic Rainbow, 1980–1989.* Berkeley: U of California P, 2000.

———. *Savage Cinema: Sam Peckinpah and the Rise of Ultraviolent Movies.* Austin: U of Texas P, 1998.

———, ed. *Screening Violence.* New Brunswick, NJ: Rutgers UP, 2000.

Ray, Robert B. *A Certain Tendency of the Hollywood Cinema, 1930–1980.* Princeton, NJ: Princeton UP, 1985.

Rebello, Stephen. *Alfred Hitchcock and the Making of* Psycho. New York: St. Martin's Griffin, 1990.

Rich, B. Ruby. "Art House Killers." *Sight and Sound* 2.8 (Dec. 1992): 5–6.

Riordan, James. *Stone: The Controversies, Excesses, and Exploits of a Radical Filmmaker.* New York: Hyperion, 1995.

Roberts, Steven V. "'Machismo' on Capitol Hill." *New York Times* 14 July 1985, sec. 4: 1.

Rogin, Michael. *Ronald Reagan, the Movie and Other Episodes in Political Demonology.* Berkley: U of California P, 1987.

Rosenbaum, Jonathan. "His Master's Vice: Fuller's *White Dog.*" *Placing Movies: The Practice of Film Criticism.* Berkeley: U of California P, 1995. 295–300.

Salamon, Julie. "Film: A Temporary Epidemic of Good Taste." *Wall Street Journal* 1 Jan. 1985, Leisure and Arts sect.: 1.

Sandler, Kevin S. "Movie Ratings as Genre: The Incontestable R." *Genre and Contemporary Hollywood.* Ed. Steve Neale. London: BFI, 2002. 201–17.

Sanello, Frank. "New PG-13 Film Rating Hits Theaters July 1." United Press International 27 June 1984.

———. "New PG-13 Movie Rating Likely." United Press International 26 June 1984.

Sanjek, David. "Fans' Notes: The Horror Film Fanzine." Gelder 314–23.

Sanoff, Alvin P. "What Is Hollywood Saying to Us?" *U.S. News and World Report* 30 June 1986: 54.

Sarris, Andrew. *The American Cinema: Directors and Directions 1929–1968.* New York: Dutton, 1968.

Schaefer, Eric. *Bold! Daring! Shocking! True! A History of Exploitation Films, 1919–1959.* Durham, NC: Duke UP, 1999.

Schamus, James. "To the Rear of the Back End: The Economics of Independent Cinema." Neale and Smith 91–105.

Schatz, Thomas. "Introduction." Schneider 1–10.

———. "The New Hollywood." *Film Theory Goes to the Moves.* Ed. Jim Collins, Hilary Radner, and Ava Preaders Collins. New York: Routledge, 1993. 8–36.

———. "New War/Old War: *Band of Brothers* and the Revival of the World War II War Film." *Film and History* 32.1 (May 2002): 74–78.

Schiff, Stephen. "Dressed to Kill." *Love and Hisses: The National Society of Film Critics Sound Off on the Hottest Movie Controversies.* Ed. Peter Rainer. San Francisco: Mercury, 1992. 36–46.

Schneider, Steven Jay, ed. *New Hollywood Violence.* Manchester, England: Manchester UP, 2004.

Schubart, Rikke. "Passion and Acceleration: Generic Change in the Action Film." Slocum, *Violence and American Cinema* 192–207.

Sconce, Jeffrey. "Trashing the Academy: Taste, Excess, and an Emerging Politics of Cinematic Style." *Screen* 36.4 (Winter 1995): 371–93.

Segaloff, Nat. *Hurricane Billy: The Stormy Life and Films of William Friedkin.* New York: Morrow, 1990.

Server, Lee. *Sam Fuller: Film Is a Battleground: A Critical Study, with Interviews, a Filmography, and a Bibliography.* Jefferson, NC: McFarland, 1994.

Shachtman, Tom. *Decade of Shocks: Dallas to Watergate, 1963–1974.* New York: Poseidon, 1983.

"Sick Films for Sick People." *Chicago Tribune* 7 Nov. 1980: B2.

Simon, John. "Lame Deer." Rev. of *The Deer Hunter. Reverse Angle: A Decade of American Films.* New York: Potter, 1982. 371–73.

Siskel, Gene. "'Friday the 13th': More Bad Luck." *Chicago Tribune* 12 May 1980, sec. 2: 9.

Slocum, J. David. "Film Violence and the Institutionalization of the Cinema." *Social Research* 67 (Fall 2000): 649–81.

———. "Introduction: Violence and American Cinema: Notes for an Investigation." Slocum, *Violence and American Cinema* 1–36.

———. "Screening Violence: Film Narratives and Postwar America." Diss. New York U, 1995.

———, ed. *Violence and American Cinema.* New York: Routledge, 2001.

Smith, Julian. *Looking Away: Hollywood and Vietnam.* New York: Scribner's, 1975.

Smith, Murray. "Theses on the Philosophy of Hollywood History." Neale and Smith 3–20.

Sobchack, Vivian C. "Afterward: The Postmorbid Condition." Prince, *Screening Violence* 119–24.

Soriano, Cesar G. "*Red Dawn* Imitated Art." *USA Today* 18 Dec. 2003, Life sec.: 2D.

Steigerwald, David. *The Sixties and the End of Modern America.* New York: St. Martin's, 1995.

Sterritt, David. "The Hollywood Horror Film Is Vanishing, Victim of Its Own Excesses." *Christian Science Monitor* 25 Mar. 1982: 19.

———. "'Rambo': Machismo, Malice, and Mayhem." *Christian Science Monitor* 23 May 1985: 25.

Stone, Judy. "Independent Spirit Triumphs: Low-Budget Features Earn High Praise." *San Francisco Chronicle* 31 Dec. 1989, Sunday Datebook: 19.

Studlar, Gaylyn, and David Desser. "Never Having to Say You're Sorry: *Rambo's* Rewriting of the Vietnam War." Dittmar and Michaud 101–12.

Swires, Steve. "How to Make a Maniac!" *Fangoria* Aug. 1980: 7+.

Tatar, Maria. "'Violent Delights' in Children's Literature." *Why We Watch: The Attractions of Violent Entertainment.* Ed. Jeffrey H. Goldstein. New York: Oxford UP, 1998. 69–87.

Taylor, John. *Circus of Ambition: The Culture of Wealth and Power in the Eighties.* New York: Warner, 1989.

Thomas, Bob. "At the Movies: *Indiana Jones and the Temple of Doom.*" Associated Press 21 May 1984.

———. "At the Movies: *Red Dawn.*" Associated Press 21 Aug. 1984.

Truffaut, François. *Hitchcock.* Rev. ed. New York: Touchstone, 1983.

"UATC Posts Warning at Windows: 'Cruising' Is X Film in R Clothing." *Daily Variety* 20 Feb. 1980: 5+.

Unger, Irwin, and Debbie Unger. *Turning Point: 1968.* New York: Scribner's, 1988.

Vallely, Jean. "Brian De Palma: The New Hitchcock or Just Another Rip-Off?" *Rolling Stone* 16 Oct. 1980: 38–39.

Vance, Carole S. *Pleasure and Danger: Exploring Female Sexuality.* New York: Routledge, 1984.

Van Gelder, Lawrence. "At the Movies: Summer in the City." *New York Times* 5 Aug. 1988: C6.

Vaughn, Stephen. *Freedom and Entertainment: Rating the Movies in the Age of New Media.* Cambridge: Cambridge UP, 2006.

Waller, Gregory A. "Introduction to *American Horrors.*" Gelder 256–64.

Walsh, Moira. "Films: *Psycho.*" Rev. of *Psycho. America* July 1960: 443.

Waterman, David. *Hollywood's Road to Riches.* Cambridge: Harvard UP, 2005.

Waxman, Sharon. *Rebels on the Backlot: Six Maverick Directors and How They Conquered the Studio System.* New York: Harper Entertainment, 2005.

Welsh, James M. "Action Films: The Serious, the Ironic, the Postmodern." *Film Genre 2000: New Critical Essays.* Ed. Wheeler Winston Dixon. New York: State U of New York P, 2000. 161–76.

Wetta, Frank J., and Stephen J. Curley. *Celluloid Wars: A Guide to Film and the American Experience of War.* New York: Greenwood, 1992.

Williams, Christian. "The Terror-Movie Boom: Why It's Making a Killing at the Box-Office." *Washington Post* 2 Nov. 1980: M1.

Williams, Linda. "Film Bodies: Gender, Genre, and Excess." *Film Theory and Criticism: Introductory Readings.* 5th ed. Ed. Leo Braudy and Marshall Cohen. New York: Oxford UP, 1999. 701–15.

Williams, Raymond. *Keywords: A Vocabulary of Culture and Society.* Rev. ed. New York: Oxford UP, 1983.

Williams, Tony. "Trying to Survive on the Darker Side: 1980s Family Horror." *The Dread of Difference: Gender and the Horror Film.* Ed. Barry Keith Grant. Austin: U of Texas P, 1996. 164–80.

Wills, J. "Blood, Guts, and Death Are Winners in the U.S." *Sunday Mail (QLD)* 11 Aug. 1985.

Wolfe, Tom. "Pause, Now, and Consider Some Tentative Conclusions about the Meaning of This Mass Perversion Called Porno-Violence: What It Is and Where It Comes From and Who Put the Hair on the Walls." *Esquire* July 1967: 59+.

Wood, Peter. "'Dressed to Kill'—How a Film Changes From an 'X' to an 'R.'" *New York Times* 20 July 1980: D13+.

Wood, Robin. *Hollywood from Vietnam to Reagan.* New York: Columbia UP, 1986.

———. "Ideology, Genre, Auteur." Grant 59–73.

———. "An Introduction to the American Horror Film." *Planks of Reason: Essays on the Horror Film.* Ed. Barry Keith Grant. Lanham, MD: Scarecrow, 1984. 164–200.

Worrall, John L. "Focusing Event Characteristics and Issue Accompaniment: The Case of Domestic Terrorism." *Criminal Justice Policy Review* 10 (1999): 319–41.

Wright, Judith Hess. "Genre Films and the Status Quo." Grant 41–49.

Wyatt, Justin. "The Formation of the 'Major Independent': Miramax, New Line and the New Hollywood." Neale and Smith 74–90.

———. "From Roadshowing to Saturation Release: Majors, Independents, and Marking/Distribution Innovations." Lewis, *New American Cinema* 64–86.

———. *High Concept: Movies and Marketing in Hollywood.* Austin: U of Texas P, 1994.

Index

Italicized page numbers indicate photographs. Film characters are indicated by (char.) following the character's name.

James Kendrick is an assistant professor in the Film and Digital Media Division of the Department of Communication Studies at Baylor University, Waco, Texas. He is the author of *Film Violence: History, Ideology, Genre* (2009). His articles have appeared in the *Velvet Light Trap*, the *Journal of Film and Video*, and the *Journal of Popular Film and Television*. He is also the film and video critic for the Web site *Qnetwork.com*.